MW01034606

BROTHERHOOD OF THE
FLYING
COFFIN

DEDICATION

To Marjorie, my life's copilot, without whom my
trips around the sun would be meaningless.

BROTHERHOOD OF THE FLYING COFFIN

THE GLIDER PILOTS OF WORLD WAR II

SCOTT McGAUGH

OSPREY PUBLISHING
Bloomsbury Publishing Plc
Kemp House, Chawley Park, Cumnor Hill, Oxford OX2 9PH, UK
29 Earlsfort Terrace, Dublin 2, Ireland
1385 Broadway, 5th Floor, New York, NY 10018, USA
E-mail: info@ospreypublishing.com
www.ospreypublishing.com

OSPREY is a trademark of Osprey Publishing Ltd

First published in Great Britain in 2023

© Scott McGaugh, 2023

Scott McGaugh has asserted his right under the Copyright, Designs and Patents Act, 1988,
to be identified as Author of this work.

For legal purposes the Acknowledgments on pp. 255–257 constitute an extension of this
copyright page.

This paperback edition was first published in Great Britain in 2024 by Osprey Publishing.

A catalog record for this book is available from the British Library.

ISBN: HB 978 1 4728 5294 6; PB 978 1 4728 5295 3; eBook 978 1 4728 5296 0;
ePDF 978 1 4728 5297 7; XML 978 1 4728 5298 4

24 25 26 27 28   10 9 8 7 6 5 4 3 2 1

Front cover: World War II glider pilots relied on bravery and bravado when flying one-way
missions into enemy territory. (Flight Officer Don D. Fritz Collection)

Index by Zoe Ross

Typeset by Deanta Global Publishing Services, Chennai, India
Printed and bound in Great Britain by CPI (Group) UK Ltd, Croydon CR0 4YY

Osprey Publishing supports the Woodland Trust, the UK's leading woodland conservation charity.

To find out more about our authors and books visit www.ospreypublishing.com. Here you will find
our full range of publications, as well as exclusive online content, details of forthcoming events and
the option to sign up for our newsletters.

Contents

Preface

For decades I walked past them in the cereal aisle at the grocery store with hardly a glance. Older men looking for the Cheerios. I couldn't have known that some were anonymous heroes who had served and unfathomably sacrificed in World War II.

When I joined other community leaders in 1996 to bring the decommissioned USS *Midway* aircraft carrier to my hometown of San Diego to become a museum, I had no indication that I was embarking on a personal mission to preserve the legacy of those who serve and sacrifice for our country. To unveil their stories on a far more personal, intimate level than most history books. A mission that has become a driving force in my life.

Brotherhood of the Flying Coffin is my 11th book on that journey, while serving the last twenty-five years first on the USS Midway Museum's board of directors, then as founding marketing director, and then again on the board. Twin passions that hopefully will inspire future generations by the estimable value of serving country and community.[1]

Novelist Ray Bradbury once said, "First, find out what your hero wants, then just follow him." Indeed, getting to know these men from their boyhood, unveiling their grit, their dreams, and discovering the invisible scars they have carried has changed my life. To share both their pain and achievements inspired me to write my first book in 2004, then the next, and the next.

I hope this latest installment will be as worthy of your time as much as it has meant to me.

Author's Notes

This book is the story of the young men who left lumber mills, girlfriends, family farms, sales jobs, coal mines, their children, parents, or perhaps college for war. It focuses on their individual legacies that became the personal mosaic of World War II in Europe, not a history of their squadrons, troop carrier groups, air wings, or troop carrier commands. Other authors already have admirably chronicled what are commonly called wartime "unit histories."

It is in that spirit I've focused more on the glider pilots' experiences, rather than unit identifications and military orders of battle. For example, focusing more on glider pilot James Larkin's four combat missions than whether he was assigned to the 84th Squadron, or if he was part of the 437th Troop Carrier Group (TCG), and whether his TCG was part of the 52nd or 53rd Air Wing. Specific references to a unit are used only when they are helpful for the reader to keep track of the pilots' experiences.

To be sure, this is not to overlook the vital contributions of various military units, but only to keep the focus on the young men's legacy.

Similarly, I steered clear of military acronyms, Roman numerals, and where or when an individual might be transferred to another unit or base on temporary "detached service" that would require explanation and blur their story. War is chaotic, and this book's aim is to stay centered on the lives of those young men from West Virginia, the Texas panhandle, and the California foothills.

Likewise, rank can become muddling at times. Glider pilots graduated as a flight officer or 2nd lieutenant. Those entering at higher ranks graduated in grade. A pilot could have been promoted between one mission and the next, or, he may have held his graduation rank of flight officer throughout the war. Extant records are not always clear or do not include what rank a glider pilot held at the precise time of a particular quote or combat experience. So, in the interest of clarity, I've included a documented rank reference generally in the first or second detailed combat inclusion and then "glider pilot" thereafter.

Again, this is not out of any disrespect for anyone's rank but keeps a laser focus on their experiences in the course of more than 250 specific glider pilot references throughout the book. In the case of senior officers (generals, captains, and majors), rank has been included when it was essential to illustrating roles, decisions, and relationships.

Glider pilot mission narratives understandably do not always match military historical documents. A glider pilot may be listed in unit records as eighth in line when taking off but reports after the mission indicated he was behind the flight leader when they reached the landing zone. In such cases, I generally relied on the pilots' personal reports.

Combat statistics and official unit narratives (and even the time of day in war) can be as fluid as a battle's front line. Official US Army primary-source documents frequently differ on how many men, the tons of equipment, or how many howitzers a glider mission delivered to the battlefield. Or how many glider landings in a designated area made it a "successful" mission. Even the number of participating glider pilots can be a moving target from one source to the next.

Again, in service to the reader, I've either used the most-cited figure or have conservatively rounded off a range of statistics to "more than" or "nearly" simply to make a point and get back to their story.

Regrettably, very few World War II glider pilots are with us today. Those who remain now are in their mid-nineties or older, making reliably accurate interviews problematic. Yet this book remains as much in their words as possible.

As the decades passed, a glider pilot may have – in various combinations – recorded his oral history for the Library of Congress or another museum, contributed his personal writing to the Silent Wings Museum in Lubbock, Texas, been included in various books over the years, and been quoted in *Stars & Stripes* in 1944, *Yank* magazine in 1945, or in a 50th anniversary article in his local newspaper in 1995. In some cases, he's told his story to a family member who has written it for posterity. In other instances, his family has kept and treasured his diary, war records, log books, newspaper accounts, and letters.

For the sake of clarity and to keep the story moving, in instances of redundant sources I have often employed a "Darlyle Watters personal account" citation with general information on the source or multiple sources of his account.

A glossary of aviation-related terms is included at the end of the book, also in the interest of keeping the story focused on these American heroes. The 24-hour, military-style clock is used for convenience.

Finally, I elected not to go into great detail about the role of British gliders in the European Theater of Operations, the ongoing research and development of American combat gliders during the war, or some of their ancillary missions, experiments, or post-battle operations. Each has been ably chronicled by other authors.

All so that the reader may sit in a glider's copilot's seat in the largest airborne assaults of the war, complete each mission, and, for the lucky ones, somehow find a way to return home.

List of Illustrations

When fields were filled with wrecked gliders, late-arriving glider pilots often were forced to land in stands of trees, into hills, woodlots, stone fences, and orchards. Extensive casualties usually resulted. (National Archives)

A glider could become a firetrap in seconds. Its fabric was flammable and cargo sometimes explosive. Burned-out skeletons were an unnerving sight following a glider mission. (Silent Wings Museum)

Gliders became the theme of several national product advertising campaigns during the war, often touting the glider pilots' bravery and "American know-how." (Silent Wings Museum)

Glider pilots not only contended with enemy fire; collisions on their final approach and in the fields were common. In an attempt to avoid this, some flew through tree lines, hoping tree trunks breaking off their wings would reduce their speed. (National Archives)

Glider pilot Thornton Schofield survived this crash after he was hit by another glider 150 feet above his landing zone. Once he hit the ground, the jeep he was carrying broke free and struck him in his back. It took several hours to extricate him from the wreckage. (Silent Wings Museum)

Elden Mueller was among the glider pilots who completed combat missions only to die far from the battlefield during routine training flights. A tow rope wrapped around Mueller's tail, forcing him to crash nose first. (Silent Wings Museum)

Propping up the tail of a glider after a successful landing enabled heavy equipment to be offloaded "downhill" out the front once the cockpit was pulled up and out of the way. (Silent Wings Museum)

It was nearly impossible to identify the snow-covered landing zones near Bastogne. As enemy fire intensified, glider pilots freelanced their way to any likely looking open space. (National Archives)

Flight Officer Richard Mercer was released just 300 feet over his landing zone. Seconds later, his Horsa crashed, killing him

Introduction

They were farm boys. Class presidents. Grocery baggers. Pranksters. Pre-med students. Shelf stockers. Reservists. They volunteered to fly an aircraft not yet invented into war; one that would be skinned with fabric but carry no guns, no engines, and no second chances. They were the volunteer glider pilots of World War II. They led the "Greatest Generation" into battle in Europe, setting standards of bravery and self-sacrifice that both frighten and inspire us to this day.

They all stepped forward for duty their officers believed would exact a fifty percent casualty rate on their one-way missions. Yet none faltered. In every major European invasion of the war – Sicily, Normandy, Southern France, Holland, crossing the Rhine into Germany, and even the Battle of the Bulge – they led the way. Ahead of the infantrymen who stormed the beaches and forded the rivers.

Brotherhood of the Flying Coffin is based on their interviews, after-action reports, journals, oral histories, photos, diaries, and letters home. The personal stories of young men like pre-med student Joseph Andrews; Don Manke who had tried to build a plane as a boy; Noel Addy, one of eight children, whose college football scholarship was scuttled when his state's national guard was mobilized; Dale Oliver, a farm boy and aspiring artist; and James Ferrin who had ridden his horse, Old Red, over to his friend's house in the Arizona desert so they could enlist together.

Readers will sit in the copilot's seat as they were towed by twin-engine planes that released them in enemy territory sometimes at only 600 feet; then endure the enemy's machine gun fire and antiaircraft shrapnel shredding their gliders and the troops they carried as they searched for a place to land. They will feel the controlled crash landings, for which some pilots had trained for only a few weeks. And upon landing, they will always be surrounded by the enemy.

Their gliders were known as Flying Coffins, Tow Targets, Death Crates, Puke Ships, and Plywood Hearses. Yet untold numbers of American glider infantry and paratroopers owed their lives to the "suicide jockeys" who flew them.

Their missions were so dangerous that glider pilots earned an Air Medal (the equivalent of a Bronze Star) for each mission, while bomber pilots had to complete five missions and fighter pilots ten to receive that same medal.

The Greatest Generation's glider pilots remain the epitome of courage, dedication, and sacrifice. Yet the story of these anonymous heroes is almost unknown. In fact, multi-volume books published by the US Air Force itself about World War II typically include only a handful of glider references. The US Army's 759-page book about the Battle of the Bulge similarly mentions the glider pilots' role only in passing.

This book begins as Americans mobilized for war, some eagerly volunteering for an unknown glider program led by a general who had been the second choice of both his father and of West Point. Yet General "Hap" Arnold developed the Army Air Corps throughout the war and would become recognized as the founder of today's US Air Force, a legacy built in part on his leadership and innovations that included glider warfare.

In the second chapter, these volunteers take off from dirt strips scratched clear among the mesquite and in the west Texas Dust Bowl. They learn how to soar above California deserts, Kansas prairies, Minnesota forests, and see friends die when tow ropes break, thunderstorms erupt, and mistakes are made.

Subsequent chapters carry readers as copilots into one major invasion after another. These new pilots unwittingly became test pilots on their first mission – the invasion of Sicily. A suicide mission of flying across the Mediterranean in a storm at night, braving point-blank friendly fire from Allied warships, and then being released too far out at sea. Dozens ditched and drowned – sometimes within a few hundred yards of the rocky coastline – along with the troops they carried. Yet no one faltered. Duty called.

Then we accompany hundreds of glider pilots leading the Normandy invasion, and then ride along in southern France when unimaginable chaos in the sky resulted in some gliders landing on top of one another. Readers are alongside more than a thousand glider pilots over Holland in the bloodiest airborne mission of the war, some of whom crashed and were hidden by the Dutch underground or became prisoners of war. They share in the tragedy encountered by nearly a thousand glider pilots who crossed the Rhine into Germany, bound for the most heavily defended region in the Fatherland, only to find their landing zones inadvertently hidden by Allied smoke screens.

By the time World War II ended in Europe, as many as 1,900 glider pilots had been towed in a single operation. They landed in America's first stealth aircraft that had been cobbled together with tubular steel, wood, and fabric. Comprising 70,000 component parts, the gliders had been built by inexperienced manufacturers, one of which had produced coffins before the war, and others who were better known for their refrigerators, food condiments, and pianos. The design and workmanship of these gliders at times proved as deadly as the Germans.

Then, as quietly as they had penetrated enemy territory during the war, they blended back into America to marry, start families, and become shopkeepers, college students, electricians, lawyers, carpenters, entrepreneurs, teachers, our grandfathers, and great-grandfathers. Yet the untold story of these intrepid heroes stands apart for their audacity, nerve, and accomplishment.

He [the glider pilot] lived to bear his country's arms. He died to save its honor. He was a soldier ... and he knew a soldier's duty. His sacrifice will help to keep aglow the flaming torch that lights our lives ... that millions of yet unborn may know the priceless joy of liberty. And we who pay him homage. And revere his memory. In solemn pride we rededicate ourselves to a complete fulfilment of the task for which he so gallantly has placed his life upon the altar of man's freedom.

General "Hap" Arnold, Commanding Officer
United States Air Forces[1]

I

Guts and Gliders Wanted

Richard Libbey was as helpless as a duck flying in hunting season.

His combat glider was locked in formation only a few hundred yards off the ground as the shadows below lengthened on D-Day in Normandy. The enemy's coal-red tracer fire seemed to walk down his tow rope from the plane towing him toward his cockpit. Antiaircraft bursts rocked the glider as shrapnel sliced through its fabric skin. By the final glider mission on D-Day, German gunners had been honing their accuracy since sunrise.

They had opened fire shortly after Libbey and other glider pilots had crossed Normandy's beaches. In only minutes, they would reach the landing zones where they would release, turn, drop, and crash-land. But not before chunks of sheet metal peeled off wounded aircraft engines coughing fire, and swatches of glider fuselage fabric fluttered away in the armada's prop wash.

The fields below didn't look like the photos Libbey had been shown in the pre-flight briefings. *Are we off course?* He watched gliders ahead of him cut loose and turn toward the ground. *Is this our landing zone? Wait too long and I'll be way into German territory. To hell with it.* Libbey released from his tow plane, pushed his glider's nose down and to the left, and looked for any place to land. *There, looks big enough.* His copilot started calling out the glider's altitude as Libbey leaned into the glider's dive.

"100, 120, 100, 100, 100, 90, 85…"

"Full flaps, Ray!" Libbey ordered.

"We'll hit the trees at the edge of the field!"

"Damn, full flaps."

"God, this is it!"

Libbey and his copilot heard the trees scraping the bottom of their glider. Slowed, they somehow cleared the hedgerow and dropped down onto the field, hard, crushing part of the landing gear and spinning to a stop.

Then the terror began.

Machine gun tracers swept across the furrow where Libbey and his copilot lay after scrambling out of the wrecked glider. Libbey froze. "I could not think. For the first time I was so scared that I could not think. In a few seconds, I started to breathe again. And we started moving … the first [glider pilot] I saw was Ben Winks's copilot.

"Where's Ben?"

"Ben's dead."[1]

Two words, yelled over war's cacophony, would haunt Richard Libbey for the rest of his life. *Ben?* His buddy had been so full of confidence and was sure he'd be coming back. Instead, he had slammed into a row of trees, crushed between them and the howitzer and quarter-ton truck he had carried a few feet behind his seat. It was his first combat mission.

In the coming nine months, Libbey would fly in two of the largest and deadliest glider missions of World War II, alongside thousands of other young glider pilot volunteers, most only a few years removed from high school dances, summer jobs, and family dinners.

The older sons of farmers, seamstresses, migrant farmhands, teachers, the jobless, policemen, shopkeepers, loggers, and plant workers stood on the threshold of manhood in 1940. Many were teenagers nearing high school graduation, working odd jobs, helping bring in the harvest, and eager to see their girlfriends. Some were in college, and a few had enlisted in the US Army or their state's national guard. More than a handful had married and started families.

But as the Great Depression's dust finally began to settle, war loomed. The only life they knew on ranches, in towns the size of a single café, and in cities could soon evaporate as America mobilized for war.

Final exams would be replaced by soloing in an aircraft with no guns, no motors, and no parachutes. Friday night larks and girlfriends might be recalled in letters sent home. Friends would be killed instead of ragging on each other while hanging out over a milkshake. Bruising tackles would be replaced by antiaircraft artillery shrapnel shredding the fuselage or machine gun fire ripping into the man sitting in the next seat. Marriage would have to wait "until this thing is over." The rest of life would stall as well.

Joseph Andrews wanted to become a doctor. A good doctor. The son of a federal government lawyer in Washington, DC, Andrews was about to graduate the pre-med program at The Citadel and was bound for George Washington Medical School. He was a studious young man who enjoyed singing and tended to come straight to the point in conversations. His sincere demeanor merited a host of friends who admired his one ambition of someday being recognized as one of the best doctors in his profession.

James Larkin had wanted to fly almost from the day in 1927 when accounts of Charles Lindbergh's transatlantic flight captivated America. His immigrant father had served in the Spanish-American War and raised his children on a fire department captain's salary in Minnesota. Larkin was about to graduate high school. The military and a war might be his ticket to becoming a pilot.

Stephen Painter was a Texas prairie farm boy outside of Joshua; the kind of farming town that relied on rain, each year's summer harvest, a bank, general store, and its train station. His family had weathered the Depression well, growing crops on flat farmland country blanketed with corn, cotton, potatoes, vegetables, and orchards between stands of post and blackjack oaks.

As he was finishing high school in Joshua in 1940, Painter's future was as blurred as a Texas dust storm. His brother's Texas National Guard unit had been mobilized in 1939 and Stephen wanted to follow, but his father refused to sign the parental permission document for the seventeen-year-old. That left odd jobs on neighbors' farms, perhaps a part-time job in town between harvests, and mowing lawns until winter arrived.

Guy Gunter sometimes went to bed hungry as a boy, growing up in east Atlanta in the 1930s. The son of a policeman and housekeeper, he rarely carried a lunch to school. In the winter, dinner after school might be vegetable soup and a sweet potato topped with margarine, his first real meal since a small breakfast each morning. He was a good student bound for Georgia Tech where he would attend school at night, while working days as a salesman for an electrical parts company. Perhaps he could begin building a career in 1940, with a college degree in hand one day.

J. Curtis "Goldie" Goldman had been a blustery boy growing up in Tyler, Texas, who enjoyed fighting, pranks, spitballs when adults were not around, and acting bigger than his size. One teacher became so fed up with Goldman that she insisted he spend the rest of her semester in the school principal's office. At five feet, nine inches tall, he was too small for the basketball team so he had begged to be its manager and tote team equipment so he could go on the team's road trips.

He had grown up in a small country house with water from a nearby well and an outhouse at the end of a crooked path. His boyhood had been marked by learning how to hunt jackrabbits in stands of mesquite on an uncle's farm, volunteering to be a batboy at a softball park near his grandmother's house so he could watch games for free, and a penchant for getting into trouble.

By 1940, he had started classes at Tyler Junior College along with another Tyler boy, Harry Loftis. A country lad, Loftis "had never been anywhere in [his] life" and had hoped for a college scholarship, but when that did not come through, a local banker loaned him $50 for his school fees. Meanwhile, Goldman was a good student but failed to make the Honor Society after he and Loftis were caught cutting a college chemistry class so they could drink sodas and play checkers at Woody's Soda Fountain across the street from school. If war and the draft came, Goldman stoked the same passion as thousands of other young men. He wanted to be a fighter pilot.[2]

Sam Baker also was a handful in school. The California native was eager to please his teachers and had been elected president of his senior class. But he had to resign his post due to poor class attendance. A series of empty jobs awaited him after high school. Clearing stands of manzanita at a logging camp made him think there had to be a better route in life. So, too, did a job as a "flunky" in a box-manufacturing plant where his father worked.

In 1939, he and a couple of buddies thought about enlisting in the military. A fast-talking Army recruiter offered Baker $252 per year, room and board, and a promise of getting out of Sacramento, maybe even to Oahu as his first duty station. Baker had enlisted with little hesitation. He was eighteen.

Jack Merrick also wanted to fly. The nineteen-year-old had built a glider in high school that was towed by a car. He had no instructions but had learned the requisite principles by "reading the funny papers, building model airplanes, you know, that sort of thing."[3] In 1940, he held a private pilot's license, had graduated junior college, and was headed for the University of Texas.

The Depression had been especially hard on Jack, his mother, and four brothers and sisters after his parents had divorced. He had lived with relatives for two years before their separation. Money and food were scarce for the five Merrick children. At times, relatives sent money to support them.

None could have possibly imagined that within a few years Henry Arnold, a man who had been the second choice of both his father and the United States Army, would send them into battle in what some later called a "flying coffin."

Herbert Arnold, a dour surgeon, had wanted his firstborn son, Tom, to attend West Point Military Academy to continue the family tradition of service in uniform.[4] The family generally thought their younger son, Henry, was destined to be a minister. But when Tom chose another college to study engineering, the onus fell on Henry. His acceptance in 1903 at the age of seventeen came only when a higher-rated applicant opted for marriage instead of West Point.

No one could have predicted Arnold would become chief of the US Army Air Forces in World War II and architect of what would evolve into the United States Air Force. That he would lead a massive transformation of aerial combat capability from generally obsolete open-cockpit aircraft to fighter jets and long-range strategic bombers. Or that his World War II airborne strategy throughout the European Theater of Operations and elsewhere in part would rely on motorless and defenseless gliders and the young men who dared fly them past the front lines to land in enemy territory.

In fact, at this point in time, Arnold was simply a likable sort who might have been forgettable at West Point, had it not been for his string of demerits that warranted frequent marches to walk off his punishments. He favored pranks, including one with fireworks which led to his confinement in quarters, a frequent punishment for him at West Point. Nearly six feet tall and about 180 pounds, he excelled neither in athletics nor the classroom.

Classmates pegged him as a minimal-effort cadet, a description that Arnold acknowledged later in life. He graduated in 1907, still as a private after an anemic academic performance, ranking sixty-sixth in a class of 111. By almost every measure, Henry Arnold was an average cadet with average prospects as a soldier.

Upon graduation, the Army sent Arnold to the Philippines on a two-year posting to map various islands. On his return to the States, promotion was his mission. Transfer to the ordnance department carried a promotion to 1st lieutenant, but he failed the admission test. Perhaps a new Army program run by the Signal Corps that barely existed was an option. Aviation?

Arnold was accepted into the program in 1911, the first year Congress funded an Army airfield and when the Wright brothers, the famed aircraft designers, were contracted to train the first cadre of military aviators at Simms Field in Dayton, Ohio. That inaugural class numbered two students, Arnold and 2nd Lieutenant Thomas Milling. It was a crash course. Arnold soloed after two-and-a-half hours of flights that averaged about eight minutes each. Less than two hours of additional flight time were enough to earn his aviator's wings.

The Signal Corps owned only two aircraft at the time, and promptly made Arnold a flight instructor in a profession in which many students died. Applying power to early aircraft sometimes caused them to dive toward the ground instead of gain altitude. On occasion, the flimsy biplanes mysteriously turned over and their pilots fell to their death. At one point, Arnold wondered if there was "an unseen hand that reaches out and turns the machines over in the air for there have been so many accidents that have never been explained," he wrote in a letter to his fiancée.[5] Yet Arnold became an innovative aviator, setting an altitude record, pioneering the use of goggles, and directing artillery fire from the air.

But the deaths of two aviators he knew well, as well as a near-fatal crash when his aircraft suddenly lurched into a gut-wrenching turn toward the ground, almost ended Arnold's aviation career. He developed a fear of flying so profound that the Signal Corps nearly relieved him from aviation duty as he battled his demons. "I cannot even look at a machine in the air, without feeling that some accident is going to happen to it," he wrote at the time.[6] His fitness reports by superior officers painted a bleak picture for Arnold. One described him as having above average intelligence yet lacking in common sense and someone who was untrustworthy. He landed in Washington, DC, with a desk job.

Famed aviator Billy Mitchell lured Arnold back into flying about three years later. After posts in San Diego, California, Washington, DC, and Fort Riley, Kansas, by the mid-1920s Arnold had found his footing in life. He had developed a growing reputation as an aviation officer with a penchant for aircraft research and development. After only three months of working together, Brigadier General Ewing Booth characterized Arnold as tireless, cheerful, cooperative, inspirational, a pleasing man and able officer. Two years later, Brigadier General Charles Symmonds was equally effusive: "An exceptionally high-grade officer. Pleasing manner, magnetic and natural leader... Possesses lots of good hard common sense."[7]

In 1936, he was summoned to Washington to become the assistant chief of the Army Air Corps. Arnold had become an accomplished aviator; had overcome disastrous evaluations early in his career; had shown a knack for organizational leadership and aviation research; and had developed friendships with a handful of fast-rising officers within the Army. Arnold had served several posts in Washington, DC, dating back to 1917, and had learned the intricacies of managing political skirmishes between senior military officers, War Department officials, the commander in chief, and Congress. He knew how to skirt strict lines of authority in the military and to encourage input by qualified civilians in the interest of results.

Two years later, he became chief of the Army Air Corps when his superior officer, General Oscar Westover, was killed instantly when the plane he was flying crashed into a Los Angeles neighborhood and burst into flames. He commanded a moribund Air Corps. Its authorized personnel strength was 26,000 and its aircraft numbered only 1,200 bombers and fighters. Some were biplanes and dangerously obsolete.

At fifty-two years of age with hair that had receded and had turned prematurely white, together with a dimpled chin, he had the pleasant look and beguiling demeanor of a college professor. He was widely known as "Hap," thought by many to be a shortened version of Happy. Yet he had suffered from ulcers for years and, as one historian suspected, had suffered a possible heart attack.

Sometimes impatient, his aides believed his swearing was mostly for effect. Historians have noted that Arnold opposed Black servicemen serving in the AAF, strictly enforced segregation regulations, supported a Caucasian officer's bigoted treatment of Black officers, and he openly criticized the French and English. Yet he also had a reputation for honesty and the ability to identify the macro issues as well as understand how they impacted aviation at the squadron level.

He took command of the Army Air Corps just as President Franklin Delano Roosevelt directed that it be expanded to an unprecedented 10,000 aircraft and that factory production capability be increased to 20,000 aircraft annually. It marked the beginning of an aviation arms race, with no real plan for gliders.[8]

In the twenty years since World War I, aircraft technology had leaped forward, creating a host of new strategic and tactical options for war planners. One was "vertical envelopment," the ability to spearhead an assault by inserting troops behind the front line in enemy territory and in advance of the main attack. Objectives could include seizing water crossings, establishing bridgeheads, disrupting reinforcement movement, creating a diversion, destroying enemy supply depots, and severing its communications network. Parachute troops offered one option. Gliders could be another. But would enough young men across America volunteer for airborne combat that was not yet battle tested and, in some cases, would rely on aircraft that did not yet exist?

When Sam Baker, Jack Merrick, "Goldie" Goldman, Guy Gunter, and other young men turned in on the night of May 9, 1940, they could not have known that German Luftwaffe gliders were releasing from their tow planes and turning toward a massive Belgian underground fortress as the sun brightened an overcast sky.

Fortress Eben Emael sat at the northern end of the Maginot Line, a network of fortifications along the border between France and Germany. The Germans' Siegfried Line to the east largely paralleled the Maginot – static front lines reminiscent of World War I. Where, when, and how would Germany force a world war following its invasion of Poland the year before? At Fort Eben Emael with gliders.

Built over several years in the 1930s, Eben Emael was a modern-day castle featuring massive artillery protected by concrete-reinforced casements. A moat encircled the fort and was augmented by flooded fields, tank barricades, steel gun and observation turrets, minefields, and machine gun emplacements. A network of tunnels connected ordnance storage, artillery crews, a power station, and barracks. With fifteen combat emplacements, it was considered the largest and most impregnable fortress in the world.

It had been designed to repel a German invasion long enough to enable Belgium and France to mobilize their troops against a traditional enemy assault that could take months and cost thousands of lives. But Eben Emael's landscaped roof nearly three football fields long could make it vulnerable if aircraft loaded with troops, weapons, and explosives might somehow approach and land on it silently.

In one of the greatest surprise raids of World War II, the German glider force landed atop the fortress and captured Fort Eben Emael and its garrison of more than 1,000 men in less than an hour, at a cost of only six dead and twenty wounded men. It was accomplished by a highly trained assault force of seventy-eight men aboard ten combat gliders. A second glider force landed nearby and captured two of three bridges crossing the Meuse River.

Within hours, German military convoys were rolling across the bridges into France. In the following six weeks, the British evacuated more than 300,000 men at Dunkirk as Belgium, Holland, Luxembourg, and France fell. The all-out conquest of Europe had begun in silence and with surprise by combat gliders. The stagnant front lines of World War I would be replaced by a flow of battle from every direction across the European continent. Stealth, mobility, and specialized forces would become vital tactical elements in World War II.

Nine months following Germany's glider assault at Fort Eben Emael, America began to look to the potential of gliders – not as a combat strategy, but as a training aid for future power pilots and to deliver cargo. February 25, 1941, became the birthdate of combat gliders when General Arnold ordered a study of their capability with an eye toward their delivery capability and potential tactical objectives uniquely suited to gliders. From the outset, gliders were envisioned for troop and light armament delivery. They would serve as airborne delivery trailers, as one historian put it.[9]

Glider pilots would be the Sherpas of World War II.

General Arnold was in a hurry. Exactly one week later, his office directed procurement officers at Wright Field – an aircraft research and personnel training base in Ohio – to begin designs for a glider that could carry twelve or fifteen men, or a combination of machine guns, artillery, ammunition, and cargo. He envisioned a glider able to deliver a combat-ready and self-contained team to the field. It took only four days for letters to be sent to eleven aircraft manufacturers for proposals to design and build glider prototypes. A key caveat stated that glider development could not siphon any resources away from the Air Corps' massive, powered aircraft program. Only four responded.[10] Others cited previous commitments, some sidestepped the experimental notion of gliders altogether, and others lacked the production capacity.

"A NEW CRETE GLIDER BLITZ" declared the banner headline in the *San Francisco Chronicle* and elsewhere on May 21, 1941, news that stunned much of America, including war planners. The day before, Germany had launched a massive air assault to take the island of Crete to complete the conquest of Greece. More than seventy German DFS 230 gliders and hundreds of troop transport planes had participated in the assault. Readers of the *Chronicle* and other papers had no way of knowing that the Germans' use of glider and parachute troops to capture three airfields had become an airborne disaster.

New Zealand, British, and Greek troops defending the airfields had been put on alert and were waiting. Machine gun fire shredded gliders and German paratroopers. Gliders were set afire within minutes of landing by the entrenched defenders. Although Germany ousted the Allies and took Crete a week later, the airborne price had become horrendous. More than 5,000 of the 13,000 German glider and paratroop forces had been killed or wounded. Half of the 350 German aircraft in the assault had been destroyed.[11] Regardless, for the second time in a year, German gliders had played a leading role in an assault that had achieved its objectives.

Meanwhile, America did not have a single combat glider in its inventory and no glider pilots fully trained for combat.

By mid-May, ten glider concepts of varying capacity had been ordered for static testing and preliminary analysis. When they arrived, the Air Corps would need trained pilots. Where would they come from? The first handful of pilots came from two civilian aviation schools, one in Elmira, New York, and the other in Lockport, Illinois.

In May 1941, Major Fred Dent, Jr, led five other officers in America's first glider pilot training class in Elmira. For more than a decade, southern New York had hosted national soaring competitions and was home to a leading sailplane manufacturer. The region's hills, deep valleys, warm summer weather, prevailing wind against rows of ridges, and thermals created ideal soaring conditions over a checkerboard of farm fields and forest.

Dent had begun his career in the Army Corps of Engineers and had earned his pilot's wings in 1930. He later earned a degree in aeronautical engineering at the Massachusetts Institute of Technology. Few men in the Army held both the intellectual and operational requisites of aircraft design, testing, instruction, and piloting skills like Dent. Within two years, Dent would direct the Army Corps' development and procurement of military gliders.

The anticipated demand for glider pilots made it clear that the Air Corps would need to quickly contract with civilian aviation schools across the country. By September, discernible progress had been made. A basic training program for 150 glider pilots had been outlined. First, thirty-three glider pilots would be trained at Elmira and, as soon as programs could be established in the South and West, the remainder would be trained. Twentynine Palms, California, became one of the first to open with a training regimen that largely relied on sailplanes.

In October, General Arnold turned to a tall, lanky soaring enthusiast in the Pennsylvania National Guard to make sense of his glider vision and get it off the ground. Lewin Barringer was a nationally renowned expert on soaring. He had flown aircraft and commercial gliders for more than a decade. He had spent two years in Iran in charge of the Aerial Department of Joint Iranian Expeditions. His firsthand broad perspective of gliders was unmatched. But perhaps it was his enthusiastic promotion of gliders that had ultimately led him to the job.

In 1938, he had written:

An experienced pilot of motorless craft is used to having every landing a forced landing ... whereas the power plane pilot is often careless about his approach and depends on his motor to lift him over ... obstructions. A pilot of an airplane who has a background of soaring experience is a far safer pilot ... because of his thorough understanding of all types of air movement.[12]

Barringer would have to make sense of the glider development program, even though its use on the battlefield was not yet crystallized and its leadership organization was largely uncertain. Only a handful of pilot instructors had been partially trained at contracted private aviation schools in civilian soaring techniques using sport gliders and sailplanes.

Meanwhile, Arnold prepared for an air war on multiple fronts – including in Washington – as his Air Corps remained far from war ready. It had grown to more than 152,000 personnel with almost 6,800 aircraft. But less than half of those planes were combat aircraft. Only about a thousand were bombers, some of which were obsolete.[13] Not only was a massive buildup still necessary, airborne strategies and the role of gliders remained a work in progress.

He also faced sustained headwinds from within the Army pilot community. A later Army analysis summarized:

There also seems to have existed ... a disinclination on the part of various Air Forces agencies to take proper responsibility for its [glider program] achievement. The basis for this situation can probably be found in the ever-present antipathy of the power pilot toward any other type of aircraft. Another cause of difficulty was perhaps that the glider program was a borderline project, a case of divided responsibility between the ground and air arms.[14]

Meanwhile, young Americans had begun registering for the draft, some with heady dreams of aerial dogfights or perhaps parachuting onto the battlefield. Few, if any, of those dreams included intentionally careening through machine gun fire into a forest or sliding to a stop among rows of potatoes deep behind enemy lines and engaging an unseen enemy who had been waiting for their arrival.

It was the Japanese attack on December 7, 1941, that would change the course of thousands of those young men's lives, putting them onto a path that would lead to risking their lives in an aircraft whose nicknames included "Purple Heart Boxes."

Lawrence Kubale sat on a ship bound for the United States on December 7. He had enlisted a year earlier and had hated his post in Puerto Rico where his buddies went swimming on Thanksgiving. He was used to skiing that time of year; maybe he would ask for a transfer. The next day, Pete Buckley enlisted at the age of sixteen without his mother's permission. When he got home, the family conversation did not go well. About six months later, he would volunteer for glider training. Joseph Andrews, the pre-med student at The Citadel, enlisted nine days later. Gordon Chamberlain was a sophomore at San Diego State University. Already he had become president of the campus Toastmasters Club and had starred in a college stage production, "The Colonel's Lady." He enlisted on December 29.

They would be joined by thousands of other young men who ultimately would rely on General "Hap" Arnold for the leadership, training, and aircraft they would need for combat. Their fate would depend on the former West Point cadet who had headed a secret club of pranksters, had been frequently late to class, and who had earned demerits for chewing tobacco in formation that cost him participation in his graduation ceremony. But Arnold was no knockabout. He had been one of the youngest cadets admitted to West Point and had demonstrated a remarkable ability to memorize mathematic tables. Almost from the outset as an aviator, he had demonstrated a mechanical aptitude as he pushed the Wright brothers to design more powerful and capable aircraft for the military.[15]

He would first send junior college dropouts, farm boys, pranksters, medical school students, salesmen, college students, and disgruntled Army privates to primitive airfields in Tucumcari, New Mexico; Lubbock, Texas; Victorville, California; Pittsburgh, Kansas; Stuttgart, Arkansas; and elsewhere. They would discover it would "take some real guts" to endure a frantic, motorless journey that would carry them beyond the front lines of the battlefields in Europe.

2

Crashing is a Lonely Sound

His torpedo ran straight and true toward the enemy battleship as he pulled up toward the clouds. Or, the enemy aircraft carrier wobbled in his bombsight as a Japanese Zero's machine gun pounded his fuselage. But he held his course, released his bomb, and turned away. Seconds later, a massive explosion rocked the sea. Mission accomplished.

Dreams of becoming a Navy pilot as imagined by Guy Gunter and others never included flying into combat in a powerless and defenseless glider.

Knowing he soon would be drafted as he drove around Georgia selling General Electric supplies, Gunter wanted to be a Navy pilot "because I could sleep between white sheets at night." When his notice arrived in January 1942, there were no openings in the Navy's pilot-training program. But if he enlisted in the Army Air Corps, perhaps after a few weeks at its flight school at Wichita Falls, Texas, he could transfer to the Navy's program. It never happened.[1]

In early 1942, the Army and Navy were scrambling to build training infrastructure and capacity, process draftees and volunteers, and procure massive amounts of warfighting equipment and supplies. All while Hitler stormed across Europe and the Japanese secured new territory across the South Pacific.

In a little more than a year, Gunter would be among the first American glider pilots to fly into combat. But first they would have to complete a training regimen over scrubby deserts and prairies. Mastering the nuances of being towed by aircrews equally green as they pulled more than three tons of dead weight about a football field's length behind their aircraft in crosswinds, through downdrafts, and at night would prove deadly.

Noel Addy had worked in Chandler, Arizona, from the age of twelve, only two years following his father's death from pneumonia after working as a field hand clearing the desert. Although his mother received veteran's benefits, eight children were a financial burden. His first job selling newspapers was followed by a paper route five miles from home. He graduated Chandler High School and was bound for Arizona State Teacher's College in Flagstaff on a football scholarship. But his national guard unit mobilized for a year's duty in 1941. December 7 ended any hopes of playing football for the Lumberjacks in the foreseeable future. In 1942, he volunteered to become a glider pilot because "flyin' into war seemed like a whole lot better than doing it by walking."[2] He joined a legion of young men as green as a high school freshman on his first day.

One day he took off from a west Texas airfield behind a Douglas C-53 Skytrooper tow plane, bound for an overnight stop in Tucson, and then on to Victorville Army Air Field in California. Addy had a copilot, and the C-53 carried a crew of four along with four Army passengers. As the sun set that day, the C-53's copilot mistakenly released Addy's glider over what he thought was Tucson. It was Blythe, California, along the Colorado River, more than 200 miles to the northwest and only about 150 miles from Victorville. Both Addy and the C-53 landed safely, intent on reconnecting and continuing their journey. But circumstance and poor training could abort flight plans, sometimes with no warning.

As Addy helped reconnect the tow rope to his glider for takeoff, he noticed the locks had not been removed from the glider's ailerons, elevators, and rudder. As he and his copilot began removing them, the C-53 pilot added power and began pulling the empty glider forward. As it gained speed, the glider knocked Addy to the ground. Seconds later, the tow plane lifted off the runway along with a pilot-less glider. Almost immediately, the tow plane turned back toward the runway. The pilot had only seconds to decide. Release the glider.

The uncontrolled glider collided with the turning tow plane. With too little power and not enough altitude, Addy watched in horror as the C-53 stalled, nosed over, and slammed into an embankment, exploding in flames. All eight men aboard died instantly.

The Army accident report noted that miscommunication caused the C-53 to begin its takeoff prematurely and Addy should have been in his pilot's seat with seat belts fastened while someone else reconnected the tow rope and checked the glider. Too frequently, glider pilots tragically learned that rigorous training for both crews and unwavering protocol discipline were necessary if glider pilots and their tow plane crews were to work as an effective team when they reached the war zone in Europe.

The prop wash of an unprecedented expansion by what became known as the Army Air Forces (AAF) threatened to overwhelm the fledgling glider program in early 1942. With no real plan in place for gliders or their use, Army Chief of Staff George C. Marshall had already approved an Air Forces proposal for 100 groups, 375 combat squadrons and 400,000 men. But that paled in comparison to the Army's overall intent to build a force of 5.4 million troops by the end of 1942.

In addition, President Roosevelt authorized production of 60,000 aircraft in 1942 (increased to 125,000 the following year), and approximately 575,000 tanks, antiaircraft guns, and machine guns in 1942. The Army's need for new facilities became voracious. Its land holdings would increase from 2.1 million acres in 1940 to nearly 46 million acres by the end of the war.[3] The glider program would have to quickly chart a course toward a meaningful role in World War II.

It would start, in part, with public relations. By the spring of 1942, Lewin Barringer, Arnold's man charged with making combat gliders a reality, and others mounted a public relations campaign within the Army hierarchy to build credibility for the concept and to recruit glider pilots. In an AAF Headquarters newsletter distributed to Army commands, he made the case for the future of gliders.

He noted General Arnold had visited the first glider pilot school on more than one occasion, had accompanied the Air Forces' first glider pilot in a sailplane, and pointed out that Arnold repeatedly said America "would have a glider force second to none." Further, glider pilots' skills were not to be taken lightly. Barringer believed pilot training for glider pilots was necessary because "[gliders] should not be considered as gliders, but as transport airplanes with remote power plants... Due to the consideration of the size of these ships and the fact that they will be towed in formation at night ... a [glider] pilot should have at least the minimum airplane training of the Air Forces primary schools or a CPT [Civilian Pilot Training] course before entering a glider school."[4]

Barringer also had allies in his campaign. The month following his spectacular bombing of Tokyo, Brigadier General James Doolittle wrote, "Some of the boys who trained for the party could not be taken along, but they were just as important as the rest of us. We're all together in this war – air crews, ground men, factory workers, and don't forget the boys without the motors – the glider pilots. They will be the spearhead of future air-borne attacks."[5]

In the July edition of the Air Forces command newsletter, an article written by Captain Herbert Johansen revealed the glider corps had not yet settled on several key aspects of glider combat. He believed gliders would release from as high as 10,000 feet, miles from a landing zone. Within a year the typical release point would be much closer to 600 feet and a pilot would only have a few minutes to find a suitable landing field. He also anticipated the cost of a glider would not exceed $12,000, a figure that nearly all manufacturers would never come close to reaching.[6]

Glider use uncertainty aside, "The 'Commandos of the Air' are no longer a promise but reality... Today the glider is as much a part of our war plans as the Flying Fortress ... the American glider is definitely ready for war," wrote Johansen.[7]

Building credibility for the glider program also included the civilian aviation community. In February 1942, Barringer penned an article in *Flying and Popular Aviation* extolling the potential of postwar gliders in commercial aviation. As he had explained in Army command newsletters, the former national soaring champion also noted that "only qualified airplane pilots would be desirable" as glider pilots in combat, given the anticipated night flying and flying in tight formations.[8]

Then in June, the Army Air Forces and US Treasury Department launched a nationwide series of air shows to sell war bonds. Fighters, bombers, and a captured German fighter were to be the stars in the "Air Cavalcade." At the last minute, a towed sailplane was added to promote the glider program. Although dwarfed by the others, its eerily silent approach and precise landing proved to be a showstopper.

General Arnold, Assistant Secretary of War Robert Lovett, and various Air Forces commands were creating and revising the glider program almost on a weekly basis. By the time the first cadre of 150 glider instructors was trained in March 1942, Arnold had abandoned his vision for a glider force of 1,000, tripling it to 3,000. He did so while acknowledging to the chief of the air staff that although glider procurement was proceeding, a refined plan and their battlefield role had not yet been finalized.

Only five days later, Arnold directed the Army's Materiel Division to deliver 4,500 gliders by July 1, 1943. That closely matched another Arnold order the same day to produce 4,200 trained glider pilots over the same fifteen months.

A daunting parallel challenge was to determine who would make a good glider pilot candidate. Would he have to come only from the Army's power pilot corps? Would a private pilot's license and flight experience be enough for admission to the glider program? What about young men who had accumulated substantial soaring experience?

When it became clear that the number of pilots needed for the air war prohibited 4,000 enlisted Army power pilots from being transferred to the glider program, the first set of admission standards was established. A glider pilot candidate had to be between the ages of eighteen through thirty-five; pass a medical examination; and have flying experience by holding a current or recently lapsed civilian airman (pilot) certificate or have 200 glider flights or thirty hours' glider flight time experience. No Army flight-school washouts would be accepted.[9]

Becoming a glider pilot proved to be a tough sell to young men who watched actor Jimmy Stewart starring in an AAF recruiting video shown in theaters. He pitched patriotism ("flying and fighting for the safety of our people at home"), education benefits, and $75 a month plus room and board. In quest of 90,000 Air Forces enlistees, he had a pitch for everyone, including high school students. No mention was made of gliders.

By mid-June, the program was expanded to allow volunteers with no flying experience and even some power pilot school washouts. Two student tracks were established. Students with flying experience would spend four weeks at a preliminary school, in part learning how to land light aircraft with no power (called "dead stick" training). Students with no experience started with forty hours of basic training and then fifteen hours of dead stick training. The two tracks then merged for elementary-advanced training in makeshift gliders or sailplanes until the combat gliders arrived.[10]

Thousands more men could now volunteer for the glider program. Prankster "Goldie" Goldman's eyesight was less than 20/20 making him ineligible for power pilot school, but he could get a waiver for glider pilot training. The day he enlisted in the Air Corps, with tears in her eyes his mother made him repeat a vow from the day he had enlisted in the Army. Because his father was a "weekend drunk, my mother made me promise … that I would never take a drink of liquor."[11]

Power pilot washout Gordon Chamberlain now had another option as well. Others, like James Di Pietro who did not like being an Army laboratory technician, jumped at the chance for a transfer to gliders.

In addition to the California and New York schools, training operations at Lamesa, Texas, and Wickenburg, Arizona, were established. Students initially completed the same training program as the first 150 flight instructors had studied. But to meet General Arnold's mandate for thousands of glider pilots by the end of the year, the Air Forces quickly stitched together a network of eighteen schools, mostly operated by civilian contractors. Some were sure to be temporary or seasonal (in North Dakota, Minnesota, and Wisconsin) while others in New Mexico, California, and Texas offered year-round flying weather.

Some schools were little more than outposts carved in the dirt which shocked fledgling glider students when they arrived. The school near Big Spring, Texas, featured a 7,000-foot dirt runway and not much else. It closed seven months after it opened when its water supply and living quarters were deemed unacceptable.

Sheppard Field near Wichita Falls, Texas, became notorious for its undrinkable sulfur water and equally foul food. The bad water offered scant relief after trainees completed calisthenics on an oiled drill field during a Texas summer. It was a place "where it would rain on your head, sand was blowing in your face, and you were standing in water up to your knees. It was a horrible place," recalled Guy Gunter.[12]

Don Manke had grown up on a family farm in Wisconsin. He had attempted to build a plane as a boy and had completed two years of college so he could enlist in the Air Corps in 1940. He transferred to the glider pilot program and was sent to Fort Sumner, New Mexico, a town, he reflected, where "it hasn't rained here in six months. This is a place where you can see for fifty miles and see nothing."[13]

The first group of 162 Fort Sumner cadets cleared mesquite for what passed as the airstrip that Manke used. Brutal winters, incessant wind, mud, tents with dirt floors, and a pit that passed for a latrine made it a miserable place to fly. Dysentery was common. Some pilots called it "Little Valley Forge" due to heavy snow that collapsed their tents. Improvements finally included tarpaper barracks with pot-bellied stoves.

Another early student at Fort Sumner was Pete Buckley, the teenager who had bucked the wishes of his mother. He volunteered for the glider program in June 1942 and reported to Fort Sumner after completing a civilian flight program in Stillwater, Oklahoma.

Many glider pilots seemed to hail from Texas where some of the advanced glider pilot schools would be established. A few years older than most glider students, C.B. "Boots" King was a realist when he volunteered for the AAF in March 1942, the same month he married June O'Donnell. He and three brothers had grown up in Texas cotton country before he volunteered for the glider program and training at nearby schools at Plainview and Lubbock. At twenty-nine years of age, King faced nearly a year's worth of training and the prospect of starting a family before he would be sent to Europe.

Plainview was typical of the pre-glider training schools the Army was establishing. Remote deserts and featureless prairies were ideal for young men learning to fly. Plainview was aptly named. The endless, flat fields of cotton, corn, and sorghum grew on land that varied by less than 500 feet across nearly 1,000 square miles. Where a hazy sky touched a horizon as flat as the ocean. Where unending wind swells rolled through the prairie grass and roiled red dust clouds across plowed fields, and where grain elevators marked country hamlets and the intersections of ruler-straight farm roads, so level they disappeared as mirages on the horizon.

It was a place of indoctrination. While every soldier learned how his actions could save or cost the lives of the man in the next foxhole, the stakes for glider pilots brought personal pressure few others experienced. "There are no reserves in an airborne invasion. If you fail to deliver your load right on the spot, you may turn victory into failure and cause a needless sacrifice of life," stated their training manual.

King and others lived in a work camp environment so primitive that residents invited them into their homes for Christmas dinner. Rows of barracks were nearly identical to those constructed in Texas prisoner-of-war camps. Residents donated to a fundraising campaign for gas stoves to heat the students' dressing area. Once oil heating stoves were installed, spilled oil made the students' clothes smell like an auto-repair shop.

A month later, Claude Berry arrived. By then the AAF had taken two floors in the local hotel. Berry shared a room with two other glider students. They ate breakfast in the ground-floor diner with Glenn Miller playing in the background before climbing onto a bus for the ride to the airfield for each day's training.

Students with flying experience were checked out by instructors to determine their flying proficiency while those with no experience were taught to fly. A future glider pilot first faced thirty to forty hours' flight instruction, with an emphasis on approach patterns that were controlled by "s" turns and slips. Dead stick landings became the first tentative introduction to gliders. They were conducted in small aircraft with the engine turned off, anywhere from 500 to perhaps 3,000 feet off the ground. Instructors told their student pilots to reduce the throttle, cut the ignition, pull up into a partial stall to stop the propeller from windmilling, find the designated landing area below, and land safely – with no power – both in daylight and at night.

The AAF believed that when glider pilots mastered the ability to "land precisely on a chalk mark on the field, they developed excellent judgment of distances and gliding range, qualities essential to proper glider pilotage."[14]

The ground school component was more problematic. Its curriculum was not mandated. Offered as a guideline by the AAF, it left plenty of room for civilian instructors to focus on what they knew best. Flying. In addition, a shortage of instructors increased the teacher-to-student ratio and sometimes resulted in shortcuts, especially in the classroom, because the instructors were paid for student flights. Overall, the Air Forces deemed glider pilots' ground school in most early training programs as inadequate.

For many students, the next phase of training included soaring in sailplanes. But soaring is premised on gaining altitude, not landing. Staying in the air as long as possible, not setting down at the first opportunity. Sailplanes with a long glide slope of as much as 30:1 held little relevance for pilots whose combat mission would be to descend immediately in a glider with an approximate 9:1 glide ratio and a sink rate of 950 feet per minute (at 100 miles per hour).[15]

Regardless, Dale Oliver, a Kansas farm boy and aspiring artist, was among many students who thrilled at the sensitive flight characteristics of sailplanes that could exceed 100 miles per hour, once he crammed his six-foot, four-inch frame into the pilot's seat. Thermals in the California desert sent him soaring almost as if he were weightless. "It was the most thrilling time of my life," he recalled. "In calm air, you could stick your hand out and turn the sailplane."[16]

Sailplanes would have to suffice until the far heavier gliders designed for combat would become available. Historian Charles Day noted the disconnect between sailplane training and combat gliders which "were, rather, low-performance trailers that had to be towed to a point almost directly over the landing area, and once over the designated spot, the real piloting skills necessary to reach the ground quickly in one piece, took over, if one wanted to survive."[17] In fact, glider pilot Leon Spencer later wrote "any power pilot could step from the cockpit of a powered aircraft into the cockpit of a CG-4A glider and feel right at home at the flight controls after suitable transition training."[18]

The culmination of training would be conducted at elementary-advanced schools where students would fly combat gliders for the first time. Where "undershooting was a capital crime" and learning how to save altitude as long as possible and then drop "like an elevator" onto a field as quickly as possible was the ticket to survival. Some infantry training would follow, but an Air Forces directive made it clear glider pilots never would be considered combat troops. "The glider pilot will participate in ground combat only in exceptional circumstance or after his glider has been wrecked in landing." The directive also instructed training centers to provide ground combat instruction, even though the schools had neither the incentive nor the instructors for infantry training.[19]

It quickly became apparent that the pace of training dictated by the curriculum and school capacities would not produce the number of pilots General Arnold wanted. On May 30, only seventy trainees had been sent to the contracted flight schools at a time when the AAF needed to produce 3,000 glider pilots by September (while allowing for a twenty percent attrition rate).

The Training Command scrambled on several fronts. A recruitment program was launched, first directed at 85,000 Civil Aeronautics Administration Airman Certificate holders. Every Army command, station, and post in the United States also received materials announcing glider pilot training transfer opportunities. Recruiters began pointing out the glamour of gliders to young men who might not be fighter or bomber pilot candidates.

By midsummer, the glider pilot tide turned. Lower eligibility standards, graduation as flight officers instead of staff sergeants as originally established, and aggressive recruiting spawned new challenges as the enrollment ranks swelled. A shortage of instructors became so acute that some newly minted graduates became instructors. As sailplanes were deemed unsuitable for combat glider training, thousands of light aircraft made by Aeronca, Taylorcraft, and Piper were modified by removing their engines to make them facsimile gliders (with more relevant glider flight characteristics than sailplanes) until the combat gliders arrived. Tow planes, however, remained in short supply.

Meanwhile, the preliminary schools were producing more students than the elementary-advanced schools could accept. For three weeks, admission to preliminary schools was suspended as hundreds of trainees were sent to "holding pools" at various Army bases until elementary-advanced schools could take them. Morale sunk as young men eager for war were told to wait and were assigned what many considered "busy work." Where were the combat gliders they were expected to fly?

On June 20, 1942, it appeared the AAF finally had its combat glider after spending more than a year developing a training program, contemplating new airborne strategies, and beginning to train glider pilots whose qualifications kept changing and whose curriculum was far from settled. The first successful test flight of a fifteen-place glider took place that day, and it passed muster when it was towed from Wright Field in Ohio to Chanute Army Air Field in Illinois and back on a roundtrip of 220 air miles.

The Weaver Aircraft Company (later renamed "Waco") had delivered its CG-4A glider prototype. It largely was the work of a

Frenchman unknown outside aviation circles. Born in Paris, Alex Francis Arcier had studied aeronautics under Eiffel Tower designer Gustave Eiffel. He had emigrated to the US in 1919, had become a citizen, and one of America's foremost aviation design experts. Arcier designed the first twin-engine and four-engine bombers flown in the US, as well as America's first all-metal aircraft. He had worked at Weaver Aircraft for eleven years. As chief designer, he led what became known as the Waco glider design team.

The other three design firms that responded a year earlier to the design request for eight- and fifteen-passenger gliders with various cargo configurations had failed. The Frankfort Sailplane Company appeared to be better at designing training gliders than battlefield gliders. The St. Louis Aircraft Corporation submitted a prototype so unsatisfactory it had to be redesigned after testing. Prototypes from Bowlus Sailplanes, Inc. failed testing so badly that AAF personnel noted "the Bowlus organization appears to have displayed more talent for salesmanship than for the manufacture of gliders."[20] An inspection of the Bowlus facility by three brigadier generals and aviation engineers discovered its factory "turned out to be a small building formerly used as a dry-cleaning shop. The building was ... just large enough for one small model glider they have built to fit in sideways ... the visible equipment consisted of a couple of drafting tables, a few drawing instruments, and a couple of carpenter benches."[21]

Waco's success marked the end of a one-year rush to find a suitable glider design and the start of a race to get it into wartime production. Construction contracts were issued before the final testing of the CG-4A prototype was completed.

The manufacturers' mission was to build a squarish, motorless aircraft more than forty-eight feet long with a wingspan of nearly eighty-four feet. The wings sat atop the fuselage and were supported by external struts. The tail stood twelve feet off the ground. To save weight and because most metal was reserved for powered aircraft, most of the glider was covered with a doped-and-painted cotton fabric, supported by a steel tubing frame. A remarkably strong, honeycombed wood floor comprising more than 5,000 interlocked pieces measured approximately six feet by twelve feet. A pilot and copilot sat side by side in a three-sided Plexiglass cockpit that opened upward to unload cargo. Atop their cockpit, a bracket was used to attach a 350-foot nylon tow rope with a coiled interphone cable wrapped around it from a C-47 Skytrain.

The controls had little more sophistication than a go-kart. A glider pilot's foot pedals controlled the rudder and the brake. An instrument panel in the center included airspeed, rate-of-climb indicator, turn indicator, compass, and altimeter. Navigation and landing light switches were nearby. Overhead were trim tabs, a parachute release, and towline release. A spoiler control lever was on each pilot's outside hip and the steering wheel likely reminded farm boys of their dads' tractors at home.

In the back, twelve combat-ready glider troops sat shoulder to shoulder on four facing, removable benches and a thirteenth sat on a jump seat near the tail. Four round windows on each side were intended to reduce airsickness. Nearby were two escape hatches and doors on each side near the tail. The CG-4A could carry more than 3,700 pounds (equal to its weight) of combined glider troops, jeep, jeep trailer with supplies, 37mm or 75mm artillery, small bulldozer, medical supplies, ammunition, gasoline, and explosives.[22]

The glider's outward "flying tent" appearance was misleading. Comprising 70,000 parts and requiring about 7,000 hours of labor to build, the Army hoped to build it for $20,000 each, less than half the cost of a twin-engine C-47 Skytrain that towed gliders and carried paratroopers, cargo, and the wounded with a top speed approaching 230 miles per hour and with a range of 1,800 miles.

Including Waco, sixteen companies (with hundreds of subcontractors) signed contracts to manufacture the CG-4A. (Quantities ultimately produced ranged from one glider from one manufacturer to more than 4,000 from another.) Waco would provide the engineering data, production methods, and patent and design rights to the others. The manufacturers could send representatives to Waco to observe its production methods and agreed not to pirate any Waco employees. Waco received $250 for each glider the others produced.[23]

Overall, however, the group of contractors was not qualified to meet General Arnold's buildup of a glider corps. Only four possessed relevant experience and just two (Ford Motor Company and Cessna Aircraft Company) had existing production facilities and organizations capable of large-scale aircraft production. Cessna was an exception to the directive that the builders of power aircraft for the AAF could not allocate resources for glider construction. Further, in the AAF's rush to get the first gliders into production and delivered first by Cessna to the glider schools by August 1942, the Army assigned a top priority for the supplies and equipment needed by Cessna.

Four of the contractors had no aircraft-manufacturing experience. From the outset it became evident they had no business building gliders. Seven months after it signed its contract, National Aircraft had only eighty-seven production employees. Ultimately it produced a single glider at a cost of more than $1.7 million.[24] Several months into its production contract, Robertson Aircraft managers were accused of "gross mismanagement," of being "torn by jealousies," and of "a lack of authority that is disgraceful."[25] Babcock Aircraft tried to build gliders in a rented circus tent until a Florida storm destroyed it. Florida's humidity led to a ninety-five percent failure rate of tested parts. Ward Furniture Company managed to build only seven gliders at a cost of about $308,000 each.[26] Conversely, however, one of the best producers of gliders proved to be the Gibson Refrigerator Company that had taken steps years earlier to prepare for military equipment production.

Each builder wove a network of subcontractors and suppliers experienced to varying degrees in wood, steel tubing, or product manufacturing that included Steinway & Sons (tail and wing assemblies), H.J. Heinz Pickle Company (wings), and Gardner Metal Products (a casket maker now fabricating metal fittings) and a host of wood-product manufacturers such as Villaume Box and Lumber Company, in St. Paul, Minnesota.

Northwestern Aeronautical Corporation was formed by three Michigan lawyers expressly for the purpose of subcontracting glider construction to Villaume and others. Villaume was typical of several wood-product subcontractors in the glider program. It quickly expanded its workforce, hiring employees with diverse backgrounds that included an ordained minister, orchestra leader, violin maker, chiropractor, undertaker, palm reader, teacher, and bartender, among others. A large percentage were women, who finished exterior surfaces by hand. AAF inspectors noted Villaume production became so efficient that Northwestern's glider assembly contractor had difficulty keeping pace. Villaume ultimately produced more than $25 million worth of glider parts, glider crates, and ordnance boxes built by 1,500 employees working in three shifts, six days a week.[27]

Ford Motor Company's vast automobile mass-production experience enabled it to convert a station wagon plant into a pioneering glider plant and quickly retrain thousands of workers. Three connected buildings near Iron Mountain, Michigan, held woodworking machinery, kilns, painting rooms, and glider assembly areas. Ford engineers developed a method that reduced wood components' glue-drying time from up to eight hours to only ten minutes by using waste steam. Ford ultimately delivered twice as many gliders as any other contractor and did so at a cost of approximately $15,400 each, the only contractor to surpass the Army's goal of $20,000 per glider.[28]

Training for Gunter, Andrews, Larkin, Goldman, and thousands of others could not proceed without the combat gliders Ford and others were scrambling to build. Cessna was expected to deliver the first gliders on August 10 but delayed their arrival to September 1. Cessna was not alone in failing to meet near-impossible manufacturing deadlines for a never-before-seen aircraft whose production plan and management were severely fragmented.

Some glider builders claimed Waco's engineering documents were inaccurate. Waco struggled to accommodate hordes of representatives from other builders observing Waco's production methods. Government indecisiveness on who could produce specialized tools required to build components slowed the process. Several glider manufacturers were already behind on pre-existing contract schedules. The desired interchangability of parts between manufacturers was considered "deplorable" by one Army inspector. Obtaining specific raw materials proved difficult in many cases, even though the gliders' production priority had been elevated from Group VI to Group I, the same priority as four-engine heavy bombers.[29]

Cessna – the only experienced aircraft manufacturer of the group – delivered only thirty-two gliders in September and 223 in October, out of the contracted deliverable of 1,500. As other manufacturers struggled as well, the prospect of making up the shortfall, plus another 1,500 by December 31, appeared dim.[30]

By the end of the year, the contract schools had graduated nearly 6,000 students from primary training programs and, overall, there were more than 10,000 students in the training pipeline, despite students learning that the AAF expected a fifty percent casualty rate in battle.[31]

James Ferrin was among them. Months earlier, he had ridden his horse, Old Red, across an eastern Arizona desert covered with saguaro cactus among dozens of old mines with names like Buster, Cat's Paw, and Dollar Bill to a neighboring farm outside Pima where his friend Gene lived. Farms and ranches defined Pima, along with a café that served burgers and beer. It was owned by a man Ferrin called "Chink" who also was the town mayor and president of the local draft board. One day "Chink" told James he would be drafted in a few weeks.

Like many young men at the time, the two friends agreed that it would be better that they both enlist if either one knew he was about to be drafted. James and Gene enlisted with an Army recruiter a few days later and told their girlfriends immediately "so we could get as much tender loving care as possible before we had to leave for the Army." Soon they were on a train bound for Fort Bliss in the Texas desert. Other than beating the draft by enlisting, Ferrin's ambition was modest when he wrote "there was about as much chance of me becoming [an officer] as there was for a snowstorm in Phoenix in July."

He simply wanted to fly but washed out of cadet school after his instructor had reportedly written "Ferrin is not well coordinated, and is occasionally dangerous in the air, not only to himself but also to others. It is recommended that he does not continue as a flying cadet." He was transferred to radio operator school and then to the Waco Army Air Base in central Texas. He hated it. When Ferrin spotted a flyer promoting the glider pilot program and noted cadet washouts could be accepted, he jumped at it. His training ultimately would take him to Lubbock on his way to combat in Europe.[32]

The wind nearly always blew tumbleweeds across the parched badlands of the Dust Bowl in west Texas. Daily springtime winds in Lubbock could reach fifty miles per hour and persist the entire day. Dust storms punctuated the brutal summer heat, followed by thunderstorms that flooded and turned the red soil into a quagmire.

But where farmers had given up, townspeople saw an opportunity in 1942. In April Lubbock's city council leased its municipal airport for one dollar a year to the Army for use as a training base. About 200 miles to the north the following month, Dalhart's mayor, hotel owner, and chamber of commerce manager successfully concluded a campaign to buy 3,000 acres and offer them to the AAF for a training airfield.

Construction began at a gold rush pace that summer before students and the CG-4As appeared in the fall. By the end of September, 225 structures were built at what became known as the South Plains Army Air Field (SPAAF) in Lubbock. At Dalhart, three runways were built, along with barracks, streets, and utility lines.

While the training headquarters for Dalhart consisted of tents in Amarillo, a tent city for students at SPAAF was necessary for several weeks. Thunderstorm flooding made life miserable until tarpaper barracks were built. They were so flimsy that students periodically had to hold onto ropes thrown over the barracks to keep their roofs from flying off. Attempts to plant trees largely were folly as some grew at a back-breaking angle away from the persistent winds.

Glider students had been training for months at several schools around the country before arriving at Dalhart and Lubbock around September. Until enough CG-4As arrived for training, boredom became the enemy. Work details planting trees, hauling dirt in wheelbarrows, and building sidewalks had to suffice. Discipline also had to be maintained. Those who overslept faced the prospect of carrying their bedding the rest of the day. "Walking tours" imposed for other infractions included lugging a fifty-pound field pack on laps around the parade ground.

CG-4A gliders began to arrive at preliminary-advanced schools located primarily in the southwest and Texas in the fall of 1942. Training for war at SPAAF and Dalhart finally could begin in earnest. Students quickly realized that flying a CG-4A was significantly different than steering a sailplane or a modified light aircraft with no engine, to say nothing of the nuances and dangers of being towed by and then releasing from a massive C-47 or C-53 tow plane and immediately turning toward the ground.

John Butler had grown up on his family's farm in Delaware, had purchased a Piper Cub, and favored startling townspeople with low-altitude loops and rolls. He had worked in a glider tow-rope factory before joining the Air Corps a month following the Pearl Harbor attack. Six months later, he transferred to the glider program. He earned his wings at Dalhart, but it would be months before he was sent to Europe. Like many glider pilot students and graduates, he continued to train prior to deployment. Witnessing death sometimes was part of that training.

One night a glider's tow rope prematurely broke free of the tow plane. The glider pilot carrying infantry troops had no points of reference in the darkness as he descended toward the closest open patch of ground. "The pilot of the glider couldn't see the ground below ... and when the pilot made his approach for his landing, his approach was in the woods. When a person stands on the ground and listens to a ship go into the woods at night, it's a lonely sound," Butler recorded in his diary.[33]

Sherfy Randolph left college to volunteer for the glider corps. After several stops, he reached Dalhart in late in 1942 and learned the dangers of the combat glider. Glider instructors explained that if a tow rope snapped, it flew back into the glider and sometimes shattered the cockpit or tore holes in the fuselage. Worse, it might wrap itself around the glider's control surfaces or the wheels. Glider pilots often died when that happened.

One of Dalhart's instructors was Flight Officer Bradford Root. He had enlisted in New Jersey in 1941 and had been known as a snappy dresser who wore his hat at a rakish angle, was fun-loving, athletic, and had wanted to be a pilot almost from boyhood. He looked older than his age and had done well during flight training. Root became an instructor upon graduation.

Only two weeks later, he took a group of students up one night on a training flight. Shortly after takeoff, the tow rope broke. Too low and slow to return to the airfield, Root had one option. Clear the fence at the end of the base and land on the vacant prairie that stretched ahead. Root had nearly set the glider down when a cinderblock building, the only structure seemingly for miles, appeared in his path. His glider slammed into the slaughterhouse. Root and four of the men he carried were killed. Two others were injured.

Far from enemy territory, learning to fly combat gliders in America was becoming a dangerous proposition. Yet young men persevered to earn the right to pin wings on their chest that were emblazoned with a "G" in the center. "It really doesn't stand for Glider," many said, "The G is for Guts."

In a few months, a handful of glider pilots would lead the glider corps' entry into war. They were destined to become part of a disaster at sea so horrific that it would threaten any future use of gliders in combat.

"Prepare to Ditch"

The Sicilian night was angry.

A boisterous wind roiled an ocean that sparkled under the Germans' star shells. They seemed to hang in the air, like street lights illuminating the Allied gliders' incoming path. In between, enemy searchlights swept back and forth, akin to a policeman's flashlight, looking for the airborne intruders.

A curtain of antiaircraft and tracer fire ahead on the gliders' approach in the predawn hours on July 10, 1943, marked the start of the first major Allied airborne battle for Europe.

A battle of nerves.

"We can't go in … release!"

"Man, we're gonna land in the water."

"That's too bad. Either you release or we're gonna release you."

With blood flowing from shrapnel that had sliced his face and leg, Flight Officer Guy Gunter flinched as the C-47's tow rope rocketed back toward his glider's cockpit. His British glider pilot, Sergeant Smith, had about a second to release his end of the rope and begin his turn down toward the whitecaps. They would never reach their landing zone on Sicily.

Not far away, Flight Officer Michael Samek and his British pilot, Vic Taylor, were not going to wait for their tow pilot to release them. The pilot had already changed course to avoid tracer fire and had flashed his navigation lights, telling them to release their glider. They were unable to see land as a headwind bullied their glider.

They could release and take control of their glider or wait for the tow plane pilot to release and then react. Taylor punched the overhead release lever. The glider swung free, turned toward land, but dropped too fast toward the sea. The infantry troops they carried opened the escape hatches, shed the heavy equipment they wore, gripped steel tubing, and waited.

The glider's nose dug into the ocean as if it were wet sand. It plunged below the surface as the sea crashed through the bottom of the cockpit and surged into the fuselage. The glider began to settle. Perhaps the wings atop the fuselage would keep it from sinking to the bottom of the sea.

Nearby, Flight Officers Arnold Bordewich, Kenny White, Paul Rau, and other American glider copilots pressed ahead through enemy searchlight sweeps, antiaircraft flak, and machine gun fire. At almost the same time, some of the Allied ships offshore turned their guns toward them as their gliders and paratrooper transports passed overhead. They flew less than 1,000 feet above the ocean, through deadly crossfire from German, Italian, and even Allied naval guns.

Sicily beckoned the Allies in 1943 following their victory in North Africa in May. Its thirty airfields two miles off Italy's southern coast that had plagued the Allies for three years in Africa would be key to invading Italy and to taking the Italians out of the war. But the mountainous island the size of Vermont was defended by an estimated 230,000 German and Italian troops.

Codenamed Operation *Husky*, an amphibious landing force of more than 2,500 ships would be supported by three nights of paratrooper assaults and glider missions. An established road system enabling the enemy mobility, mountainous terrain, and sand bars made it a dangerous and potentially disastrous amphibious proposition.

On the night of July 9, more than 225 aircraft would deliver more than 2,000 paratroopers of the 82nd Airborne Division inland, designated *Husky I*.

The next morning, two amphibious landings would take place. Elements of General Bernard Montgomery's Eighth Army would make the primary attack on the southeast coast and advance north toward the port city of Syracuse. Meanwhile, General George Patton's Seventh Army would come ashore on the south coast and advance in a northerly direction across the island toward Palermo. From there, he would turn east along Sicily's northern coast and link up with Montgomery's forces near Messina on the northeastern tip of the island. At that point, the Germans and Italians would face surrender or retreat off the island to Italy.

But the linkup would take place only if Montgomery's force could first reach Syracuse after coming ashore. Troops and combat supplies delivered by gliders were critical to seizing the Ponte Grande Bridge over the Anapo River in a southern Syracuse suburb in advance of Montgomery's approach. Failure to quickly seize the bridge could slow the Allied assault and cost lives. The gliders' mission – codenamed Operation *Ladbroke* – was critical to the Allies' first major invasion in Europe.

Once the beachheads were secured, another parachute regiment would be dropped onto the battlefield in *Husky II*. Gliders would begin flying supply missions to captured airfields. Then in the final phase, Operation *Fustian*, a 135-aircraft airborne mission would include nineteen gliders delivering artillerymen, artillery, and jeeps.

Operation *Husky* had been in the works for more than six months. A detachment of 110 American glider pilots had arrived in Egypt on February 1 after a six-week voyage aboard the SS *Mariposa*, a converted luxury liner carrying 5,000 troops. Two months later, half of them had been transferred to Casablanca to supervise the CG-4A gliders' arrival and assembly, and then ferry them to six Tunisian airfields. The other half would prepare those gliders for the resupply flights to Sicily from Tunisia.

The glider pilots were awaiting their gliders' arrival when General Montgomery shocked nearly everyone by changing the battle plan. British glider pilots now would spearhead the assault the first night by carrying glider infantry troops and supporting equipment. Their objective would be to seize the Ponte Grande Bridge to enable

General Montgomery's troops to advance north. To do so, British glider pilots would have to take off a few hours before sunset in Africa in unproven gliders, fly across the Mediterranean through the night, cross over the Allied fleet in the dark, release from their tow aircraft thousands of yards offshore, and descend through enemy artillery fire toward their landing zones inland. Paratroopers would follow an hour later in the US sector.

A more dangerous plan for gliders could hardly be conceived. Gliders that had never flown in combat by pilots who were equally inexperienced. A handful of American volunteers could determine if General Arnold's vision for combat gliders would become reality or folly.

British Major General George Hopkinson, commander of the 1st Airborne Division, delivered the news of Montgomery's glider decision to Lieutenant Colonel George Chatterton who commanded the British 1st Battalion Glider Pilot Regiment.

Shock and concern washed across Chatterton's face. He believed a glider pilot should be as fully trained and equally proficient as a combat soldier. But this mission smelled of suicide. There were far too few British gliders and not enough tow planes for a single lift, forcing a series of airborne missions over several days. In addition, Chatterton was short of pilots and those he had in Africa had not flown in months.

He would have to rely on American personnel to train his pilots in American gliders that would be towed by American aircraft. The American glider pilots had not flown in combat and only some of his tow plane crews had flown missions in the recent North Africa campaign. He would have only a few weeks for the recently graduated American glider pilots to train his men. Strangers would have to become a cohesive combat unit quickly. And some of those Americans would need to volunteer as copilots to fill out Chatterton's British glider pilot ranks.

Chatterton had a choice: accept the new battle plan or risk being replaced. Chatterton got to work on the new plan.

Meanwhile, Major General Matthew Ridgway, who commanded the Americans' 82nd Airborne Division and who was a believer in gliders, had similar concerns. Not only did he think the night glider mission should be changed to a daytime mission, but he also had serious reservations about Montgomery deciding the Americans would tow the gliders to Sicily. The 51st Air Wing had no experience in towing gliders. Further, every plane towing a glider was a plane unavailable to deliver more than two dozen combat-ready paratroopers or three tons of supplies to an inland objective. The gliders' route over the Allied invasion fleet offshore in the dark reeked of friendly-fire risk. But his appeal for mission changes to General Dwight Eisenhower's Allied Command headquarters was denied.

Conversion training from the British Horsa gliders to the American gliders could not begin without the CG-4As. The Horsa glider dwarfed the CG-4A and was less maneuverable. It carried twenty-eight passengers or more than 7,000 pounds of cargo. The Horsa was as long as a B-24 bomber. Horsas were the ponderous big brothers of the nimbler CG-4As.

Although 500 CG-4A gliders had been shipped to Africa by April 23, most still were not yet ready to fly in mid-May. Logistics personnel apparently had routed glider crates haphazardly to various ports, bases, and depots. Assemblers found they did not always have everything necessary to complete a glider's assembly. The five shipping crates containing a glider might be in hand, but the five crates containing its components had been shipped separately and were elsewhere. Specialized tools to complete assembly often were missing as well.

And for those who had all the parts they needed, glider assembly carried a low priority. At one base, about twenty-five gliders ready for assembly were assigned to one officer and twenty enlisted personnel. Assembly proceeded at a snail's pace for a glider that required six men working an entire week to complete assembly. In addition, many of the early arriving gliders now suffered from lackadaisical maintenance in the brutal North African desert. By May 25, only thirty of 240 gliders were operational.

But when it was announced the gliders would lead the Sicily campaign, the Army bureaucracy mobilized. Assembly became a top priority only a few weeks prior to the mission. By mid-June, nearly 350 gliders were airworthy, enough for training and operational needs.

But invaluable training days had slipped away before practice maneuvers finally began in mid-June. "I think we lost three in the drink last night," wrote 2nd Lieutenant Ellsworth Dewberry. "I thought that would finish that crazy bullshit about night landings coming in from the sea. But then along came the British and the invasion of Sicily, and I'll be goddamned if those silly bastards weren't serious all along."[1] Only two daytime rehearsals of more than fifty aircraft were conducted, with the gliders spaced two minutes apart as they landed at airfields. By the time the gliders were moved to their Tunisian fields in early July, the British pilots had accumulated about four-and-a-half hours of flight time in learning the differences between the Horsas and CG-4As.

Months earlier, a call had gone out to the American glider pilots that volunteers were needed for a mystery mission. Some were said to have drawn straws, others raised their hands, and others had reported to their commanding officer when they saw a note on a bulletin board. Ultimately forty-two American glider pilots volunteered for mission training. Later, twenty-two of them received assignments to fly as copilots in Operation *Ladbroke*, the first night's glider mission in Operation *Husky*. As time had run out for more training, their inexperience might have cast a pall on the prospects of the mission, if it were not for an undercurrent of optimism and, in some quarters, an eagerness for combat.

Many combat pilot teams train together for weeks, even months, before a major mission. Each had to know what the other was thinking and what his instincts would command in every possible emergency. A mission could be jeopardized if either hesitated, misread the other, or simply paused for an extra second of uncertainty. Or they could die.

Shortly before takeoff, British glider pilot Victor Taylor was already sitting in his cockpit seat when Michael Samek approached his glider that shuddered in nearly gale-force winds, an ominous backdrop to the coming mission. Samek climbed aboard and settled in, without a word.

An Austrian native, Samek had moved to the US only four years earlier. He had volunteered for American military service in 1941. As a shortage of glider pilots had developed, Samek graduated the first glider pilot class that did not require its students to previously hold a pilot's license.

Taylor, on the other hand, had completed a more robust British training program that included combat training. He had first tried to get into Britain's air corps, but there had been a waiting list. So, he had reported to an infantry training camp and then for Signals training. He ultimately had been assigned what he came to believe was the best job in the British Army, battalion dispatch rider (on a motorcycle). But when openings in the air corps training program appeared, he jumped at the chance for a transfer.

Like many glider pilot/copilot tandems in future missions, Samek and Taylor were total strangers.

Samek had learned at *Ladbroke*'s morning briefing that he would be flying with Taylor in glider number thirteen. He had looked forward to the mission as he waited to report to his glider. Days earlier, rumors had swept through the ranks. The Europe invasion was on. Greece? Sicily? Mainland Italy? Samek and most of the others did not care. Full of confidence coated with braggadocio, it was, he believed, the first step toward Rome and then Berlin. That was all that mattered, after at least a year's worth of training, transfers, more training, waiting, and still more training and waiting.

He would be among the 144 gliders on the mission. Several American copilots would be bunched near the middle of the takeoffs in Tunisia and presumably would be within sight of one another as they flew into enemy fire. Others would fly farther back in the airborne force. They harbored no hope of surprise when they reached their landing zones.

Some shared a brief greeting with their British counterparts when they reached their gliders while others, like Samek, simply nodded. Sometimes last-minute changes took place as the pilot teams prepared to take off in gusting winds that were driving walls of desert dust the color of a stone wall. Flight Officer Ruby Dees's British pilot, a fellow named Leadbetter, asked him to fly the glider, given Dees's experience. He agreed, even though the glider would be battered by winds approaching forty knots, nearly half the strength of a major hurricane.

Many pilots double-checked their cargo or glider infantry before strapping in. They knew a well-secured and perfectly balanced load was critical to getting off the ground, much less flying across the Mediterranean in brutal wind. Sometimes heavier glider infantrymen were asked to swap seats with smaller men to help balance a glider's load. Flight Officer Bob Wilson found a trailer lashed down in his glider filled with canvas bags, tags, and wood crosses. They were supplies for those who would die in a few hours.[2]

Some of the volunteers not tapped to fly were furiously disappointed. "If they pull this invasion and don't count me in on it, they can take the whole Army and shove it," wrote 2nd Lieutenant William Knickerbocker in his diary the day before the mission. When he learned he was not on the list to fly in Operation *Ladbroke*, Knickerbocker offered $100 cash to anyone who would let him take his place on the mission list. "Those that might have been willing to accept this offer couldn't afford to sell out because of the loss of face," Knickerbocker wrote.[3]

As the glider pilots prepared for takeoff, the tow aircraft crews did the same. At another Tunisian airfield, navigator Paul Gale approached his C-47 Skytrain that would soon tow a glider across the Mediterranean. As he leaned into the wind he knew the mission was in trouble before the first engine fired off. Gale's coordinates for the release point of his plane's glider over Sicily were based on winds less than one-fourth of the Tunisian gusts. If the weather over Sicily was anything like what Gale now faced, his glider would never get close to its objective in the absence of high-wind release coordinates. It might not even make it ashore.

At about 1848 hours on July 9, gliders began lifting off their runways, seconds ahead of their C-47s reaching flight speed. Ninety minutes later, they were all airborne. Once the C-47s assembled in their grouped formations over their airfields (called "serials"), they began their 200-mile leg to Malta, only a few hundred feet above the ocean to avoid enemy radar. After a sharp left turn to the north, Sicily would be only seventy miles away.

Almost immediately, adjustments had to be made. Dees could feel heaviness in his glider's right wing and tail. He shifted some of his glider infantry to one side and had the biggest men move forward. Other pilots faced far more dire complications. Six C-47s returned to their airfields when their gliders' loads shifted. One returned to base when the jeep in its glider broke free. Farther out to sea, three gliders broke loose from their tow planes and vanished without a trace. Two other C-47s got lost and turned back toward Africa. The mission was losing gliders with the enemy still hundreds of miles away.

The remaining British and American glider pilots found themselves atop a veritable rodeo bronc. Gale winds, sea spray, and prop wash from their tow planes knocked them about, forcing many to take turns at the glider controls with sweat-slick hands in a tag team battle against fatigue. The glider infantry sitting on benches in mostly windowless, darkened glider fuselages suffered from a mix of airsickness, persistent queasiness, relentless sweating, nerves, and fear. Several men had worn out the bottoms of their paper airsickness bags after eating tinned herring sandwiches before takeoff. If any were complaining about how their anti-nausea pills weren't doing any good, it was impossible to hear them.

British Lieutenant Arthur Royall was not happy sitting in the back of Guy Gunter's glider. Only half his platoon fitted in the CG-4A, the other half in another glider. Had they been flying a larger British Horsa glider, the entire platoon and its supplies would have been together and ready for immediate combat, assuming they survived a landing zone that was small, rock strewn, and bordered by stone walls.

Meanwhile, like dozens of other C-47/glider tandems, navigator Gale discovered the intercom system between his C-47 and its glider's cockpit was not working. Apparently, the intercom wire wrapped around the tow rope had been damaged when it was dragged during takeoff or had broken when the tow line had stretched under tension. Now the tow plane's crew had to fly in tandem for more than four hours across the Mediterranean at night through the remnants of a storm with outdated release coordinates and no way to talk to one another.[4]

Samek and the other Americans unwittingly had become test pilots on their first mission. They trailed along helplessly when their C-47s sometimes drifted dangerously off course as their crews searched for the navigation beacons on the island of Malta. Gale had little more than a magnetic compass to keep his tow plane on course to its release point. His drift meter would have been helpful, but that required visual contact with known landmarks. The cloud cover made that impossible.[5]

As the stream of tow planes finally approached the Sicilian coast, aircraft overtook some of the formation's lead planes that struggled. Gale's pilot and others quickly gained altitude, creating a layered formation to avoid collisions. Meanwhile, their crews peered through the darkness, hoping to spot Cape Ognina and Cape Murro di Porco that marked the southwest and southeast boundaries of their release points off Sicily's southern coast. Two parallel glide paths between the capes would take the glider pilots straight toward enemy strongpoints with antiaircraft batteries on three sides of their approach.

After hours of flight, the arrival timing of too many tow planes had been thrown off and too many were changing their approach routes at the last second, so that too few remained on course and on time. The glider pilots' designated release point of 3,000 yards from shore guaranteed a long, slow approach into the enemy's crosshairs. Including the distance to their landing zones inland, the glider pilots faced an approximate two-mile, low-altitude approach to their objective – assuming their gliders were released where and when they should be.

"What do you want me to do?" the C-47 pilot asked his navigator.

"You've got to move up," said Gale.

"Well, I can't move up. There are planes over me, there are planes under me, there are planes alongside of me."

"If you move up, they will move up because everyone is flying on everybody else. Otherwise, cut [the glider] loose here. We might as well drown here if we are going to drown. Do you want me to go back and get a boat? Stuff it!"[6]

Gale's pilot added altitude as the C-47 pressed ahead. Others were equally anxious to cut their gliders loose.

"You see those fireworks ahead? I believe you're close enough."

His tow pilot's message over the intercom was hardly necessary. Flight Officer Irvin Kinney knew the enemy's artillery barrages meant that he was nearing Sicily's coastline and that he had no chance for a surprise landing.

The shore was invisible in the darkness, despite the exploding antiaircraft fire and the enemy's searchlights on both sides of his approach. He could barely make out the mountaintops on the far side of the island, but not much else. When his British pilot released from the C-47, the glider slowed from 100 miles per hour nearly to stall speed. That would cost precious gliding distance.

Kinney and the others now crossed through a cauldron of exploding flashes and swarms of flak on all sides, doomed to ditching at sea.

Descending through flashes on both sides, Kinney hit the water tail first nearly within sight of the beach. The ocean cascaded into the glider through window openings and an emergency door, so fast that Kinney was underwater before he could release his seatbelt. One by one, the pilots and glider infantry popped up at the surface as the glider settled to its wings.

As a searchlight found his glider and the enemy began firing tracers in Kinney's direction, his tow plane turned back toward Tunisia.

Up ahead, Samek and Taylor could see Flight Officer Kenneth Hollinshead's glider as everyone prepared for release. A flash startled Samek. *What was that?* Samek's friend Kenny White had taken off from the same airfield only three gliders ahead of Samek. *Had something happened to White? Or Hollinshead? Maybe one of the other gliders?* Ninety-eight gliders had taken off ahead of Samek so he couldn't be sure. Focusing on his tow plane remained Samek's priority.

The American glider pilots quickly learned they were at the mercy of their tow plane crews, particularly those pilots who perhaps fought a private war with their nerves.

"Get ready to release!"

"Bullshit, we're not even close to the LZ [landing zone]! We haven't even crossed the beach for Chrissakes."

"You either release now, or we're going to release you!"

The last thing Samek and Taylor wanted to see was a 350-foot nylon tow rope (or the bracket attaching the rope to the tow plane) flying toward their cockpit if the C-47 released it from its tail prematurely. It could wrap around a glider's wings or tail and turn it into a flying brick. Or it could remain attached to the glider's nose and wreak havoc when the glider crash-landed.

Samek and Taylor decided to release their end of the tow rope almost right away when they saw the plane flashing its navigation lights, the signal to get ready to detach. The glider pilots could not see land and knew the tow plane pilot had changed course shortly before the release. Worse, the howling offshore wind had made it a certainty that they would have to ditch at sea and get their glider infantry out before the glider filled with water. Ditching protocols became critical to their survival.

"Everyone, get your gear off. Anything that's heavy. Get those escape hatches open."

Taylor and Samek worked to hold the glider steady, letting it drop toward the whitecaps. It came to a quick stop when its nose dug into the two- and three-foot swells, its tail rising briefly and then settling into the ocean. Samek later reflected it had been a remarkably smooth landing under the circumstances. Then again, it had been the first time he had landed at sea. But the plywood at Samek's feet had split on impact. The sea began to fill the glider. The water level rose as the infantry troops pushed through the incoming current at the escape hatches. Before long, only about a foot of trapped air remained in the fuselage.

Samek kicked through the fuselage fabric near the cockpit and scrambled up onto a wing as others clambered out into the dark sea. Taylor was not far behind. Fortunately, the glider appeared to be floating. Soon its crew and most of the glider infantry found handholds and relied on their inflated lifebelts (little more than "water wings," reflected one soldier later) or climbed as best they could onto the wings' top side.

Six men were missing. Were they still in the waterlogged fuselage? Several had been airsick in the hours leading up to the crash. Inside, the fuselage was slick in some places with vomit. Perhaps they had been too weak and had drowned only feet from the benches where they had sat.

The fuselage now floated just below the surface as dozens of other gliders descended, as if they were giant, spent flat-winged dragonflies drifting down toward a creek and oblivion.

Samek, Taylor, and their infantry now faced a new enemy. Exposure. When the clouds broke, the setting quarter moon dimly revealed the coast about three miles away. It would be a long swim into a headwind toward enemy positions. They could swim toward shore in a race against exhaustion or stay with the glider and hope it would stay afloat long enough to give them a chance at being rescued after sunrise. Taylor decided to stay with the men and wait to be spotted. An infantry officer and Samek decided to take their chances and paddle toward the beach.

Samek recalled:

I had the idea to swim to shore... I kept the canteen and a tube of condensed milk. I started in the direction of the shore as I remember[ed] it. Before too long, I saw another glider maybe thirty or forty yards away... I swam to it and noticed someone, totally submerged in the left pilot's seat. I was convinced that I could recognize [Flight Officer] Joe Capite, one of my squadron mates, in the dim moonlight, probably because I saw an ammo bandoleer over his shoulder and I knew that Joe had insisted on carrying a Thompson [submachine gun] and ammunition.[7]

As he swam toward shore, Samek spotted another glider with men sitting on it. He realized he lacked the strength to reach the beach, assuming he had not already drifted far off course. He decided to stay with the second glider through the night.

"Here's where you get off," the tow plane pilot suddenly told Kenny White and his British glider pilot, Lieutenant Stevens.

White's tow plane pilot had promised to inform him of their position prior to releasing the glider. That became impossible more than ten miles from shore when the pilot abandoned his straight-line course for Sicily and "made several sharp turns, climbed, dived, and made things very difficult for us," White later reported. Yet the flak was still five miles away.

When his glider was released, White could not see Sicily's coast. Stevens set the glider down into the rolling waves. Emergency exits were opened and the infantry and crew clambered out and found handholds on the floating glider. Two, though, were missing. Little could be done for them as the glider began to break up. Each man searched for a floating piece he hoped would keep his head above water until dawn. But not everyone could wait.

Hands stiffened and hopes dimmed after several hours spent gripping glider flotsam in the surprisingly cold ocean. Three men began swimming toward a ship they had spotted far off on the blurred horizon. White did not think they would make it through the waves. Not long after, another soldier lost his war with fright. He began drinking sea water, became delirious, and swam away. He, too, was never seen again. White hung on with the others, riding up, over, and down each wave, waiting for daybreak.[8]

Some glider pilots like Paul Rau carried particularly critical passengers. Half of a battalion's headquarters staff sat in his thirteen-passenger glider. British glider pilot William Buchan was at the controls when he released from a tow plane that had made several course corrections and now was on an incorrect approach in a glider with an intercom that had ceased working. Rau estimated his glider was two-and-a-half miles offshore at 1,400 feet as it turned toward the beach and a maze of searchlights and antiaircraft fire.

"Prepare to ditch," announced Buchan. Few heard him in the rear of the glider. The forward emergency doors were jettisoned, but the rear doors remained locked at impact. Everyone climbed out of the glider once it settled in the sea, amid a floating glider graveyard.

Not far away, Lieutenant Colonel George Chatterton, the commander of the British Glider Pilot Regiment who had opposed the glider battle plan, floated alongside his glider. Nearby, three other senior commanding officers of the airborne assault force awaited rescue as well.

Guy Gunter's glider had shuddered from artillery near-misses just before it hit the water with a resounding thump, knocking the British pilot unconscious. The sea filled the cockpit, the water level rising to the pilot's chest and soaking a deep leg wound Gunter had suffered. After Gunter had pulled himself free of the glider, the British pilot came to and reached for his commando dagger to cut a hole in the glider's roof. He couldn't risk swimming back into the glider toward an emergency door that might be jammed shut.

"Here he is!" Several men pulled him up onto the top of the fuselage. He had survived, but had left his equipment in the waterlogged glider, including a flask of whisky. Another man had lost his glasses and his lifebelt had failed to inflate. His buddies began grabbing him when waves threatened to wash him off a wing when he became exhausted. Meanwhile, some began to assess their options as they scrambled from a wing to the tail and back again when each began to submerge.

"We want to swim ashore," some of them told the British colonel who was among the passengers now holding onto the glider.

"I can't say that. What do you think, lieutenant?" Gunter was surprised when a colonel asked him for advice.

"If they can make it, let 'em go." Three men headed toward shore, betting they could beat both wind and tide.

Countless others – glider crews and the men they carried – who were stranded atop their gliders faced a similar decision as searchlights swept the sea's surface and locked onto glider silhouettes. The first Allied glider mission of World War II had become a disaster.

Like so many others in the first few hours of July 10, Arnold Bordewich faced a gut-wrenching decision as he clung to floating glider debris. How does a man save his life? He could trust in God and prayer. Or assess and then act. *The Old Crow is pretty torn up. Is she going to sink to the bottom? Maybe I should start out now and hope the waves and tide push me in the right direction before my arms give out.* His decision might depend upon whether he was a man whose instincts to take charge and assume responsibility, regardless of rank, trumped his faith. *Some of the guys look like they're in bad shape. What if some of them want to go with me? And what happens if one of 'em can't make it? What do I do then? Gotta settle on a plan. Make a decision.* Perhaps it would boil down to whether Bordewich could ignore the danger – even the prospect of death – by believing he could recast long odds into opportunity.

Meanwhile, for those who made landfall, the enemy imposed a different set of odds of survival.

An enemy machine gunner almost missed Flight Officer Samuel Fine seconds after Fine veered into a tree with his left wing to spin to a quick stop before hitting a stone wall. Somehow the antiaircraft fire had been relatively light as his glider approached its landing zone. At the request of his British pilot, Lofty Wilkner, Fine had flown the glider across the Mediterranean, had argued with his tow pilot on when, where, and at what altitude the glider would be released, and then had selected the field where they had set down.

Before he could release his seat belt, two bullets grazed Fine's shoulder. Another hit one of the glider's soldiers in his lower back. The others returned fire, enabling the pilots and remaining soldiers to disengage and head toward their objective, the Ponte Grande Bridge about two miles away.

The only other American glider pilots to make landfall were Flight Officers Morris Kyle and Russell Parks. Kyle landed nearly three miles from his landing zone while Parks was able to join Fine on the way to the bridge. Parks's glider pilot also had argued with his tow plane crew which had diverted to a route over Syracuse Harbor on the east coast where the antiaircraft fire was even more sustained than on the approach route from the south. British glider pilot Jack Barnwell had come in too fast and had slammed through two stone walls and trees before coming to a rest, partially blocking a dirt road. By Sicily standards, that was a successful landing as Parks and the others climbed out and joined Fine's group. When enemy fire from an inland lighthouse threatened their advance, Parks and some of the men attacked while Fine and the remaining infantry bypassed the skirmish and pressed ahead.

When they reached the bridge, Fine discovered that British paratroopers had seized it and had cut wires leading to explosives that would have destroyed it. The next morning, Fine and the others prepared for an enemy counterattack when expected reinforcements had not yet materialized. It came at 1000 hours. The eighty-seven defenders were outgunned and outmanned from the outset. When Italian infantry launched a mortar attack and then added artillery firepower, the defenders' casualties mounted, and their perimeter shrank. Fine and others were nearly out of ammunition after several hours' fighting.

Only twenty men who were not wounded remained when they withdrew to a nearby ditch. While the enemy advanced almost to point-blank range, some escaped while others became perhaps the briefest prisoners of World War II, Fine among them. As Fine and the captured British troops were marched toward Syracuse, a British captain appeared on the trail, about fifty yards ahead. He darted behind a tree, pulled out a pistol, and shot the prisoners' lead guard dead. Unseen British reconnaissance troops nearby opened fire.

Chaos reigned within the prisoner detail. Fine and others grabbed weapons from the startled Italian guards in the mayhem. He tossed one weapon to a British paratrooper "and the two of us shot every fascist we could see." The rest promptly surrendered. Fine had been a POW for about an hour. They returned to the bridge.

Fine saw Parks later in Syracuse. Wounded a third time in the bridge battle, Fine declined treatment for his wounds when he saw wounded soldiers in far worse condition needing treatment.[9]

Long before the sky began to brighten on July 10, the massive armada of ships stretching for miles out to sea began to move toward the beach. It remained windy, threatening the smaller craft as thousands of troops waded ashore, within sight of waterlogged and shattered gliders less than a mile or two from shore, floating among dead bodies. Elsewhere, mangled gliders lay across rocks in the shallows, their backs broken and noses pointing upward toward the beach as if they had died crawling toward safety.

By mid-afternoon, an estimated 150,000 men came ashore along with 600 tanks, surprising the defenders who had thought a landing impossible in such wind-driven conditions.

After twelve hours in the water, the incoming tide had pushed Paul Rau's glider to shore. He and the others climbed to the top of a nearby peninsula to join British paratroopers. Eventually he was evacuated to ships offshore. "It was an experience I shall never forget. And now that it is over, I'm glad to have been part of it," wrote Rau later.[10] Few shared his point of view.

The pain from Guy Gunter's leg wound had raged through the night. The three men who had decided to swim for shore were never seen again. The official report listed those three and the glider's British pilot as missing. Gunter and the others who had decided to hang onto the glider were picked up by a Greek destroyer the following day. Gangrene soon took hold of Gunter as a knot grew in his groin and purple streaks stretched down his leg. He narrowly avoided amputation. It took a month for his wounds to heal.[11]

Arnold Bordewich and three others had decided during the night to swim for shore. About thirty minutes later, a survivor who had stayed with Bordewich's glider had heard cries for help. A man clinging to the glider waived a flashlight in the direction of the panicked voices. But he couldn't tell if they were getting any closer. Maybe they were slowly closing the distance to the glider in a race against fading energy and panic? Then, a choking noise. Then nothing. Bordewich was never seen again and listed as killed in action, somewhere between a fragile glider floating in the ocean and the enemy waiting on shore.[12]

Michael Samek was picked up the next morning by a Dutch Navy ship and then transferred to a British destroyer. Joints stiff with cold and shaking uncontrollably, Samek thought he had survived the night in decent shape. "It was not until I got safely up on deck that I realized my degree of exhaustion and hypothermia. I was shaking like a leaf... I will never forget the taste of the first cup of tea I was handed by the Brits."[13]

As a British ship approached Kenny White's glider, only seven of the fourteen who had climbed aboard in Tunisia remained. They were taken to the ship's sick bay for a check-up, warm clothes, and a meal.

Colonel Chatterton had made it ashore during the night and had linked up with British Special Air Service troops. His belief that his glider pilots must be combat trained proved prescient when they advanced up the face of a cliff and neutralized several enemy strongpoints. Once the sun rose, his group joined other combat troops and advanced inland.[14]

Parts of gliders floated on a sea now at rest, their victims soon to break the hearts of their families in a telegram or at a stranger's knock on their front door. The parents and families of five American glider copilots would get the news that their sons would never come home from Sicily.[15] Arnold Bordewich had landed four miles out at sea. Flight Officer Giuseppe Capite drowned when his glider crashed at sea two miles from shore. Flight Officer Gus Petroulias, who had earned pilot licenses while a teenager, did not survive his first combat mission. His tow plane had dived to avoid flak, costing Petroulias critical gliding altitude. He crashed at least three miles out at sea. Flight Officer Charles McCollum simply disappeared in the night.

The fifth was Kenneth Hollinshead. After Michael Samek had found his friend Kenny White back at their base, they suspected that it was Hollinshead's glider that had exploded in midair a short distance ahead of their position. Samek and White had seen Hollinshead release from his tow plane prematurely and so violently that it rocked the C-47. Hollinshead had been hit by flak and the glider had soon exploded. They researched the glider mission's records and saw that Hollinshead was carrying block TNT.

Samek and White later packed Hollinshead's personal belongings, a sobering moment when Samek realized that "by His Grace" it could have been Samek's personal effects being shipped home.

"I'm as sure as I can be that I am correct and I am equally sure that Kenny did not suffer," Samek later wrote to Hollinshead's aunt, Isabel Hollinshead Yates.[16]

Charles McCollum's body was never found in what became recognized as an epic glider mission failure. More than 600 officers and men died, more than half of them by drowning. Of the seventy-three gliders that were released farther out than the 3,000-yard release point, only one in sixteen made it ashore. Of those released inside 3,000 yards, about eight in ten made landfall. Poignantly, every C-47 tow plane in Operation *Ladbroke* made it back to North Africa safely.

Only four American glider pilots flew the following Operation *Fustian* on the third and final night of the airborne invasion. This time, the British tow-plane crews on the daytime mission were ordered to fly all the way to the landing zones and not attempt to evade enemy artillery fire. Only the glider pilots would release from the tow ropes when they recognized the landing zone.[17]

These changes in mission orders for *Fustian* notwithstanding, one of the great tragedies of Operation *Husky* was "friendly fire." The gliders and paratroopers had flown through fire from Allied ships on the 9th, the American naval fleet had inflicted serious damage to American paratrooper aircraft on the 11th, and the British Navy had fired on its airborne forces on the 13th. The rage within the airborne forces over friendly-fire losses and the actions of tow plane crews in Operation *Ladbroke* in particular would persist long into the war, and in many cases for a lifetime.

The Allies captured Sicily thirty-eight days later. They pushed 100,000 retreating Germans and the remnants of a battered Italian Army back to Italy. During the campaign, Italy's fascist dictator, Benito Mussolini, was removed from power.

Regardless, Operation *Husky*'s recriminations spread like wildfire through the Allied senior command. Montgomery was foolish to rely on unproven glider warfare. American gliders had arrived too late for tow plane and glider crews to get acquainted, much less train and then practice adequately. The gliders' route across the Mediterranean was too long and too complex. Gliders should never be used at night. Allied combat ships mistakenly shooting down Allied tow planes and gliders, due to poor communication and coordination, was excusable. Perhaps the entire concept of massive airborne assaults was simply too complex, too vulnerable to complications, required too many resources, and was far too deadly.

Michael Samek wrote an analytical letter criticizing the glider mission's premises and planning, and circulated it throughout his chain of command. He later refused to wear his Operation *Ladbroke* US Air Medal on his shirt in protest. Others shared his anger and resentment after seeing friends blown up, and others floating face down or sitting strapped to their seats underwater.

Many glider pilots believed that C-47 aircrews had doomed their mission, even though the aircrews had been ordered to stay outside the enemy's artillery range. The British glider pilots' anger was so great that they refused to be towed by American crews during the later stages of Operation *Husky*.

Meanwhile, Allied Headquarters Command in North Africa made sure the parents of Gunter, Samek, Fine, White, Rau, and the other glider pilots knew nothing of what their sons had endured. Some reports were outright lies.

They read about "Hitler Probably Chewing a Rug" in newspapers like the *New Castle News* in Pennsylvania.

Allied gliders slid down out of the misty night onto Sicilian targets without great losses. Parachutists followed without becoming clay pigeons for Axis marksmen, despite the numerous antiaircraft guns, machine guns and searchlights… Towed into target zones at low altitude, the Allied glider pilots, undeterred by searchlights and flak, maneuvered their gliders into the most advantageous currents toward their targets. They discharged their loads with such rapidity that the air-borne troops … storm[ed] forward to seize their objectives before the enemy garrisons could collect themselves for hold-out resistance.[18]

Military pool reporters filed stories that appeared in newspapers across the country. A reporter who was with Fine on the bridge recounted,

> Our men fought magnificently during Friday night before the Allied seaborne invasion ... the full story of which I am too exhausted to write immediately... We had been under the concentrated fire of four-inch mortars and heavy machine guns for some hours... For 15 hours we fought with almost no cover... Within an hour of our capture, all of us who had survived escaped – when a British reconnaissance unit shot our Italian guards.[19]

But the public version of Operation *Husky* could not mask the Allies' internal debate over the future of gliders that would unfold in the coming months.

D-Day at Normandy was less than a year away. No one knew if the risks and losses endured by glider pilots over Sicily were a harbinger of what they would suffer in future assaults. Were the gliders worth the potential tactical advantage they theoretically offered? Perhaps paratrooper forces would be enough to accomplish the same objectives. Some senior officers believed airborne operations should be limited in scale to smaller battalions, not divisions.

The next five months would be critical to whether the glider pilots would continue to play a role in World War II when the buildup in England for the Normandy invasion began. If gliders were to stay in the game, they would have to be part of that mobilization, including the necessary infrastructure, personnel, living quarters, supplies, and equipment on a nearly unimaginable scale.

Meanwhile, young glider pilots were training in California, Texas, and North Carolina, some of them dying before they earned their wings. "We [had] a job we had agreed to do... We suppressed fear with a little braggadocio ... but no heroics," Samek wrote fifty-nine years later.[20] But in mid-1943, it was unclear whether Michael Samek, Kenny White, and Guy Gunter would return to battle, or if James Larkin, "Goldie" Goldman, Jack Merrick, John Butler, and thousands of other young glider pilots in training would ever reach a battlefield.

General Eisenhower had a critical decision to make. He and other senior officers openly questioned the wisdom of massive airborne operations. And there was the matter of whether gliders could be combat effective without an exorbitant cost in casualties and resources. Their Sicily experience certainly did not bode well for their future.

Eisenhower's decision might dictate whether the Allies could establish beachheads on France's northern coast in Normandy.

4

Pea Patch Savior

Recently dug patches of barren dirt marked graves near wrecked gliders in tomato fields, on the sides of hills, and alongside stone walls that had been crushed. The bodies would be collected later. Nearby, some gliders resembled dead creatures, but still smoldering after fires had consumed everything but their steel tubing frames.

Some glider pilots and the infantrymen many had carried remained missing at sea. Perhaps the tide had carried them into timeless anonymity as casualty lists became the macabre scoreboard of Operation *Ladbroke*.

> This glider struck trees of approximately thirty feet in height … leaving the entire left-wing tip in the top of the trees. The glider was cartwheeled into a hard nose landing … the fuselage broke in half, doubling the tail section under… From the debris found around this wreckage, the jeep carried in the glider was also damaged. There was but one grave to indicate the fatality in this landing.
>
> […]
>
> [Glider] landed in boulders and rocks on side of hill. This glider struck head-on into a large boulder demolishing it. Nose completely crushed in and both wings folded forward on either side of boulder. There is definite evidence of fatalities.[1]

The War Department had sent 2nd Lieutenant Rolland Fetters to assess the preparation, role, and fate of the gliders on and near Sicily. His field assessment of thirty gliders that had reached Sicily read like a medical examiner's autopsy: "eight troops went through their plywood seats," "glider is completely burned," "passed through two stone walls," "at terrific speed causing the floor to almost completely disintegrate."[2]

His analysis painted a grim future for glider pilots like Clayton Cederwall who were in the glider pilot training pipeline. In 1942, being a fighter pilot held most of the glamour. That certainly appealed to Cederwall, a farm boy, but there were no openings, according to the Navy recruiter. Disappointed, he returned home to help his father milk the family's cows. Later, he heard about a new Army Air Corps glider program and jumped at the chance to fly.

Cederwall and others would be towed by the C-47s that Fetters thought were impractical due to their lack of self-sealing gas tanks and armor. Although he recommended thirty glider design changes, he believed gliders had a future, given the overall success of the Sicily invasion. Others were not so sure, and some believed they knew who should be held accountable.

The man in charge of the British Glider Pilot Regiment, Lieutenant Colonel Chatterton, blamed the American tow pilots for what he considered was borderline cowardice for releasing their gliders so far from shore. But American tow pilots had been ordered to release their gliders over the ocean at a relatively low altitude and to stay outside antiaircraft artillery range. Factoring in the brutal wind, that had doomed Michael Samek and the others to ditching at sea.

At the same time, many British tow pilots had released their gliders at an altitude that enabled them to reach their landing zones.

Samek blamed the battle plan. Glider pilots had not been trained to approach over the ocean and land at night. Guy Gunter was at the mercy of a tow plane pilot who might make two or three passes through enemy fire because he was off course. Kenneth Hollinshead perhaps could see Allied ships firing at him because the ships' orders were to fire at any approaching aircraft that could not be readily identified. If Kenny White had reached his landing zone, there would be no visible markers because there were no advance pathfinders on the mission.

Meanwhile, General Eisenhower and others questioned whether airborne operations of regimental size (at least 1,000 men) could deliver enough troops in an adequately concentrated area to be combat effective. Yet despite Sicily's horrific carnage, Chatterton and others remained proponents. "The glider has undoubtably proven itself. It was tested to the limit against every obstacle, lack of interest, poor training facilities, bad weather, and a formidable operation. The glider pilot ... [who] is properly trained can pull off any type of landing by day or night."[3]

A subsequent American investigation in September produced additional recommendations. Meanwhile, General Arnold's glider vision remained mired in a fog of unreliable glider construction, a paucity of tow planes, a gold rush of glider pilot volunteers, and no clear vision of how to train and what to expect of his glider pilots. As Gunter healed and the McCollum family grieved, time to make sense of it all was running out.

In the months leading up to the Sicily operation, glider pilot recruitment, training, and equipment situations had remained fluid, some said disorganized, and they suffered from a lack of a master plan. War in Europe was on the horizon and would be dependent on massive amphibious invasions supported by relatively inexperienced airborne troop carriers filled with paratroopers, supplies or towing gliders. Yet, there were far too many glider pilots in training, too few and often deficient gliders available, a shortage of tow planes, chronic alterations to the training regimen, and infighting between the glider training and troop carrier commands.

In January 1943, nearly 9,000 men were in training programs to become glider pilots. But only about 3,000 were actively training while almost 6,000 were in "pools" at various Army bases, waiting for vacancies to open at their next level of instruction. Recruitment had become so successful that glider trainee morale had become a major issue when enrollment far outstripped training capacity. No one had volunteered to sit around for months between training programs and read "Rommel Driven in Full Retreat" headlines in the newspaper.[4]

Boredom produced pranks and prowling. Unauthorized jaunts into town and the nearest bar after a day's training were not uncommon. Stories – not always confirmed – spread about the glider pilot who drove an unattended locomotive one night and the trainee who yelled "Timber!" out his glider's window moments before he plowed into a fence.[5] One pilot recalled driving across the prairie when off duty, trying to run over prairie dogs.

Not only did morale become an issue, but pilots also lost their flying proficiency, flying only two or three hours a month. Spending their days maintaining small airplanes, learning Morse code, and standing guard duty were poor substitutes for honing flying skills.

Hard decisions had to be made about the futures of young men whose boyhoods had been defined by family, the Great Depression, and the prospect of war. Men like Elbert Jella, Robert Horr, Sylvan Lucier, T. Bleecker Ripsom, and the other glider pilot students. They represented a microcosm of an America preparing to send its young men and women to war.

Elbert Jella was too old for pilot school. "They gave me a choice, gliders or they showed me something called a helicopter. One look at that thing and I told them, 'gliders would be just fine.'" His pilot's logbook reflected a meticulous notetaker with a neat hand, one who had a penchant for sketching glider approaches and towing configurations, and who highlighted admonitions of "Know where your wind is from at all times … *do not under shoot*."[6]

Robert Horr had grown up in Iowa and had a girlfriend, Mary Elizabeth Cullen, back home. His training in a year's time reflected how fragmented the glider pilot program had become. His 1943 pilot's logbook listed flights at Alabama's Bates Field in February and Maxwell Field in March; Little Rock and Laurinburg-Maxton in April; Sheppard Field, Texas, in August; Lubbock in September; and Stuttgart Army Airfield, Arkansas, and Bowman Field, Kentucky, in November. A seemingly endless tour of training, transfer, and more training. He found time, though, between assignments for trips to Iowa to court Mary.

Sylvan Lucier had been an accountant in North Dakota before joining three brothers who were already in the military. T. Bleecker Ripsom had earned a Dartmouth College degree before going into the airport-hangar sales business and taking flying lessons. An avid skier, he had dreams of serving with mountain troops. But he joined the glider corps and a training regimen that would take him to twenty-eight bases around the country.

At a February 1943 conference and in subsequent orders issued in August, senior officers overhauled the program. About 5,000 glider trainees had to be transferred or released from service. More than 7,000 glider pilot students were interviewed by officers of the Glider Pilot Training Survey Board to determine who would continue training, and who would be transferred out of the program, or be released from the military. Afterward, less than 2,000 remained in the program, plus those already in advanced training. Among those culled from the program were "a number of men who under other circumstances would have been eliminated on the basis of improper attitude or the lack of flying ability."[7] (When it appeared later that more glider pilots would be needed, the program was reopened for volunteers. Some who had been reassigned returned to the program.)

In addition, contract glider training schools would be closed, and advanced training would be consolidated at SPAAF in Lubbock. For those who remained, a combat training program for glider pilots would be established, and their advanced training flight time in combat gliders would be nearly doubled to fifteen hours.

The Glider Pilot Combat Training Unit was created for "the production of a precision pilot, a tough soldier, and an officer."[8] Up to 400 glider pilots at a time would be trained in six- to eight-week courses that would include at least fifty glider landings. Weapons training would include the M-1 carbine, submachine guns, rocket launchers, mortars, bazookas, grenades, and field tactical training, among other aspects such as developing a hatred for the enemy.

Lieutenant Colonel Ellsworth Curry was assigned to develop the combat training regimen at Bowman Field, Kentucky for glider pilots, in part because they would need it and in part because hundreds of pilots waiting for advanced training vacancies had little to do in the "holding pools" at various army bases.

Idleness was causing serious morale issues, including "[increased] VD rate ... ill-advised marriages, poor money management, too many hot checks, and run-ins with civil authorities."[9] Curry initially thought that glider pilots only needed to "see lightning, hear thunder, and have two natural teeth." But as he began training hundreds of glider flight officers for battle in Normandy, he realized they were "some of the finest officers I ever served with."[10]

They would not only learn to fly gliders, they would also need to learn to hate if they were to survive war. Hate was necessary to combat, according to Private Frank Sargent of the 34th Infantry Division who had written an analysis of battalion and regimental personnel training.

> Americans have never had to drag the torn bodies of loved ones out of smashed buildings or fight for survival... The American soldier is ... fair minded and thinks that the enemy will be fair to him. He does not really want to kill, because he does not hate ... he thinks of war as a game where the umpire's whistle will stop it before it gets too rough... After you have seen your buddies killed; after you see bodies, or what's left of them, piled up for burial; when you realize that they are after you, too; when it finally connects in your mind that moral code does not exist in this way, you will begin to hate, and want to retaliate... Until he hates the enemy with every instinct and every muscle, [the American soldier] will only be afraid.[11]

The realities of war in North Africa and Sicily's horrors reached into every corner of the Army. Only three weeks after Operation *Husky* in Sicily, Frank Sargent's analysis of battlefield reality and the implications of training for hate was so impressive that it reached General Eisenhower's desk and then was circulated to every Army command. Glider pilot training, too, was evolving as units prepared to board converted cruise ships bound for England

and the increasingly intense buildup toward D-Day in Normandy, codenamed Operation *Overlord*.

To meet revised training and combat needs, the 1943 plan called for 6,200 gliders to be produced by the end of the year. But the combat glider was still being invented to a great degree. In late 1942, nearly all operational gliders had been grounded due to structural tail failures. Then in May 1943, an estimated seventy-five percent of training gliders had to be grounded for inspection. Designed for a single combat mission or two, gliders were logging as much as 400 hours' flight time by pilot trainees. While additional design changes were suspended, the heavy use of inconsistently manufactured gliders in training sometimes had disastrous consequences.

On August 1, Robertson Aircraft Corporation held a public celebration of delivering its sixty-fifth glider to the AAF. Robertson and other glider manufacturers in the St. Louis area were a badge of civic pride. Thousands gathered at a local airfield for an afternoon demonstration that had been rehearsed earlier in the morning.

The sixty-fifth glider was towed into the air, filled with some of the city's most influential leaders. When it reached about 1,500 feet, it released from its tow plane. Almost immediately, the glider's right wing tore away from the fuselage with a loud *snap*. The glider turned nose down. The two pilots sat helpless as the ground rushed toward them, their straps holding them back in their seats. Perhaps the VIPs back in the fuselage screamed. Maybe some prayed. The impact demolished the glider and killed all ten men instantly.

They included the president of Robertson, the city's mayor, and the president of the local chamber of commerce. An investigation discovered a wing strut component manufactured by a subcontractor (that had previously produced caskets) was only one-fifth the prescribed thickness and that there were additional deficient fittings ready to be shipped to Robertson and another glider manufacturer.

Other gliders being ferried from factories to AAF bases had suffered wing failures as well. In one instance, when a glider pilot leaned up against a wing while talking, it fell off.

Anger soon replaced shock. "What most people don't know is that … the entire U.S. glider program has been woefully neglected," wrote national columnist Drew Pearson who also questioned whether the program had been properly developed. He cited the example of a prospective glider manufacturer pitching the AAF for a contract earlier. When asked the name of his company, he replied, "I'll tell you in the morning."[12] Nearly five months later, a federal grand jury held the War Department partially responsible for the St. Louis crash due to its "uncertainty and looseness" of manufacturer inspections, though no indictments were handed down.[13]

Six weeks after the St. Louis disaster, Colonel Norman Olsen, the commanding officer of the AAF's primary CG-4A glider school in Lubbock, watched a glider piloted by Frederick Dillingham and Oscar Dyson – both advanced glider students – as it lifted off the runway. In an instant, the glider's left wing folded at a perpendicular angle. To Olsen's horror, the right wing did the same. Gyrating madly, the glider pulled on the C-60 tow plane's tail so viciously that the C-60 pitched upward to become nearly vertical. When it stalled at only about 300 feet off the ground, both the glider pilots and C-60's crew had no options.

Both the glider and the C-60 turned nose first and dove straight into the Texas dirt, about 100 yards apart. The C-60 burst into flames. Olsen found Dillingham lying on his back near the glider's tail section, his parachute wrapped around the tail structure. A witness reported that Dillingham had tried to jump clear of the glider, but his parachute had fouled on the tail and pulled him to his death. Dyson's body was still inside the glider. The examiners of the bodies from the tow plane and glider called it "blunt force trauma."

A subsequent crash review board discovered two wing fittings had failed, one of several chronic problems in 1943. The glider fleet's structural failures had included the landing gear, tail section, control push rods, wings, and rudder control mechanisms, among others. It appeared strengthening one component was increasing stress on other components that were failing and killing glider pilots.

Olsen had had enough of the CG-4A glider. "After careful consideration and investigation of present and previous difficulties experienced with the CG-4A glider, this office recommends that the use of this glider, both in training and tactical use, is discontinued immediately," Olsen wrote.[14]

In some military circles, such a written proclamation by an officer that flew in the face of the AAF's commitment to the CG-4A glider might have been what officers called a "career ender." But in the months following the Sicily debacle, glider pilots were training in a glider whose accident record remained worrisome at best, atrocious at worst. Regardless, the AAF remained committed to the CG-4A, an experimental aircraft that was being revised and redesigned as glider pilot students strapped themselves in to train for war.

Hard landings and crashes at pilot schools across America and in the sea off Sicily revealed the belly of gliders was especially vulnerable to damage – to the glider, cargo, and passengers. An early improvement was the addition of a wooden, ski-like reinforcement under the cockpit. Only four feet long, the idea was to keep the front of the glider and its pilots from "digging in" and to clear minor obstructions on the ground. But the real improvement came in October 1943.

Roger Griswold II designed a steel truss structure that resembled a spiderweb. Incorporated into the front of the glider, the "Griswold nose" absorbed energy when the glider hit the ground and deflected ground obstacles away from its path, much like a train's cowcatcher. It quickly was incorporated into glider construction, in time for several hundred to be retrofitted onto gliders destined for the Normandy invasion. It likely saved more lives than any other CG-4A glider modification in World War II.

Yet as modifications to gliders continued, aircraft crashes haunted the glider program and reached the highest level of those responsible for training glider pilots. Four months before Sicily, the man in charge of the program, Major Lewin Barringer, was returning from an inspection trip in England. Somewhere over the Caribbean, his plane vanished without a trace. It was a deeply personal loss for Arnold who again turned to the civilian aviation community a month later when he appointed Barringer's friend and fellow soaring enthusiast, Richard C. duPont, to take charge as Special Assistant for the Glider Program.

Five months later, duPont was at the controls of an experimental glider that could carry fifteen soldiers. While being towed at 3,500 feet, the glider became unstable, broke free of the tow plane, stalled, and plummeted in a flat spin. DuPont leaped from the glider, but his parachute had only begun to open when he hit the ground. He died instantly.[15]

Glider pilots were dying from Sicily to St. Louis to California's high desert to Midwest farmland, even as improvements in training were being instituted. "Now that the Army Air Forces glider program had been in operation for two years ... it remained for the worth of the glider as a tactical weapon to be established conclusively," summarized a later Army analysis.[16]

Thousands of young men like 2nd Lieutenant Stratton Appleman had staked their lives on the vague concept of combat gliders. Like so many others, he had fallen for a recruiter's string of promises that he would be promoted to staff sergeant upon graduation, then promoted to lieutenant six weeks later, would be part of a secret mission, and if he survived he would hold the rank of major within a year. That sounded awfully good to the flight-school washout. He had grown up in Aransas Pass, Texas, a shrimping and fishing town in the shadow of Corpus Christi. He had attended Baylor University before entering the service. He had earned his glider pilot's wings more than a year earlier but he remained nowhere near a battlefield. It would be up to a handful of glider pilots whose night flights on hot North Carolina nights might determine if he would see combat.

Turbulent air along the glider's reinforced fabric fuselage surrounded Flight Officer Arthur Furchgott, Jr, as he peered into moonless darkness on August 4, looking for a particular North Carolina cow pasture. He had glided nearly eight miles since his release from the tow plane. Somewhere below, on "a night as dark as an ace of spades," there should be a flashlight wrapped in a handkerchief to shield it from General "Hap" Arnold and other observers who were waiting for the glider landing demonstration. Furchgott had descended three-quarters of a mile in the midst of other gliders, each pilot working to keep his glider in position and on time.

There! Just keep it steady. Two gliders should already be in the field and three more are behind me.

Furchgott was too old to become a power pilot in World War II. But at thirty years of age with a degree in mechanical aeronautics engineering, the glider corps had gladly accepted him in 1942. A year later, he became one of six glider pilots whose skill might keep gliders from being grounded permanently.

Less than a month after the Sicily debacle, Major Mike Murphy, a renowned stunt pilot and barnstormer before the war, planned a two-day glider demonstration for General Arnold and other senior officers at Laurinburg-Maxton Air Base to showcase new landing skills that Murphy had taught to a cadre of about two dozen hand-picked glider pilots. Murphy had been flying since 1928 but had graduated from glider pilot school only about a year earlier.

For more than a year, glider pilot students had been learning to land on long airstrips carved out of prairie grass and desert sand. In combat, they needed to come to a stop within 400 feet on various patches of open ground – likely surrounded by trees, the enemy, stone walls, houses, or barns – by digging their glider's nose into the dirt or clipping trees with their wings, if necessary.[17] Murphy began teaching a technique that relied on a longer and slower approach that was more controlled at seventy miles per hour to replace fast descents and longer runouts in the absence of obstructions that could demolish gliders.

The combat glider mission was to reliably deliver men and cargo to the battle, even if it required a slower approach and far greater exposure to enemy fire. If confidence in gliders was to be restored following Sicily's scars, Murphy had to showcase new techniques and glider reliability in a way that would merit attention and restore confidence at the highest levels of the Army Air Forces and War Department.

Following dinner the first night, Arnold and others were escorted to an unlit pasture bordered by silhouetted trees on three sides. Furchgott and other glider pilots were headed toward the same pasture.

What was that? It sounded like a wheelbarrow being pushed over hard ground. Or maybe a farm wagon far off in the distance. Then another. And another. Almost overlapping one another, it seemed. *Can't be a tractor this time of night. Maybe something out there sliding or rolling on the ground?* The gliders rolled to a stop almost alongside the observers, their infantry passengers jumping out, and in some cases mixing with the observers before their gliders were spotted. Their stealth drew gasps.

Earlier that day, twenty-two gliders had landed nearly in unison in front of hundreds of reporters and Army observers – some coming to a stop only a few yards away – and unloaded glider infantry that conducted a mock attack on the enemy in the next field. "Two landing gears had been washed out. The tail of one glider had been cut off. One had a wing split so deeply by a tree that it would hold a large man in the gap. But ... every man and every fighting arm had emerged without damage and gone to work on the 'enemy,'" wrote one reporter.[18]

In another daytime demonstration, a tow plane approached a field only about twenty feet above the ground with an extended tailhook that snagged a glider's attached tow rope that had been stretched between the tops of two ten-foot poles. The ability to "snatch" an undamaged glider in a field and yank it into the air showcased the gliders' inherent ruggedness when they weren't being piloted into crash landings. Another demonstration entailed gliders landing on water with flotation devices.

Successful stealth and precision landing defined the daytime exercises. But Murphy wasn't finished. Ten more glider pilots the following night had been assigned to deliver a *coup de grâce* to any remaining skeptics alongside a field that had been a pea patch before the war.

Lights were extinguished, cigarettes crushed, and conversations became whispers after General Arnold and others once again had been ferried out to another field, waited, and wondered what Murphy had in store. Glider pilots awaited their release signal miles away as Murphy was making his pitch to the audience.

Second Lieutenant Clayton Cederwall stared at the dim silhouette of his tow plane, almost straight ahead. *There it is.* Upon the release signal, he turned toward where he thought the pea patch would be, along with the other glider pilots who were releasing at two-minute intervals. A hole had been dug at the front edge of the field to conceal a flare pot. At the far end was a man with a flashlight, equally shielded. One after another, Cederwall and the others spotted the two beacons and glided in.

Murphy concluded his pitch with a call for "Lights!" Floodlights instantly revealed the gliders only feet away. Most had landed within a few feet of the startled entourage. And to drive the point home, the camp band marched out of one glider playing the AAF's fight song. (One reporter thought he had faintly heard the band playing "On a Wing and a Prayer" as its glider neared the pea patch.)

"Everything worked like it was supposed to that night and I got to shake the hand of a general. We never did tell them that we had a flare pot hidden at the other end of the field," recalled Cederwall.[19] It became known as the "Pea Patch Show," the night when a barnstorming stunt pilot had proven that well-trained glider pilots at the very tip of an invasion force could reliably deliver troops and supplies, even at night.[20] But could glider and paratrooper operations on a large scale be honed quickly enough to become an effective fighting force in combat conditions?

Two additional paratrooper and glider exercises in the North Carolina woods later in 1943 were conducted to convince Secretary of War Henry Stimson, General Arnold, his chief of staff, General George Marshall, and others that airborne warfare by paratroopers and gliders on a large scale not only was feasible, but was also strategic.

In December 1943, glider and paratrooper regiments conducted a massive training exercise. Paratrooper and glider aircraft flew several hundred miles to deliver men and gliders to their drop points and landing zones, then flew resupply missions for several days in deteriorating early-winter weather, and in simulated combat conditions.

"I was prepared to recommend that airborne divisions be abandoned," wrote General Leslie McNair who led Army Ground Forces to Major General Joseph Swing (11th Airborne Division) afterward. "The successful performance of your division has convinced me that we were wrong, and I shall now recommend that we continue our present schedule of activating, training, and committing airborne divisions."[21]

D-Day at Normandy was less than six months away.

The scent of war hung in the air when Flight Officer Richard Mercer descended the gangway off the cruise ship RMS *Mauritania* in Liverpool. Bombed-out warehouses and other buildings smoldered along the waterfront in a country that had been at war since 1939. He had stepped into another universe, far from Wichita Falls, Texas, where he had grown up. He had entered the Army two years earlier on December 30, only ten days after marrying Norma Jo Pierce and three days after celebrating his twenty-first birthday. He had earned his wings learning to fly gliders over the rice fields of central Arkansas.

He was among the hundreds of glider pilots and troop carrier ground personnel arriving at United Kingdom ports in early 1944 on cruise ships, usually six men packed in a stateroom designed for two. Some had been miserably seasick for a week or more, particularly those whose ships had taken a northern Atlantic route to avoid prowling German submarines.

For many, there was a tingle of excitement at finally reaching England. A three- or four-hour train trip, and then perhaps an hour in a truck would deliver them to their assigned AAF bases in England. Some had been training for two years to reach the edge of war.

But culture shock soon gripped many glider pilots who, only yesterday it seemed, had been high school students, busboys, aircraft hobbyists, and fieldhands. They had never seen stone hand-washing troughs in breezy men's bathrooms. *Geez it's cold here, why are the Brits running around in shorts and open shirts? And what's this about serving godawful orange marmalade practically with every meal?*, mused 1st Lieutenant Milton Dank and others.[22]

Their living quarters in Quonset huts were always cold in the British midwinter, prompting Cederwall to sleep in his sheepskin flying suit in search of warmth on a straw-filled mattress atop a steel cot. Heating fuel rationing led to the mysterious disappearance of nearby farmers' fences at night as some glider pilots sought an alternative fuel source for their Quonset huts' stoves.

Few recognized the British version of coffee and thought warm beer odd, to say the least. Tea apparently had to be strong enough that "you could float a spoon on it." And getting used to the Brits' rations of creamed chicken on toast, Brussels sprouts, powdered eggs, and fried spam paled in comparison to many pilots' distaste of mutton. Some men snared rabbits at night and fried them in their barracks while dysentery struck in some quarters.[23]

Many pilots, meanwhile, faced another wait for lack of aircraft. Beginning in May 1943, more than 2,000 CG-4As had been shipped to England. But fifty-one of the first sixty-two assembled by British contractors were deemed unflyable. Six months later, only 200 of a quota of 600 CG-4As were assembled. With no light aircraft for dead stick practice as an alternative, there was plenty of time for pilots at bases near London to take a train into the city for a dinner and show or perhaps visit Piccadilly Circus, which was said to be full of prostitutes.

Once the C-47s and American troop carrier squadrons' glider mechanics arrived, more than 900 were assembled by the middle of April and training had begun in earnest.

Mercer, Captain Norman Aigner, 2nd Lieutenant John Whipple, and others learned how to fly the British Horsa, a massive glider that many American glider pilots came to detest. Far larger and not nearly as nimble as the American glider, the pilot and copilot had to master a control wheel and rudder controls mounted on two-by-fours. As they reached the edge of their landing zones at about 800 feet, they pulled full flaps and "dumped" the glider's nose downward, so it aimed at the spot where they wanted to land. Slow to respond, "it felt like trying to change the Queen Mary's course in a high sea," according to Flight Officer James Ferrin.[24]

Many thought "the monster" was too large and tiring to fly hundreds of miles and then land in a small clearing. Many British glider pilots, on the other hand, were not enamored with the Americans' CG-4A and considered it "jinxed," given the Sicily disaster.

By May, glider training had intensified considerably, including night formation training and landing zone exercises. Rumors swept through the ranks about the invasion everyone knew was coming at some point. Escape and evasion lectures were delivered by military intelligence personnel. There were other useful tips as well. "Women in whorehouses, we were told, were known to be more likely to help downed Allied airmen than any other single element of the French population," recalled one glider pilot.[25]

They didn't know that RAF Air Marshal Sir Trafford Leigh-Mallory, in charge of Operation *Overlord*'s air operations, believed that as many as nearly three out of four gliders and fifty percent of the troop carrier planes and their paratroopers would be shot out of the air over Normandy. "I cannot guarantee the safe arrival of any definite percentage of troops or equipment ... a large proportion will be lost," he wrote in a memorandum on May 29, 1944.[26]

The First US Army Corps General Omar Bradley, meanwhile, believed the stakes were so high in getting the infantry divisions ashore that he was willing to risk more than 15,000 101st and 82nd Airborne troops, including their gliders, to ensure success of the Normandy landing.

By the end of May, American airfields in England were home to more than 1,200 troop transports, more than 1,000 CG-4A gliders, 300 Horsa gliders, and thousands of glider pilots, C-47 transport crews, and paratroopers.[27] One pilot likened England to a huge aircraft carrier.

Meanwhile, some families checked their mailboxes for letters from England, while others looked for letters from air bases in Texas and North Carolina. No one could predict when their sons and husbands would first fly into combat, but few doubted they would be at the tip of the spear, "swooping down behind enemy lines in huge, Waco-designed gliders with jeeps and field guns, these tough fighting men [will] strike as quickly and quietly as lightning … with deadly effect … very likely that's the way it will be happening soon all along the road to Berlin and Rome and Tokyo," according to a Waco advertisement.

They read glowing war correspondents' accounts of early-war battlefield victories in which combat heroism overlooked body counts. Perhaps that had bolstered the hopes of fathers who had sent their sons to war.

I had the news within the last five minutes from your mother that you have your call from Uncle Sam. While I can honestly say that I am proud of you beyond words, I must also say that it has put a lump in my throat. You are a good son in any way that sons can be measured, and you will always be such a son, I know. There is also no doubt in my mind that you will be a good soldier, since you have long felt and understood the meaning of fighting for the right. May I say that in putting on the uniform of the United States Army you are doing it for all of us and our prayers for your safety will be with you wherever you go… Only thing I am sorry about is that I couldn't be there to say g'bye.[28]

The barbed wire became a sure sign that war was near. By the first of June, it had been installed on the perimeter of American air bases in England and military police were marching glider crews to and from their mess halls and briefings. They were told not to talk to anyone not involved with the upcoming invasion. America's invasion forces were on a lockdown worthy of a maximum-security prison.

Everyone waited and wondered. *When? Where?* Some men crafted carefully worded letters for their families. Others added entries in their journals. Perhaps some had premonitions of their fate.

2nd June, 1944
This has been quite a day. I was to get the glider out today and let General Pratt's aid [sic] paint a picture on the nose of it ... they restricted all pilots at noon, which caught me... I hope you get these books, because there are a few things in it you might like to know. But I sure hope I get to give it to you instead of them sending it to you. My watch is at this address: Goldsmith's, F.W. Gibons, Lon. Co. Ltd., Newbury, England.

3d June, 1944
This is the last day before D-Day. So, I will put this away, and if anything happens, maybe you'll get it.

Close with love ...[29]

War beckoned.

5

Popcorn Popping

I am walking out ... to a line of 50 Horsa gliders... Take-off in
an hour... It makes my stomach tighten... This is what ... we
have worked for, sweated for, cussed, and lately prayed for. This
is our day, the glider pilot's day... Ray shows up [copilot Ray
Salkeld]. He looks white. I climb in the cockpit, give the controls
a last-minute check. She's O.K., perfect in fact. [Another glider
pilot] comes over from his glider. "Hi Lib, watcha doin?" "... see
ya in France." "Right you are, I'll be right on your tail!" He has
a big cigar in his mouth... It's time [as] the [C-47] engines are
beginning to roar...[1]

Captain Richard Libbey was among the hundreds of glider pilots
who battled a firestorm of emotions on June 5, 1944, the eve of
D-Day at Normandy. Once they climbed into their gliders, the
pilots' route over the English Channel would take them across
a broad marsh to a quilt of small, squarish fields bordered by
hedgerows. Below, more than 150,000 American, British, and
Canadian troops would be headed for five beaches aboard more
than 5,000 combat and landing ships in Operation *Overlord*.

Libbey, Robert Horr, John Hanscom, Jimmy Metchicas, and others
facing combat for the first time knew they had to crash-land their
gliders in the fields on the 6th and 7th, alongside 13,000 pathfinders
and paratroopers of the 82nd and 101st Airborne Divisions. Their

objectives would be to block German reinforcements moving toward the coast and to capture the causeways leading inland from the beaches. The airborne operation, designated Operation *Neptune*, would be the largest airborne mission to date and the first large-scale American military use of gliders.

Tens of thousands of infantrymen wading ashore would be relying on the paratroopers behind the German defenses to attack from the rear. And within a few hours of landing, those paratroopers would be dependent on the reinforcements, vehicles, artillery, supplies, and ammunition delivered by the glider pilots. The glider pilots' role reminded some of an anonymous proverb of how the lack of a nail led to the loss of a shoe, horse, rider, and ultimately the battle. For the paratroopers supporting the infantry coming ashore, the glider corps could become the nail of the Airborne's Operation *Neptune*.

The Germans knew an Allied amphibious assault would come from Britain. At Calais? Or nearly 175 miles away in Normandy? The Germans' 2,400-mile line of defense along Europe's northern coast comprised more than six million mines, thousands of concrete bunkers, and a concentrated string of heavy artillery emplacements. Although some were undermanned, thirty-six German infantry divisions and six panzer divisions were positioned to thwart the Allies' invasion.

Fifty thousand Germans were dug in at Normandy to defend the deep-water port of Cherbourg on the Contentin Peninsula. A few miles inland, antiaircraft artillery and heavy machine gun nests stood ready to send a curtain of deadly fire skyward at incoming paratrooper aircraft, tow planes, and gliders. Hundreds of clearings, farm fields, and cow pastures had been mined, flooded, or studded with upright tree trunks, up to about a foot wide and ten feet tall, a mutant picket fence, nicknamed "Rommel's Asparagus," to demolish gliders skidding to a stop.

Jack Merrick, Richard Mercer, Dale Oliver, and the others piloting CG-4As and Horsas would arrive in three waves of gliders bound for landing zones about six miles inland from Utah Beach where the Americans' 4th Infantry Division would wade ashore.

Three glider landing zones paralleled the coast, from the Hiesville area running northwest to Sainte-Mère-Église, and were designated LZ-E, LZ-W, and LZ-O.

One hundred gliders in the first wave, designated Operations *Chicago* and *Detroit*, would touch down in LZ-E and LZ-O at 0400 hours on June 6. Both had been switched from day to night missions only days before to avoid a long, daytime approach over enemy gun emplacements. Then a second wave of more than 200 gliders in Operations *Elmira* (LZ-W) and *Keokuk* (LZ-E) would approach over those feared emplacements on the same day, arriving at about 2300 hours.[2]

On D+1, another 200 gliders in Operations *Galveston* and *Hackensack* would arrive in the third wave at LZ-W with more troops, artillery, ammunition, and supplies at 0700 and 0900 hours. The six missions would span only thirty hours. Intrepid glider pilots would enter combat for the first time, landing in the predawn dark, under a morning sun, and as sunset arrived. Each carried unique threats and dangers but would bind hundreds of glider pilots by the horrors of war experienced only by combat veterans.

The glider operations could prove critical to whether the 4th Infantry Division could establish a beachhead, whether the Germans would be stopped from quickly reinforcing their frontline troops to pin the Americans against the sea, and to how many Americans would die in the sand and surf.

The glider pilots would fly what British Air Chief Marshall Sir Trafford Leigh-Mallory considered were glider suicide missions and deemed airborne operations "unsound in principle." He noted the gliders' three-hour flight from England would be spotted long before their destinations, would be over enemy territory at less than 1,000 feet under a full moon or in daylight, and would "fly over or near enemy flak, searchlights or ground troops, and particularly those that wander, are likely to suffer heavily."[3]

Andrew Bates, Irwin Morales, Edwin Blanche, and other glider pilots would have to ignore their long odds of survival as they prepared to be towed across the French sky and then descend toward enemy artillery and machine guns.

Guts had tightened in the final days before the three waves of glider missions took off from seven airfields west and southwest of London. Final briefings at the squadron level were conducted in huts, mess halls, tents, or any other location that afforded a decent-sized group of men and a focal point as maps and photographs were unveiled. Pilots and copilots often sat together, exchanging looks and maybe a wink as the squadron or troop carrier group's commanding officer ran through the details which might reveal where the glider pilots would face the heaviest enemy fire.

James Larkin, John Butler, and Evans Ittner would be among the first to land on D-Day, after a long flight before sunrise. They had sat through several days of workshops, lectures, and demonstrations. They reviewed first aid techniques, zeroed in their weapons, sat through lectures on mines and booby traps, and went over how to deploy and use a life raft.

Maps, charts, routes denoted by strings, and recon photos defined most briefings. The aerial photos of potential landing zones could be deceptively bucolic or dangerously outdated. A farm field full of potatoes one day could be riddled with wide ditches, studded with wooden poles, or flooded with several feet of water a few weeks later.

Regardless, the paratroopers would be carrying limited ammunition when they dropped. Successful, on-target glider landings would be critical to meeting the invasion's inland objectives.

The commanding officer then walked through the sequence of takeoffs and arrivals over the landing zones – much like a football coach reviewing the playbook, blended with a pep talk, just before kickoff. By now it should be more reminder than new information. For many, the most bone-chilling part of the briefing came when officers from the 82nd or 101st Airborne Division told the glider pilots what to expect from the enemy once they exited their glider in the middle of a clearing, holding only a pistol or a carbine.

Some glider pilots, grim faced, broke eye contact to stare at their hands clasped in their laps. Some sat frozen, with a thin grin that failed to reach their eyes. Each one was lost in his thoughts.

By the time the officers had finished their briefing, a heavy dose of reality had been mainlined into every pilot. Most glider pilots believed they would come back but couldn't help but wonder who might die. Second Lieutenant Merrick would fly the next-to-last glider (fifty-first) in the first wave, and his good friend 2nd Lieutenant Larkin would fly as "tail end Charlie" behind him. Hardly ideal positions to avoid enemy fire and find enough space to land. They had to figure their odds of survival would not be as good as the glider pilots up front.

For many, crosscurrents of uncertainty, obligation, fear, responsibility, and duty churned their insides as they waited for the word to head out to their gliders. One way to pass the time was to review their pockets' contents, escape kit, and pack repeatedly.

Do I have everything I'm going to need? I've got my long woolen underwear, two pairs of thick woolen socks, my wool shirt, wool olive drab pants, shoes impregnated against mustard gas, and my field jacket with a small flag sown into the right sleeve. Don't forget the gas detector, my steel helmet, gas mask, and the ammunition belt. Still filled with ninety-six rounds of ammo? Good. There's my rifle, bayonet, .45 automatic pistol, a few hand grenades, and a trench knife strapped to my calf. Plus, a first aid kit, canteen, cup. Maybe check my escape kit one more time. It should have two thousand French francs, terrain maps, small saw, compass, passport pictures, and foreign language guide, and whistle. The flashlight, chewing gum, notebook, pencil, cigarettes, and matches are all in my pockets, right? Where's my pack?

A pack contained a blanket, shelter half, mess kit, food powder, matches, extra socks, two K-rations, six D-rations, two heating units to warm the rations, sewing kit, a second first aid kit, insect powder, and halazone powder for water purification. *Okay, got it. How much longer before we head out to our gliders?*

Others, like 2nd Lieutenant John Hanscom, settled gambling debts and said their goodbyes to buddies they had met only a few months earlier or perhaps to some whom they had trained with back in the States. It would soon be time to check their glider loads and perhaps argue with ground crews to keep the gliders from being overloaded by hundreds of pounds or even by as much as a thousand pounds.

The C-47 tow plane crews who every glider pilot relied upon conducted final checks for the invasion as well. First Lieutenant Louis Emerson, Jr, a tow plane pilot in the first wave, had to prepare as if he was his formation's navigator. Only the lead plane in a serial carried navigation equipment. If it was damaged, every pilot in the formation potentially became a navigator (mostly by dead reckoning) across the English Channel and over France toward his landing zone, sometimes in the dark.

After years of training, Emerson knew his C-47 – an aircraft designed for civilian use – was a deathtrap for his aircrew. Unlike other military aircraft, his fuel tanks didn't have an interior sticky coating that sealed punctures to stop fuel leaks. His plane had no armor, other than a steel plate a buddy had scavenged from a bomber that had been welded under Emerson's seat. If Emerson's plane took a direct hit, he had to signal his glider pilot to release, order his crew to bail out, unbuckle from his seat, clip a parachute hanging on a wall to his harness, and run through a possibly smoke-filled fuselage about sixty-five feet back to the sole exit door. Presumably while his plane was out of control and possibly in a dive.

Family had weighed heavily in the minds of the glider pilots and tow plane aircrews as their bases had been locked down, armed guards patrolled, and aircraft were painted with their identification markings. Important matters foreign to most young men back home had to be addressed.

Emerson coped with his unknown fate by writing a letter to his wife, Marilyn, and one to his unborn son, Dick. Another to his parents. Then maybe a nap just before heading to his plane? Not a chance. Only unending review and reflection blended with speculation. *What was flak really like? What to do if my plane's hit. What to do if the glider is hit. What to do if I'm hit. Am I frightened? I don't know.*[4]

Flight Officer Jimmy Metchicas had grown up in Greenville, South Carolina, a popular boy who loved flying. He had completed the Civilian Pilot Training Program before enlisting in 1942, about the time his mother suddenly had died. As D-Day approached, Metchicas had written his will, naming his father and stepmother as beneficiaries.

Others had written letters to their families, to be sent only if they did not return from Normandy. For some, confronting possible death was best expressed with a fountain pen. As 2nd Lieutenant William Brown listened to the final brief for the first wave of gliders, he had already written a letter he hoped his family would never see.

Dear Little Robert,
... [in three weeks] your father will have been in the Army for two years, and most of that time has been spent away from home, you and Mother... I have missed you and Mother every minute of that time more than either of you will ever know ... even though I seemed at times to be too serious about the military part of my life ... there was never a greater love in the world than the love I have in my heart for you ... if you should have to go through life without me ... I go with the prayer that I will be permitted to return to you and Mother, and if it should work out otherwise, it will have been the will of God that I make the sacrifice.

I love you and Mother,
Daddy Bill[5]

About half of the 2,000 glider pilots who had arrived in England learned they would not be flying the Normandy mission. They would remain on the sideline, after training for as long as two years, having endured a string of training delays, and yet having "stuck with it" after falling for the glowing pitches by recruiters in their hometowns. Pilots who had lived with the ghost of Sicily's slaughter for nearly a year. Instead, they would be sitting this one out, praying their best friends would return.

Flight Officer "Goldie" Goldman, the renowned prankster, had scanned his squadron's fly list. No Goldman. He had appealed to his glider pilot operations officer, offering to fly in place of one of the married pilots. There was no joy, though, when he was told he was too irresponsible to be given that chance. Pranks and stunts had finally caught up with Goldman. "I missed D-Day, which is still one of the biggest disappointments of my life, even unto this day," he wrote sixty-four years later.[6]

Glider pilot James Ferrin and 2nd Lieutenant John Lowden were among those scheduled for flights in the days following the invasion. Some were scrubbed at the last minute, not always to the glider pilots' chagrin. "Knowing how badly the British top brass had used glider-borne troops during the invasion of Sicily, I was sure we were in for a killing day," reflected Lowden.[7]

They stood aside, mesmerized by those preparing to fly, jump, or glide. The 82nd Airborne paratroopers, with their faces blackened, erect Mohawk haircuts, and faces contorted into the scowls of killers, frightened Goldman. They gathered near their planes for speeches by their officers, including one who told them that some would die, that they all were expected to kill the enemy, and who then led the young men in chants of "Kill! Kill! Kill!" that reached a crescendo that could be heard a football field away.

For the others with a mission to fly, the airfields in England soon would resemble the tightly choreographed flight deck of an aircraft carrier as the waves of gliders took off as quickly and efficiently as possible. Timing over landing zones about 125 miles away was critical. That meant assembly in formation over English airfields and then arriving in France on time was vital. Trust, timing, and teamwork between glider pilots and tow plane aircrews were critical to getting each mission off the ground. So, too, was controlling a man's fear. Last-second checks of men and aircraft soothed a man's nerves and perhaps might increase his odds of survival.

The time came to report to their gliders.

Many glider pilots knew they would be flying overloaded gliders into combat. Man and materiel were the priority, to the point of risking a glider crash before takeoff. Flight Officer George Williams knew he was in trouble when he pulled down on the tail of his Horsa glider. The strength of resistance told him it was overloaded. That would make it a more dangerous takeoff.

Small groups stood near their gliders, lost in huddled conversations between glider pilots and sometimes with the infantry they would carry. Some joked in an unfunny way, others affected a transparent aura of confidence that neither convinced nor reassured. Each man confronting an unfathomable fate. After a sleepless night as it rained outside, 2nd Lieutenant Byron Sharp approached his glider and surveyed his passengers. "All these [infantry] guys were sitting there with their painted black faces and camouflage stuff on their helmets. I acted like I'd taken off that way every day of my life. I walked up to the front and said, 'Let's go.'" Concise, business-like exchanges between glider pilots and the men they carried were oddly settling for some men.[8]

Each man coped with the prospect of death privately. First Lieutenant John Devitt checked his aircraft on the runway, huddled with his crew one last time to synchronize watches before takeoff, and finished a cup of coffee supplied by the Red Cross. When he climbed aboard, he found a crewman kneeling in prayer. Devitt calculated the odds of his survival, putting it at somewhere between ninety-five and eighty percent. That worked out to anywhere from five to fifteen planes out of every 100 could be shot down, perhaps exploding in the sky, or spiraling out of control toward the ground.

"I will say of the Lord, he is my refuge and my fortress; my God, in him will I trust. Surely, he shall deliver thee from the snare of the fowler and from the noisy pestilence. A thousand shall fall at thy side, and ten thousand at thy right hand; but it shall not come nigh thee." Glider pilots like Merrick who weren't particularly religious stood politely at the edge of the runway as the chaplain read to the group of glider pilots. Silence wrapped Merrick once the chaplain finished. Perhaps the whisper of a breeze, but nothing else. Then the pilots gathered in small groups, buddies who would be taking off one after another, chatting and privately wondering who they were seeing for the last time.[9]

Runways across the south of England sat filled with gliders and tow planes. Many glider pilots marveled at the pre-launch formation when they reached their runway. The runway had been converted into a parking lot with gliders positioned so closely that their wings overlapped. On each side in a single file, the C-47s were parked and angled toward the runway with their wings also overlapping. Each glider's tow rope was attached to its tow plane off to the side. At other airfields, the gliders were parked wingtip to wingtip on both sides of the runway, their C-47s filling the runway nose to tail, their tow ropes snaking off to the runway's edge where their gliders waited.

In the final minutes prior to their takeoff, some glider pilots carrying infantry could smell fuel and oil mixed with the nervous sweat of their passengers as they had settled down on their benches and buckled in. Everyone waited. Some wondered and others worried until their C-47's left propeller began to turn, spewing a cloud of black smoke. A sputter, the report of a backfire, "and then she lit up, just-a-singing like a lark," one glider pilot reflected later.[10] Then the right engine. Together they blended into a continuous roar with no ebbs, no flows, simply increasing volume and ferocity as the engines warmed and the airstrip's fine dirt and dust billowed. The pervasive growl crescendoed, swallowing ground personnel, pilots, and passengers alike. Aircraft handlers stood or sat in jeeps, waiting for the signal. *There!* A flare arced across the runway. *Let's go!*

The first plane of each wave slowly pulled forward, straightening the glider's coiled rope as if it were a snake slithering forward. When the plane reached the runway personnel who had been carefully positioned ahead and off to the side, the pilot knew the slack had been taken out of his glider's tow rope. *Power!* The tow planes shuddered under the strain as they and their gliders slowly gained speed. Once the glider lifted off the ground, the tow plane could accelerate faster and hopefully lift off before running out of asphalt. Meanwhile, another C-47 was already taxiing to the point of tow-rope tension.

Glider pilots and copilots each had specific responsibilities the moment their glider began to roll. John Hanscom who flew later on D-Day wrote:

Bill and I watched in fascination as the [tow] rope slowly inched out knocking pebbles right and left as it [straightened]. The go-ahead signal was given, and the pilot in our tow ship began easing his throttles forward.[11] We moved slowly at first, then faster, ever faster … the nose wheel of our landing gear was kept slightly off the runway surface … to prevent the terrific vibration which inevitably resulted if all three wheels were kept on the ground … the noise of the wind about our Plexiglass enclosed compartment rose to a shriek… I shouted the speed figures for Bill's benefit so that he would not attempt to pull up the big ship before it gained flying speed.[12]

Airspeed quickened in the climb toward the prescribed altitude while turning left so the others on each mission's serial could take off and catch up. Each serial took about fifteen minutes to become airborne. Usually about an hour later, all the serials had got off the ground and had formed up at the "Initial Point" at 1,500 feet. The formation now could increase speed to 125 miles per hour and head toward battle. Each wave of glider missions followed the same general pattern and, once in formation over the English countryside, knew to follow the navigation beacons on land and on ships to the point that they crossed the French coast, only minutes away from their landing zones.

Each glider pilot in the three waves of the Airborne's Operation *Neptune* would face unique enemies as he went "feet dry" (crossing the French coast), threats he could not have anticipated when learning to fly gliders back in the States.

The mission's senior glider officer and now a lieutenant colonel, Michael Murphy, had insisted on flying Operation *Chicago's* lead glider on D-Day. His serial flew at 2,000 feet across the Channel after taking off in England at 0100 hours. They dropped a bit before bypassing the German-occupied Guernsey and Jersey Islands. As his glider made a wide turn toward the coast, a ribbon of tow planes' blue navigation lights stretched out behind him for miles. As he dropped down farther to 600 feet, bright red tracers erupted from the countryside below. Surprise had been lost as Murphy and the other pilots watched the tracers arc across the night sky, reminding some of July 4 fireworks.

The glider armada pushed ahead on a straight line through the tracers and antiaircraft artillery. *What's that? Sounds like popcorn popping?* It was the enemy's groundfire tearing through Murphy's fuselage fabric, narrowly missing Brigadier General Don Pratt, the assistant commander of the 101st Airborne Division, his aide, 1st Lieutenant John May, and the copilot, 2nd Lieutenant John Butler, the young man who had thrilled his hometown neighbors with airplane stunts over Main Street and who had been haunted by a glider crashing into the woods during training.

Murphy and Butler needed to land as quickly as possible and clear the landing zone as fast as they could because up to fifty other gliders were inbound, looking for the closest field to land in. Murphy had ordered everyone to land from any direction they could – as fast as they could – to unload their cargoes and glider infantry. The paratroopers had landed about three hours earlier and it was likely the enemy still controlled many of the fields.

Only about fifteen minutes behind Murphy's *Chicago* armada, 1st Lieutenant Evans Ittner and Flight Officer Richard Levering were already battling in the air. Nearly forty gliders in Operation *Detroit* had flown into a cloud bank thick enough that some glider pilots lost sight of their tow planes. As they approached LZ-O not far from Murphy, the formation had disintegrated in the cloud bank. Some C-47 pilots had tried to fly above the clouds while others held steady. Speeds varied. The glider pilots no longer could cut off from their tow planes in the sequence and at the pace they had practiced for months. Worse, as Ittner and Levering had crossed the coast, their communication line with the tow plane had been cut.

They knew to keep a steady watch on their tow plane's astrodome. When the communications wire between a C-47 and glider broke on takeoff or was cut by enemy fire, a plastic bubble about two feet wide on top of the tow plane became critical. A crewman could communicate by flashing colored lights out the astrodome back to the glider. Steady red: We're on approach. Green: Release! Blinking red: Don't release, we're going around for another pass.

Up ahead, it "looked like five guns were pyramiding a cross fire and we had to fly through it. We were hit often," reported Ittner afterward. Then what Ittner thought was a German fighter strafed the glider, shooting away the controls of his right aileron and hitting the tow rope, causing it to unravel. By now they were within range of groundfire which "blew off our rudder control." Ittner and Levering were within seconds of disaster as they cut off from their tow plane.[13]

Somehow, they were among the thirty-seven gliders that reached the LZ-O area in Operation *Detroit*. They carried about 200 glider infantry, jeeps, trailers, antitank guns, and ten tons of equipment. Most released at least a mile short of LZ-O. Chaos and improvisation marked the sunrise of America's first daytime glider mission.

While the first predawn wave on D-Day had preceded the amphibious landing, a fully prepared enemy greeted the glider pilots in the second wave close to sunset in Operations *Elmira* and *Keokuk*.

John Hanscom's ponderous glider had been painted a dull black, "suitable for such flying coffins," he mused on his first combat flight. As he settled into his seat, behind him sat 82nd Airborne troops and a trailer filled with communications equipment. Hanscom and his copilot, 2nd Lieutenant Bill Meisburger, would be carrying about five tons of combined payload that promised a hard landing.

Perhaps because his glider was overloaded, glider pilot George Williams's tow plane lifted off the runway before he did. The C-47 pilot stayed only ten feet off the ground, at full power, and finally lifted Williams's glider off the ground. Disaster avoided, the aircraft and glider finally, slowly, began to gain altitude. His life may have been saved while still over the runway.

The air generally smoothed for some glider serials over the English Channel while others battled turbulence, especially the glider pilots flying the massive Horsa gliders. Some glider pilots in CG-4As succumbed to a nervous tic of periodically tapping their instrument panel, not overly confident that each dial was reliably working. Several glider pilots and their copilots in Horsas and CG-4As alternately took the controls on the three-hour flight to battle. That would be a good time for one of the pilots to unbuckle and turn toward the tail to check on the glider infantry he carried. It had been much rougher in the back of the glider.

"They looked up with dull, listless eyes and then hung their heads back over their helmets [held upright in their laps]," recalled Hanscom.

> I couldn't see what was going on in the back of the trailer [closer to the tail]. Since the riding was even rougher back there than up front, I could well imagine what the sight was like. I went back to my seat feeling thankful that I was helping fly this winged hearse and not riding in that stuffy compartment. No matter how rough the air got, I had never known a glider pilot to suffer air sickness while flying.[14]

Second Lieutenant Andrew Bates and the others dropped down to 1,000 feet near the French coast as the daylight ebbed.

> The moon lit the English Channel just like a searchlight. Visibility was really good. As we approached the French coast, I could not believe my eyes. There were boats of all shapes and sizes as far as the eye could see. What an armada… We could see the occasional flash from the ships but most of the fighting there was over. Our flight took us right over Utah Beach. You could see that there had been lots of action down there. There was stuff still burning, thick black smoke was billowing up from the hulks, but you couldn't make out what they had been. We then descended to four hundred feet so we could avoid the heavier antiaircraft fire, but we could see plenty of tracers coming up to greet us from small arms fire. They were just like dozens of fireflies flying up towards us.[15]

Bates flew one of more than 200 gliders in Operations *Elmira* and *Keokuk* that reached the battle zone minutes apart at about 2300 hours. The glider armada had benefited from the Allied air cover over the Channel but discovered portions of the LZs had not been cleared of the Germans. Paratroopers below tried to warn the glider pilots by waving yellow flags and using orange smoke in the shape of an "F."

It was too late, as glider pilots looked down at flooded fields only 200 yards long.

As some pilots of wounded C-47s struggled to stay on course, many glider approaches would have to be steep and fast into clearings where fighting had raged for more than eighteen hours.

First Lieutenant Eddie Elkin constantly scanned his tow plane's instruments as he approached his glider's release point. When he was about to signal his glider's release, his left engine's oil pressure plummeted. Perhaps antiaircraft flak had hit it. He tried to feather the prop (adjust the blades to minimize resistance) but had to shut the engine down before "the prop ran away," broke free, and sliced through the aircraft. Flying on only one engine, he fought his C-47, holding a hard right rudder, giving it right trim tab, and slowed to ninety miles an hour. When 2nd Lieutenant Samuel Welch released his Horsa glider, Elkin turned back toward the coast, wondering if he could reach the English Channel.[16]

Second Lieutenant Noel Addy was the third tow from the lead tow ship in Operation *Elmira*. Up ahead, the lead C-47 took a big burst of enemy fire. As flames spread, it started to descend. Too fast. The tow plane crew released the tow rope, but it remained secured to the glider. Clearing trees with a 350-foot "anchor rope" dangling below his glider was every glider pilot's nightmare. Meanwhile, the second tow plane promptly had released its glider as well. Now Addy figured he had no choice, even though he was not entirely sure he had reached his landing zone. He reached for the overhead lever to release his tow rope, without looking down to see if he could land.

Farm fields offered the prospect of soft soil. He might tear the wheels off his glider and bury his nose, but digging out was better than a head-on collision with trees. Cows always were a good sign, indicating a field had not been mined.

Dead ahead, he spotted two small fields with a small opening in a stand of trees between them. *What the hell? The recon photos showed rows of hedges between the fields. Some of those suckers are fifty feet tall!*[17]

The opening was small but maybe, just maybe, if Addy touched down in the first field he could plow through the opening in the trees, break off both wings to reduce his ground speed, and survive in the second field. He touched down just as he had planned, but the trees didn't break off his wings. He rocketed into the next field, much too fast.

Others faced decisions they had dared not contemplate when training back in the States.

"You'd better pancake it in!"

Flight Officer Oliver Faris's idea couldn't have been appealing to his pilot, 1st Lieutenant John Jackson, as their glider settled after taking a direct hit from a flak shell. Machine gun fire had forced them toward a small field ringed with trees. They would only make it if they got over the field as low as they could and then dropped onto the ground hard and fast ("pancake") as they dared to shorten their runout and hope the glider didn't flatten from impact.

The glider plowed into the trees at the far end of a field, the sound of impact as terrifying as a car crash when a tree split their cockpit in two, passing between Faris and Jackson as the glider stopped.[18]

Throughout the day, a glider's tail slamming onto the ground signified a successful landing for the glider pilots who had put their glider up on its front skids to stop and risk a somersault. Some glider pilots felt as though they had survived a prize fight. Pinned by their seat belts, they had slammed against the side when a wing had been ripped away by a tree. Others had been yanked up and down as the glider had plowed across the field's furrows. An immediate, pounding headache, blurred vision, and queasiness probably signified a concussion. Some had descended so quickly that their ears had not yet popped. Battle sounds at first were fuzzy, yelled conversation unintelligible.

Then, it seemed someone had turned up the volume of war. Groans filled some glider fuselages. Someone yelling "Medic!" outside the shattered cockpit Plexiglass. Machine guns spitting. Rifles popping. Mortar whumps. Artillery explosions. Now a chorus of calls for medics. Somewhere nearby, a soldier might be sobbing in a whisper, a buddy kneeling over him knowing he was about to die. Another, his face and hands burned, squealing in agony, reminding one glider pilot of a hog being butchered.

Then adrenaline took hold. *I'm alive! Where's this blood coming from? Cockpit's wrecked. How are we going to get the howitzer out? Where am I? Where's that machine gun? Stay here? Take cover. Where's everybody? Who's that yelling? God no, is that Johnny? That one was too close. Stay here? Where is everyone? What will they tell my family? Don't be a coward ... move!*

By midnight on D-Day, about 600 glider pilots and copilots had reached Normandy. Most had endured terrifying final approaches to their landing zones. Paratroopers had been shocked at their hard landings. "One of the most sickening things I remember... I can still hear those gliders hitting the hedgerows, tearing off wings, smashing equipment, and mangling and killing the crews," 82nd paratrooper Spencer Wurst later wrote.[19]

Casualty lists would come in the following days. One last wave of glider pilots on D+1 would have to find room in fields littered with wrecked and smoking gliders.

The next morning, on June 7, a brief calm settled over many glider pilots in the third wave's Operations *Hackensack* and *Galveston* as they crossed the English Channel. Allied P-47 Thunderbolts, Spitfires, and P-51 Mustangs flew as escorts – called "delousing patrols" by some glider pilots – on all sides. They peeled away as a hazy French coast appeared on the horizon. Hundreds of ships along the shoreline below pointed in every direction, some of them aground, others lying on their sides in the shallows, and still more swinging at anchor. Up ahead smoke, like from oversized funeral pyres, rose from burning villages as well as from German and Allied positions and mixed into a deathly gray haze over the French landscape.

The fighter escorts had pulled away when Flight Officer Dale Oliver was stunned by "a dead landscape" as he released his glider. Images were important to the former Kansas farm boy. He had studied art and carried a sketch book with his flying gear. A vast expanse had been flooded by the Germans. "Horsa gliders and CG–4s [sat] shattered or half submerged from the previous day's landings... Every field was ringed with those ever-so-tall grotesque trees, like some Neanderthal hands ... reaching skyward to ensnare you...." Suddenly a huge white star appeared in his cockpit's overhead window. Another glider, only feet away. Oliver pulled hard into a tighter descent to avoid a midair collision.[20]

By 1200 hours on D+1, the gliders' arrival in Operation *Neptune* was complete. Hundreds of glider pilots had faced down their darkest demons in the six Normandy missions for which they had trained for years.

But the reality of combat on the ground would bring new horrors amidst crossfire ambushes, broken bones, torn flesh, buddies dying and disappearing, and the prospect of becoming prisoners of war.

6

"The Germans Are Coming!"

Practiced glider landings over American flatland had become a distant memory. Glider pilots saw their best friends horribly maimed in mangled gliders as others yelled for medics. Some landed within a few yards of a German machine gun emplacement. For others, it became a one-way trip into a German POW camp, where survival inched from one day to the next.

> big day!... flak heavy, strings of red beads, orange golf balls... I'm scared!... released in wrong territory, dark, can hardly see, still shooting at us. Little field. Watch those trees, pull up Doc! Ohhh. Not a bit of the nose left, only part of center of fuselage. First out, feet through floor. Doc pinned against something, pulled him out. Sgt. Davis next, two bad cuts behind knee. Slim Smith went out through the side. Rogers and Rappey dumped out rear... Gliders crashing all around, horrible sounds. Look out, there's one on top of us. No, went over and hit trees on other side of field. Where is that sulfa powder. Can't find any. Give Davis a hypo. Finally bandaged up... Expect to be shot any minute. Adam Bone & Ben Winks [glider pilots] lying down the road, dead. Gunfire getting closer. Let's get out of here. Where are we?[1]

Second Lieutenant Zane Graves's journal reflected the panic, horror, and resolve in battle that glider pilots endured over the two days' missions in Normandy. Where glider pilots and paratroopers blazed America's path into Europe.

Second Lieutenant Pete Buckley had always been a go-getter, even if it meant that the sixteen-year-old had to forge a birth certificate to become a glider pilot, likely making him the youngest glider pilot in the Army to enter combat. His pre-invasion training had included some night flights in England, but they had consisted of only two or three gliders at a time, landing on runways that were illuminated with flares. But on D-Day, there had been no guarantee that the advance pathfinders would take control of the landing zones in time to set up beacons for Buckley and the other incoming glider pilots. In fact, poor visibility had kept the pathfinders from marking the landing zones as thoroughly as had been planned. Buckley never spotted a pathfinder light after he had cut off and dropped toward the ground.

Buckley and the others had to make decisions fused with instinct and perhaps panic as they released in the dark over the Cotentin Peninsula. For some like Buckley at the back end of the first serial, there was no element of surprise.

Up ahead, Lieutenant Colonel Michael Murphy and copilot John Butler in the lead glider of Operation *Chicago* had cut loose under a full moon and broken clouds near Hiesville at about 0400 hours and looked down at fields that appeared identical in the darkness. An unexpected twenty-seven-mile-per-hour tailwind sent Murphy's glider sliding crosswise on a small field that turned out to be a pasture of wet, lush grass. Skidding much too fast to stop in time, the glider had slammed into a hedgerow, obliterating the cockpit, and mangling the fuselage. Perhaps Butler heard the trees demolishing the glider a split second before his head was fractured and body crushed by the imploding cockpit. His parents later would receive his diary that told them where to retrieve his watch from a London jeweler.

Whiplash broke General Pratt's neck, killing him instantly as well. His aide sitting in the rear of the glider survived the crash.

A German patrol on a nearby road stopped near the hedgerow shortly after impact. Two Germans briefly inspected the wreckage and the bodies. They soon left, apparently believing all were dead.

Murphy somehow had survived when his upper body and left leg tore through the fuselage fabric while collapsing steel tubing crushed his right leg. Still strapped to his seat, he had suffered two fractured legs and two broken ankles. A medical officer who was among the first Americans to reach the wreckage did not expect Murphy to survive. In an instant early on the first day, the invasion had lost two of its senior glider and infantry officers who were critical to the Normandy mission.

A few miles to the north and only about ten minutes behind Murphy's *Chicago* armada, thirty-seven glider pilots in Operation *Detroit* had faced a different challenge. Thirteen gliders that had taken off in England had already been lost. Now a mass release of those remaining near Sainte-Mère-Église resembled a cascading free-for-all for survival.[2]

With their controls shot out, glider pilots Evans Ittner and Richard Levering had little chance of forcing their glider to a stop before crashing into a ditch, embankment, stand of trees, or from sliding up to an enemy's machine gun. They hit hard. The jeep they carried broke loose and lurched forward, pinning Ittner and Levering against the glider's nose and an embankment. Two airborne troops, a captain and corporal, had been sitting in the jeep. The impact was so severe that it pinned both in their seats and snapped the captain's bones. Once the area around the field was cleared of Germans, it had taken more than an hour to extricate the captain by cutting a hole in the glider's roof and using its aileron as a stretcher.

Several hours later, Ittner and Levering found their way to a nearby command post (CP). Meanwhile, a Frenchman with a horse and buggy had taken the captain there. He had suffered a broken hip, crushed knee, broken leg, crushed chest, and face contusions. Many glider pilots became impromptu and improvisational medical aides as the sun rose on D-Day.

Some glider pilots weren't sure they would have a chance to land, knowing the C-47 towing them was as vulnerable to enemy fire as their glider. Flight Officer Glen McPherren's glider had been towed by 1st Lieutenant Louis Emerson. McPherren had been the best man at Emerson's wedding. Flames had erupted from Emerson's right engine three miles from the coast. A German antiaircraft shell had exploded only feet from his aircraft. The engine's power evaporated, and the fire began to melt the fuselage's plastic windows nearby.

Now what? thought Emerson. *The glider's got a howitzer in it. If I release Glen, he'll sink like a rock. I think we can make the LZ and still have 300 feet left. Maybe that will give Glen enough to survive a crash landing. Maybe get there, release the glider, and then get back to the coast where we can ditch near one of our ships?* Emerson had pressed ahead, trailing flames.[3]

After McPherren had released from Louis Emerson's crippled C-47, Emerson instead had to find a place to land as quickly as possible. Was there a pasture large enough for a C-47? As Emerson searched, an enemy machine gunner killed his remaining engine. Emerson now flew the equivalent of a dead-weight glider. He pushed the plane below the tree line and leveled, hoping the snapping limbs somehow could slow his fifteen-ton aircraft. Not much. Finally, he spotted a clearing and nosed in at 120 miles per hour. He bounced the plane off the ground, bleeding a little more speed. Down again. *Drag my wing this time to slow this thing down!* Emerson pushed his right wing tip onto the ground and at the last second veered to one side, so the aircraft caromed off a tree, its wings taking the brunt.

Horrifying screeches of grinding metal suddenly stopped. Silence. Trees lay shattered while the right side of the plane burned. Pistol flare cartridges began exploding. Emerson and the rest of his aircrew crawled out of the plane toward a sheltered area. The plane, broken into two pieces, continued to smolder. Emerson (broken ribs) and his copilot (compound leg fracture) had to find glider pilots or paratroopers to help both get to an aid station in the dark. Dozens more gliders, meanwhile, had been inbound with less than a minute before their forced landing, perhaps in fields where fresh hulks burned or lay broken.

The paratroopers of the 101st and 82nd Divisions had badly needed the personnel, vehicles, heavy weapons, and ammunition carried in the first glider wave. But only six of *Chicago*'s gliders had landed in the designated LZ. Ten others were up to a mile away, and seventeen others were listed as up to two miles away. *Detroit* glider pilots had fared little better. Only about half of those who reached Normandy were in or near their landing zone. Nearly half their gliders had been destroyed by the enemy, hedgerows, Rommel's deadly wooden "asparagus," and in one case a herd of cattle. Only half of the jeeps carried in *Detroit* were operable following the hard landings and hedgerow collisions.

"Hedgerows." Likely one of the greatest misnomers of World War II. The hedgerows that separated Normandy farm fields were nearly impregnable. Rather than a line of modest bushes as many American pilots assumed, many were parallel five-foot-high dirt embankments that separated the fields. Bramble thickets covered most embankments, as well as dense stands of mature trees, so large that the canopies of one embankment reached those of the parallel embankment. They sometimes formed a tunnel over a centuries-old path, wide enough for enemy ground troops, personnel carriers, mobile artillery, and even tanks to quickly change positions.

The hedgerows were so prominent that each field became an independent battlefield. It was impossible for glider pilots to know who was in the next field, whether buddies were being killed, or whether enemy reinforcements were approaching.

Usually there were only one or two access routes through a hedgerow into a field, so the enemy knew precisely where to direct its firepower by machine gun squads that had dug into the embankments in the fields' corners for a maximum sweep of fire. That had proven devastating to the glider pilots in the morning wave and would be equally so for those yet to arrive.

With many of the first wave's gliders spread across enemy territory, paratroopers had faced nearly twenty hours of combat until the second wave's arrival. A fully alert and locked-on enemy was ready for those glider pilots.

Second Lieutenant James Di Pietro and Flight Officer Ben Ward looked for a place to land their Horsa and unload their infantry in D-Day's twilight. For hours across the English Channel, Di Pietro had listened to a Greek soldier he was carrying tell him how he intended to pay back the Germans for invading his country. Finally, two small fields appeared, divided by a hedgerow. *Maybe there. Maybe we could increase speed, touch down on one field and hop over the hedgerow to the next.* They hit the field at nearly twice their landing speed. Both pilots pulled back on the wheel. Nothing! The overloaded Horsa had no agility. The nose refused to rise as seconds slipped by. Closer and closer to the trees. Ward turned the glider sharply to the left on the ground, the left wing scraping the dirt just before the Horsa broadsided a tree.

The glider split open on impact, just behind Di Pietro's seat. It rolled, ejecting most of its occupants, including Di Pietro who landed several yards into the next field. He remained attached to his seat and remarkably suffered only a few scratches. Ward hit his head but was only dazed while some of the glider infantrymen had suffered broken bones.

One of the infantrymen was missing. He was found dead, in a heap at the base of the tree. The Horsa had hit the tree exactly where the Greek infantryman had been sitting. Payback to avenge the loss of his countrymen and homeland had died with him.

While nearby medics tended to the wounded, Di Pietro and Ward were on their own. They joined an infantry unit where everyone had assembled on a roadbed, always looking for enemy snipers. They had to find the nearest command post. That's where the real-time combat decisions were being made, as well as directions back to the beach. There were about 200 men in the group looking for the CP.

After avoiding a German tank, they reached the CP and awaited orders for evacuation from the beach along with the wounded, guarding prisoners while they waited. Then bad news arrived. The Germans had retaken a key village up ahead. Di Pietro, Ward, and the other glider pilots had two choices: join the airborne troops and dig in, fight, and hope an enemy unit comprising tanks and fighting vehicles in the area somehow missed them, or head for the beach and fight their way through, if necessary. Nearly 100 glider pilots joined the column of wounded being taken to the beach on litters strapped to jeeps.

Di Pietro's glider had been among the more than 200 that arrived over adjoining landing zones at dusk in Operations *Keokuk* and *Elmira*, bringing badly needed reinforcements for the 101st and 82nd paratroopers.

Some glider pilots and ground personnel from the morning's wave had cut down trees to clear portions of the second wave's two landing zones and pathfinders had marked at least one with yellow panels and green smoke. But the Germans still controlled a significant portion of the landing zones and had learned to hold their fire until the glider pilots released and started their descent. Last-minute attempts to wave off approaching gliders from some areas that had not been cleared of the enemy largely failed.

The next morning, on D+1, the final wave of nearly 200 gliders in Operations *Galveston* and *Hackensack* arrived at the same landing zones at about 0900 hours. Those that were released at 600 feet in *Hackensack* were far more likely to reach their landing zones than the *Galveston* glider pilots who were typically released too soon and too low. Like the others the day before, their wrecked gliders soon littered the landscape.

Some clearings looked as though gliders had simply been tossed from the clouds, sitting at every possible angle, their backs shattered, wings ripped from fuselages, and some with their fabric skin stripped away, leaving their ribs exposed like a hapless animal stripped by scavengers. Some British Horsas, whose fuselages were designed to be separated at mid-fuselage to facilitate unloading, looked as if a giant cleaver had neatly sliced them in two.

Foxholes pockmarked the field, mounds of dirt circling each and many of them only a few yards from a glider. Cartridges littered the ground like spent cigarettes, testimony to the intense firefights that had erupted even before the glider pilots had unstrapped themselves and raced to the closest vegetation patch or ditch.

Many of the carcasses were not easily spotted from the air. Some had burrowed nose first into stands of trees, only their tails visible from the side. Others seemingly had tried to land on unpaved roads. When their wings snapped off, the fuselages sometimes rolled over into a roadside ditch, as if a tractor-trailer rig had toppled to its death.

Others sat forlornly in a clearing, alone and on their bellies. Their wings mangled, much of their tails shot away, as if a giant bird had been shot high in the sky and then had bellyflopped onto the ground, spread-eagled and now silent. Open doors hinted that perhaps glider pilots and passengers had somehow survived.

A few gliders apparently had hit so hard that they looked dismembered. A tail sat thirty yards away from one fuselage, both wing tips touching the ground after their support struts had fractured. In some cases, a jeep or howitzer sat alone in a field, perhaps abandoned by the glider infantry, or possibly having jettisoned through the cockpit or the glider's fabric.

Remarkably, Normandy glider pilot casualties over two days were relatively light. However, the glider infantry casualty rate – mostly men in the Horsa gliders that tended to disintegrate when landing – was considered high at eleven percent.[4] Overall, daylight missions with acceptable losses were validated when ninety percent of the troops carried by gliders had been ready for combat within two hours.[5]

More than 4,000 infantry troops of the 101st and 82nd Airborne, as well as critically needed equipment, supplies, jeeps, and artillery had reached the two divisions aboard gliders.[6] But both CG-4A and Horsa gliders had taken a beating. By one account, ninety-seven percent of the gliders were no longer combat capable and were "left to rot in the narrow pastures in which they landed," becoming fodder for scavengers.[7]

Yet for many glider pilots, Operation *Neptune* was far from over. Some would be haunted by what they had witnessed over two days. Some would have to step over the grisly gore of war's detritus on their way to the beach and a boat ride back to England. For others, their mission would stretch for weeks under enemy fire, a nightmare seemingly with no end.

After enemy fire finally had subsided in his sector, Flight Officer Bob Horr could assess the damage to the glider he had crash-landed early on D-Day. The glider pilot had felt the heat of bullets narrowly missing him as they tore through his glider. Sitting at a cockeyed angle in a Normandy clearing near Hiesville, the "Mary E" had been destroyed. He counted eighty bullet holes.

Horr had climbed out of his glider onto a battlefield of mayhem. Glider infantry had piled out of dozens of nearby gliders, had dug in, and were returning the fire of enemy snipers, machine gunners and mortar crews. Bullets and slugs had ricocheted off unseen rocks and the gliders' metal tubing. Some slammed into embankments, tree trunks or bodies.

The wounds suffered by some glider pilots had made it impossible to kick out the windows of their cockpits, drop to the ground, or race for cover. Horr's best friend, Claude "Buck" Jackson, had been shot just after his glider had released from its tow plane only 500 feet over the battlefield. He and his copilot had just thirty seconds to find a clearing, turn toward it in a broad circle while slowing to about seventy miles an hour, and slide to a stop.

Jackson had landed not far from Horr.

Horr scrambled to his friend's side. He could see that Jackson had been badly hurt. Pain flooded Jackson's face as Horr reached for the morphine syrette in his pack. A little relief until a medic arrived. But Horr couldn't stay. German mortars were landing too close and machine gun bursts split the air. He had to leave "Buck" behind.

He had spotted men from the 82nd Airborne and joined them. Once the Germans had been driven back as afternoon shadows lengthened, he dug in. As the sun set, nerves became the enemy between sudden bursts from unseen snipers. Later, the moon's soft glow brightened Horr's position well past midnight. He had to stay alert after an exhausting day.

"I learned more in five minutes than the army taught me in two years," Horr later wrote.[8] The first lesson was that there were two US Armies. Structure, discipline, and inspections marked the stateside Army. Overwhelming uncertainty, improvisation, and confusion under enemy fire defined the battlefield Army. The colonels in charge of battalions were more important to a man's survival than faraway generals. Aim just above the flashes of an enemy gun. And know that when you fire your weapon, your position is illuminated as well. Keep your weapon in your hand. A man not holding his weapon "is as useful as a dead man." Don't die with a full magazine. Cowards often die without firing their weapon.

Unlike training, battlefield lessons were unforgiving. Combat taught men that they couldn't know how long they would be in the foxhole they dug. A foxhole deep enough to avoid getting crushed by a passing tank might be ideal, but near-misses by enemy artillery could collapse the sides of a deep foxhole onto a man's face. Tree roots often limited too many foxholes to perhaps one foot deep, little more than a trench. And all were vulnerable to enemy artillery detonating in trees overhead, the tree bursts sending deadly timber daggers into a holed-up glider pilot.

Also, it wasn't a good idea to stick around a burning American tank. Billowing smoke provided a convenient target for German artillery crews hoping to hit nearby troops. Hit the dirt after an artillery near-miss and wait. If a man is hit by shrapnel, even seriously, at first he might feel only numbness. Feel around for any wounds before re-engaging.

Horr's pocket Bible brought comfort, as did a string of prayers and some heartfelt promises. A photo of his wife, Elizabeth, standing on her front porch or grinning alongside her friends, always drew comfort tinged with worry as well. He thought of her endlessly, perhaps reciting new vows of how things would be with her after the war. Memories of his mother and father while growing up in Iowa's Mount Pleasant surfaced. Horr wrote in his pilot logbook later that at one point he had killed a sniper. That reminded him of his father who liked to hunt woodchucks: "you have to wait for them and then pick them off." It brought no real joy. He only wanted to survive.

He hadn't bothered with collecting souvenirs on the battlefield after the fighting had stopped, even though turned-out pockets of dead American soldiers meant they had been looted by the enemy or local residents. "What's the use?" he wrote. "I'm no glory grabber. Just end this war and let me come home." Reflection and resolutions often carried a glider pilot through the night as he lay in the dirt waiting for sunrise. The Normandy mission was his first. Horr later heard that "Buck" Jackson had died. If Horr received a citation or medal from his actions that day and night, he knew he would send it to Jackson's mother.[9]

It had not been a smooth flight for 2nd Lieutenants Stratton Appleman and Walter Cobb before dawn on D-Day. They had trailed their formation by fifteen minutes across the English Channel after their glider's nose catch had failed to hold the tow rope. The front of the glider tended to pop open when the tow rope released. It took time to wire it shut before takeoff. Despite being towed at a faster-than-normal 145 miles per hour, they were late to a clearing with their howitzer and three airborne artillerymen.

Yet it was still dark on D-Day when they had landed, bending the glider so badly that the howitzer couldn't be removed. Rather than burn the glider to keep the artillery piece from falling into German hands, they hid its firing mechanism in the woods. But, like many glider pilots in the crush of battle, they weren't sure of their location. Appleman decided to reconnoiter the area around his glider, hoping to find Americans to help him unload his glider's artillery. Gunfire erupted instead as Appleman jumped into a foxhole.

When several Germans approached and looked down at Appleman, a choking terror rose from his gut:

if I had tried to get out myself, I'm sure I would have fallen on my face … my knees were twitching… I was afraid. It was the kind of fear a child has in a nightmare … the power of flight and even of speech is taken away… I was more afraid of being afraid and had suppressed the whole idea of fear so that I had behaved foolishly and recklessly since the mission began … suppressed it so strongly that while crawling through the grass under fire towards the foxhole, I became overwhelmingly sleepy.[10]

Appleman and at least ten Normandy glider pilots became prisoners for the rest of the war, but not before escaping from a poorly guarded train bound for Germany. Appleman hid with help from the French resistance for three weeks before he was stopped by German soldiers and could not produce identity papers. He would spend the rest of the war at Buchenwald and Stalag Luft III.

Meanwhile, for most glider pilots, exhaustion had ruled the battlefield on their first night of Operation *Neptune*. Paratroopers had been awake for nearly twenty-four hours and tank crews almost as long. An airborne captain rounded up glider pilots John Hanscom, William Meisburger, and others to stand guard on a group of Sherman tanks so their crews could sleep a few hours. The night regularly was punctured by the distinctive sounds of Allied and enemy weaponry. Close, but not too close.

The next day, the two glider pilots were added to a patrol assigned to knock out a German artillery emplacement. When they reached it, they found it had been deserted and rigged with mines and booby traps. But what struck Hanscom on his way to the artillery site was the fate that other glider pilots had met, perhaps some of them in his squadron.

In front of the emplacement were three gliders, one Horsa and two CG-4As. One of the CG-4As was completely burned; only the skeletal structure of the steel tubing remained. The Horsa was a mess of kindling wood. The other CG-4A had apparently made a perfect landing, but directly into the face of enemy machine gun fire. The two pilots sat stiff and cold in their seats.[11]

Later, Hanscom learned three of his squadron's pilots had been killed, some injured so badly they would never fly again, and two were listed as missing in action.

Glider pilot Byron Sharp remembered the movie *Baptism of Fire*, an army training film that had been shown to troops going into battle for the first time. Nominated for an Oscar, it was particularly graphic, with close-ups of American GIs who had been shot through the eye or whose eyes stared vacantly after being shot dead.

Those scenes had flashed before Sharp on his way from his glider to the glider pilots' assembly point when he had come upon another glider pilot. "Well, I'm the only survivor," the pilot told

Sharp. "The Germans came in the glider, and they thought I was dead." Sharp could see why. The glider pilot had been filleted from his neck almost down to his waist. The gaping wound revealed much of his rib cage. Sharp took him to a nearby aid station where other glider pilots were being treated.

A short time later, Sharp spotted a glider pilot he thought he knew. But something was wrong.

"Butler, is that you?"

"Who said that?"

"Well, I'm Sharpy."

"Sorry, Sharpy. I can't see you."

Butler had a hairless face. His eyelashes, eyebrows and hair were gone. After landing, he had moved to the back of his glider that was filled with ammunition for the infantry. A sniper's bullet detonated it in Butler's face. Sharp couldn't believe the guy had survived and heard later that his vision had returned.[12]

Glider pilots often spent the night, and sometimes days at or near a CP before walking or hitching a ride to the beach and boarding a ship headed back to England. They often stood posts guarding German prisoners, watched as medics treated the wounded as they came in, and when the shooting stopped listened to the stories told by paratroopers. Anger often fueled the paratroopers' reports from the battlefield.

Paratroopers told Flight Officer John Mahe that they had seen other paratroopers hanging from trees with their throats cut. There was a rumor that the Germans had used flame throwers against some Americans. Medics apparently were left alone until they reached an aid station so that German spotters could call in mortar attacks on both the medics and their wounded. It also was dangerous to pick up an abandoned German machine gun. There had been reports of American infantry firing at the sound of German machine guns, only to find out they were in the hands of other American troops.

The infantry and some glider pilots who accompanied them had also learned to be wary when chasing retreating German units. The word spread that suicide snipers sometimes were left behind in trees to pick off advancing Americans. Glider pilot Meisburger cringed at the sight of German soldiers hanging upside down in tall trees. They had tied themselves to the trunk or a large limb. They now hung head down with arms outstretched, a breeze rocking them back and forth. Meisburger counted five and wondered if they would be left for the buzzards. He didn't count the dead Germans floating in fields that had been flooded to prevent glider landings as he walked by.

Second Lieutenant James Campbell had been awed by a chaplain praying in the door of a C-47 back in England minutes before he had taken off. The sea of heads bowed in prayer had stuck with him as he approached his landing zone, cut off, and followed another glider down, passing over a glider that perhaps had hit a mine. Flames were eating it whole, making the prospect of survivors little more than a hollow hope.

Later, Campbell saw undeniable death when he walked along a road. Germans had been "freshly killed," he recalled, "and already had an awful yellow color to their skins. That color combined with the dirty gray of their uniform added to the picture."[13] All along the road, "Minen" signs reminded Campbell he had been fortunate that he had not landed in a field laced with mines as others had.

Soon modified "tank dozers" would push vehicle hulks and perhaps bodies off the roads. Shreds of skin and tissue, bits of uniforms hanging from fences, and sometimes boots with feet inside were all that remained of those who had taken a direct hit, leaving little for the graves registration teams that would follow later.

As he was nearing the beach for his evacuation, Meisburger and others dove into bushes alongside a road when a mortar shell passed overhead. It had landed only feet away from a jeep a short distance ahead of them, the blast throwing the driver to the ground. "Keep moving!" their commanding officer yelled as they walked by the blood-soaked American lying in the dirt. He looked to be about twenty years old and had a pepper mill's worth of freckles and reddish hair. His glazed eyes were opening and closing in slow motion. Haunted by the prospect, Meisburger was sure the boy died shortly after the group passed.

A young German lying in a hedgerow struck glider pilot Pete Buckley similarly.

> He was making his last gasps. He had about the same coloring as I had … it sobered me up. It was the first dead German I had seen this way. The fact that I couldn't do anything for him really shook me up, too … but later on I began to get very mad at [the Germans] … because I had seen what they had done to some of our paratroopers.[14]

Meanwhile, American squads were collecting their dead. Richard Mercer was a young glider pilot who had joined the army ten days after marrying his sweetheart, Norma Jo, and only three days following his twenty-first birthday. He had been released only about 300 feet over his clearing. He had less than one minute's gliding time to land his Horsa in a field surrounded by trees.

It appeared Mercer had lost control, perhaps from enemy fire or from plowing through a hedgerow. He slammed onto the ground so hard the glider broke apart and came to a stop in only about sixty feet, resting on its roof. Mercer and fourteen of the infantrymen he carried were killed. A photograph of eight shrouded dead men side by side on the ground, feet toward the camera, with the wreckage in the background became one of the iconic photos of World War II.

Eventually, hundreds of exhausted glider pilots made their way to the beach and a boat ride back to England. Like many others, glider pilot Noel Addy had survived his impossibly hard landing and ultimately returned to his base. "On the ship [back to England], they gave me a bunk and said dinner would be ready in about two hours. I lay down to rest a few minutes and when I awoke I asked if dinner was ready. 'No.' …it was the next day already. I had slept 28 hours straight."[15]

Other glider pilots faced a different kind of fight, including a Native American from the San Diego area who found himself fighting to save the life of a French village.

Several days after the invasion, everyone in the village of Graignes had gathered in the pews of its ancient stone church when a woman burst through the front door of the refuge that was guarded by 2nd Lieutenants Irwin Morales and Tom Ahmad.

"The Germans are coming!"

Four days earlier, they had flown across the English Channel in the first wave of gliders, but their C-47 was off course so far that they had landed in a marsh about ten miles south of their landing zone. They had spotted the church's steeple on a nearby hill, as did more than 180 paratroopers who also were too far behind the front lines to chance anything but regrouping in Graignes.

Morales, Ahmad, and the paratroopers had organized a defensive perimeter stout enough to hold off a panzer-grenadier division until American troops advancing from the beach reached them. Could they hold out that long with only a few days' rations and ammo? Could they retrieve additional supplies that had been dropped into the marshland between the Vive and Taute Rivers? By nightfall on D-Day, Morales was guarding the left flank of the church's perimeter while Ahmad was stationed with others closer to the church.

Days had passed as sabotage and scouting patrols from their makeshift outpost by Morales and the paratroopers tested the Germans' positions and firepower. They also destroyed bridges, ambushed enemy truck convoys, cut communications lines, and took German prisoners. But by June 11, Graignes had become surrounded by Germans retreating from the beach along with reinforcements driving forward.

Casualties had mounted under relentless artillery barrages as Morales, Ahmad, and the remaining paratroopers nearly ran out of ammunition. That night, the beleaguered Americans were overrun. Morales and most of the others fell back into the marshes, farm fields, and causeways to regroup. They hid by day and sneaked toward the beach at night, exhausted after the German assault on Graignes. Ahmad had remained behind with a group of paratroopers guarding the church and villagers. They were taken prisoner.

Finally, ten days after D-Day, Morales reached Allied troops. He didn't know what had happened to Ahmad who had been his copilot. Morales had fought as an infantryman for more than a week.

The Germans had suffered more than 1,200 casualties in taking the village. They exacted a horrific revenge by executing the church's priests, dozens of townspeople who had helped the American soldiers, and those they had taken prisoner at an aid station near the church. Some were shot and dumped in a river, others were shot and left along a roadway. Thomas Ahmad was among those who were marched into a field and shot to death. The Germans burned the village to the ground, leaving only two of 200 buildings unscathed.

Two men in a glider, one from Wisconsin and the other from southern California, had flown into battle as glider pilots, had fought as infantrymen, and had met fates fully understood only by the American soldiers who shared their battle scars and sometimes nightmares for decades to come.

Others who had dug in near the LZs had learned to dread the silence that followed an artillery barrage and the sense of doom in the next attack. *When? Where?* Some had been gripped by a paralytic fear. After mastering the ability to control a combat glider, on the ground many felt as helpless as a newborn when watching a buddy die; his eyes filling with tears, blood bubbles escaping from his mouth as muffled gargling sounded as though he was drowning. Quivering breaths becoming faint pants, and then wheezes. Blinking eyes slowing as if sleep loomed just before his eyes rolled back into his head toward stillness, his mouth frozen open. No stateside training prepared men for that. They had been trained to fly, not die.

Operation *Neptune* proved to be a key contributor to the success of Operation *Overlord*. Beach landings with airborne support suffered fewer casualties than those without. Glider payloads totaled nearly 100 pieces of artillery, five tons of explosives and mines, almost 300 jeeps, and nearly 240 tons of cargo. The glider pilots' performance assuaged the lingering glider wounds of the Sicily debacle and validated their potential as war planners plotted the Allies' advance into Europe.

Yet glider warfare remained a work in progress. Reconnaissance photos proved to be of questionable value. Tow planes were vulnerable to enemy fire. Night missions were nearly suicidal. Releasing at the designated altitude was proven critical to survival. Pathfinders securing landing zones were vital to preventing widely dispersed glider landings. Horsas required different landing fields than CG-4As. All were pointed out by glider pilot comments in their post-mission reports.

Meanwhile, the echoes of war stretched far beyond France.

Associated Press reports of 2nd Lieutenant Rollin Fowler's combat heroics were carried in newspapers across the country. Fowler reportedly killed nine Germans in a firefight minutes after his glider landed. Then, knocked unconscious by a grenade, he was captured but later managed to kill two more and then flee back to American territory on a German motorcycle. Depicted as the modest war hero, "All I'm waiting for now is the next tow job," he reportedly said.[16]

Meanwhile, loneliness was an ever-present enemy, fought in letters addressed to "My Beloved," "Sweet Baby," "Darling," "Dearest," "Honey," and "Baby Doll," and filled with expressions of love. "Your voice sounded like heaven." "I did nothing but think of you." "That telephone conversation we had. It was a peach, wasn't it?" "I can't wait to start our family, a boy and a girl, I hope." "To the sweetest girl in the world, I can't wait to take you again into my arms. I can't begin to tell you how much I love you." "I feel like having a good cry… I haven't heard from you in four days … [my] every love thought as fresh as spring grass." Written on a battlefield of despair fueled with hope for the future.

> I feel more in love now, then before we were married – hope you don't mind – then I guess it was just something that you dream would come true and now it is something that has come true. Something that has been very beautiful and fine. Something that you want to get back to, and above all something that you don't want anything to happen to. Words don't come easy and grammar and etc. aren't exactly what they should be, but every thought is as deep rooted as the "mighty oak" and as fresh as spring grass. Hear my heart as it sings the old, old love song and I will be with you always.[17]

Second Lieutenant Edwin Blanche had responsibilities foreign to most other glider pilots. The Canadian native was thirty-six years old, married, and the father of three daughters. Like most glider pilots, he wrote home almost as soon as he returned from his Normandy mission. Post-battle letters home often were a sanitized blend of risk and relief, of facing fate but buoyed by optimism for the future. Rarely did they reveal the horrors and revulsion of war.

Alece Dearest,

Well, we got back last night from the "big adventure," ... with a fully loaded glider (TNT and dynamite) so darn nerve-wracking it was such a relief to cut loose ... would have made a perfect landing except for a small ditch across the field that took off the landing gear with a big jerk... My glider had a big Alece on the nose for the sweetest girl in the world & I'm sure God brought me thru for you ... so you see, honey, as long as we have control of the air, I am not in a lot of danger, & you don't have much to worry about... Loads & loads of love to you all, darling, I'm thinking of you always. Keep praying for me.[18]

For others, the clank of the mailbox lid on a family's porch marked the start of a different kind of Normandy nightmare.

June 5, 1944

Dear Mother:

This is the type of letter I had hoped would never have to be written. I will be flying a glider in the airborne invasion of Europe and this will be my farewell letter to you for some time. I will write again as soon as possible to let you know I am well and safe.

I am leaving this with our squadron intelligence officer together with 39 English pounds that is to be sent to you in the event I do not return. Believe my other affairs are in order. As you know, you are my sole beneficiary.

I owe you and Dad so much it is the least I could do. Don't think anyone could ask for better parents and want you to know I have been eternally grateful that you chose me.
My love to you all,

Dick[19]

Captain Dick Hoag had died when he crash-landed under enemy fire in the twilight of D-Day.

For other families, the sight of a uniformed Western Union messenger boy, perhaps riding up a path to their porch on his bicycle with a pouch over his shoulder, brought a different kind of agony.

THE SECRETARY OF WAR DESIRES ME TO EXPRESS HIS DEEP REGRET THAT YOUR		
SON	CAPTAIN	NORMAN L AIGNER
(RELATIONSHIP)	(RANK)	(NAME)
HAS BEEN REPORTED MISSING SINCE		
6 JUNE		OVER FRANCE
(DATE)		(LOCALITY)
WHEN DETAILS OR OTHER INFORMATION ARE RECEIVED YOU WILL BE PROMPTLY NOTIFIED		

The "Casualty Message Telegram" arrived more than a month after Captain Norman Aigner had disappeared on D-Day after releasing from his tow plane. Other glider pilot families received similar fill-in-the-blank telegrams. It became the first shot in their war of heartache, uncertainty, hope, speculation, and tears. Weeks, often months, passed before the families of some missing glider pilots learned of their fates.

Three weeks after first reading the telegram, Aigner's father wrote to the AAF, explaining his family was "so anxious" to know more. Aigner had released from his tow plane, turned left, and encountered heavy machine gun fire. No one saw him hit. No one saw him crash. No one apparently knew anything more.

Then, a few weeks later:

THE SECRETARY OF WAR ASKS THAT I ASSURE
YOU OF HIS DEEP SYMPATHY IN THE LOSS OF
YOUR SON CAPTAIN NORMAN L. AIGNER WHO
WAS PREVIOUSLY REPORTED MISSING IN ACTION.
REPORT NOW RECEIVED STATES HE WAS KILLED
ON SIX JUNE IN FRANCE. LETTER FOLLOWS.

J.A. ULIO
THE ADJUTANT GENERAL

Nearly fifty glider pilots were killed in action in Normandy. While the deaths of some may have been clean and sudden, the heartache carried by their families back home would last beyond the end of World War II. Fathers would never play catch with their sons; parents would never share another holiday dinner table or read their children's report cards. There would be no more anniversaries to celebrate. No more birthdays.

For other families, they could only wait, hope, and pray for those who remained missing in action or who had been taken prisoner.

Meanwhile, another glider invasion loomed, only two months away. Cots needed to be stripped and personal belongings boxed for shipment to devastated families. Replacements for those killed, wounded, or who had disappeared would have to be introduced and integrated into the squadrons, training flights back in England would resume, and mission planning would have to be completed for an assault in a land of vineyards and Germans.

7

"Our Men Were Lucky"

Flight Officer Arnold Wursten knew he would be leading with his chin, flying near the front of the first Allied glider mission since Normandy.

He had "expected the worst" after he had scanned the red dots designating German antiaircraft emplacements on a map displayed at his squadron's briefing. The Normandy veteran knew each could draw a bead first on his glider and then the others behind him.

Operation *Dragoon*, the invasion of southern France on August 15, 1944 – only six weeks following D-Day at Normandy – was critical to the Allies driving the German armies east toward the Rhine River and out of France. The Germans knew the Allies were bound for the Riviera and had dug in for months. Intelligence reports indicated there were approximately fifty antiaircraft emplacements along the coast and three radar stations that would be "the greatest threat to Troop Carrier operations in the area."[1]

Would it be as bad as what Wursten had endured in Normandy? He had learned not to rely on everything that he had been told at the briefing. Especially the reconnaissance photographs. Their quality had proven laughable in Normandy. And lethal. Instead, he had tried to think of every contingency based on his Normandy experience. *How about we loosen the glider's nose latches ahead of time, so if we crash and the jeep we're carrying comes flying forward, the cockpit will swing up and we'll go with it and be out of the way.*

But he encountered no enemy fire directed at his overloaded glider as he approached his landing zone about eighteen miles inland. He had not needed the bag of dirt he was sitting on, hoping it would have slowed a bullet. No need for the flak jacket, either.

But after he landed, headed toward a command post, and then as the day's mission unfolded, unexpected death surrounded him.

> I ... noticed some of our boys dead in their crashed gliders. Some had their heads ripped off, blood all over... I learned one of my friends [2nd Lieutenant Richard McFarland] was about to die... I hurried to the Red Cross station. I thought he might want me to do something for him, but I was too late. He was lying on the operating table under a blanket, dead. They had tried to operate on him. The doc told me he died from concussion of the brain... I also ... saw friends there ... one fellow had both legs cut off. Yes, I was lucky indeed.[2]

Luck and chaos would greet more than 600 glider pilots in Wursten's wake during Operation *Dragoon*.

The thirty-six American divisions that had come ashore following the Normandy invasion now required more than twenty-one tons of supplies daily. A second port, on the Mediterranean, was critical to supplying the two million troops on the continent. If VI Corps led by Major General Lucian Truscott, Jr, could establish a Riviera beachhead, the port of Marseilles was only sixty miles to the west. In addition, an infantry advance up the Rhone River Valley would create a massive, Allied pincer attack from Normandy and the Riviera that could push the Germans back to the Rhine. There was even the possibility that the German armies in western France could be cut off from easterly retreat routes, or that German troops might be withdrawn from Normandy to meet the new threat in the south.

Like Normandy, the vanguard of Operation *Dragoon* would be the Airborne's pathfinders, paratroopers, and glider pilots supplying men and supplies. They would land in the Argen Valley – generally surrounded by hilly terrain – between Le Muy and Carnoules in one of two landing zones, designated LZ-A and LZ-O, to block German reserves from moving toward the beaches and to capture strategic high ground.

The glider pilots would support the invasion in two waves. First, three teams of pathfinders would depart at 0100 hours for their two-hour flight. They would have only about an hour to set up "Eureka" guidance devices in the DZs (drop zones) and LZs before the paratroopers arrived, followed closely by the glider pilots. At about 0600 hours, two serials of gliders, one comprising the larger British Horsas (flown by British glider pilots), and the other comprising CG-4A gliders, would take off on Mission *Bluebird*. At 0730 hours the naval bombardment would commence as troops headed toward beaches. The amphibious assault would begin at 0800 hours, about the same time that the first wave of gliders was scheduled to land inland. Then at about 1800 hours the first of nine glider serials in Mission *Dove* would arrive over the battlefield.

The two glider missions were assigned key roles in the airborne assault that would ultimately total 10,000 men delivered to the battlefield by air over the course of about fifteen hours.

It didn't look to the Normandy glider pilots that flying over enemy territory a second time would differ much from their horrors in Normandy. Would German General Friedrich Wiese's 19th Army be as well fortified as the enemy they had faced in Operation *Neptune*? The meticulous and adept battlefield tactician had risen from battalion to army commander in only five years. With only a few months' notice, his orders had been to fortify the 400-mile coastline of southern France. Hundreds of concrete bunkers had been carved out of hillsides, thousands of mines had been planted, antiaircraft emplacements had been established, and the beaches were studded with crossfire emplacements.[3]

But he commanded a sickly, demoralized, and understrength army of seven divisions. Many of his soldiers were either inexperienced boys or broken-down veterans from the Eastern Front. Others were prisoners who had been captured and did not speak German. His army's vehicles faced a critical fuel shortage and some units relied on horse-drawn carts, wagons, and bicycles.

He couldn't be sure if his men would fight with backbone, or bow to the coming onslaught.

The invasion of southern France was so widely expected that delays had forced the Allies to change its name from Operation *Anvil* to Operation *Dragoon* in the hope of throwing the Germans off the scent. Few believed, however, that surprise would be on the Allies' side.[4] Nerves grew taut as everyone pondered, planned, and looked for signs that the invasion was near.

Compared to the lockdown in the days leading up to Normandy, preparation in Italy was remarkably casual at nine Italian airfields where more than 600 glider pilots had been sent to prepare for the second France invasion. They were free to move about, the few guards at the various bases notwithstanding. Trips to the beach, sightseeing, and flying when opportunities surfaced resembled a vacation more than war duty.

But combat loomed and survival was on everyone's mind. Glider pilot James Ferrin had heard Normandy stories about glider pilots' vulnerability to small arms fire up through the cockpits. On his first combat mission he was determined to lessen those odds. He and some buddies found an abandoned Italian railroad car and used torches to cut out metal seats for retrofitting into his glider.

But idle speculation dimmed when the word spread. "The invasion is on August 15!" Like Ferrin, it would be glider pilot William Knickerbocker's first combat mission. When he had been drafted in 1941, he was managing a California oil field supply store. He figured he would be assigned to the quartermaster corps. Instead, Knickerbocker was sent to the infantry. With his previous civilian pilot experience, he volunteered to become a glider pilot at the first opportunity.

Now he had three days to prepare for his assignment. That included "homework" such as studying a four-page document, "Terrain Analysis," of his assigned landing zone. It described each of twenty-five fields in the zone. He figured not much of the info would be particularly helpful, except the section on recognition from the air. Although he might be assigned a field within the landing zone, Knickerbocker would have his own plan, just in case.

"Look for a field that might be too short, maybe some other problems with it. That's the one I'll take. There'll be less competition for that one. Besides, I could study the LZ for a year, but as soon as I cut off all my plans might go out the window."[5] His philosophy would prove clairvoyant.

First Lieutenant Richard Fort also studied the photo of the field he had been assigned. On his first combat mission he would be carrying troops, a trailer, and was paired with another glider that would be carrying the trailer's jeep. Ideally, the two gliders would land in the same field. *Mine looks pretty smooth, maybe pasture or grain stubble. That's good. Looks like vines, brush, maybe a few trees along the edge. Let's see if we can land on the right side, far end, close together. We'll unload the jeep first, use it to pull the trailer out, and those guys will be on their way.* Fort's plan, and those of other glider pilots, soon would prove illusory.[6]

Some glider pilots knew improvisation a few hundred feet off the ground likely would become more important than a plan conceived while sitting in Italian barracks days before the mission. Normandy veteran Jack Merrick recalled the reconnaissance photographs that had failed to alert the glider pilots to the dense hedgerows of tall trees. He had been knocked unconscious when his glider hit one of those trees, knocking loose the jeep he was carrying a few feet behind his seat. The photographs for Operation *Dragoon* looked suspiciously familiar to those in Normandy. Taken from a high altitude at midday with minimal shadows, it was nearly impossible to judge the height of structures, trees, and vegetation. Merrick also thought they looked out of focus at best or outright blurry at worst.

Merrick and the other Normandy veterans had their own pre-flight routine in the face of another long tow to their landing zone. In addition to his flak jacket, Merrick wore a helmet with cutouts for his headphones. Those helmets had been designed primarily for bomber crews. For others, sitting on their flak jacket might ward off groundfire. Removing the side window in the cockpit might make it easier to get out after landing, the added noise in flight be damned.

The final hour or two before takeoff would be filled with last-minute adjustments, double checks, introductions and waiting. Knickerbocker would be carrying chemical mortar personnel and their equipment into combat. Like many of the other glider pilots carrying personnel, nervous greetings were exchanged alongside each glider but little more. There were last-minute checks to make, and perhaps gestures extended to settle nerves and instill hope. Knickerbocker disdained using his gas mask, figuring he would be landing in enemy territory and that the Germans would not poison their own troops.

As the glider pilots reported to their aircraft tightly packed in runway marshaling patterns on August 15, an Allied armada comprising 2,500 ships and about 145,000 troops was in position off the Riviera.

The gliders' mission started as a "milk run" from Corsica toward the Riviera, one pilot remarking "we couldn't hear anything except the wind on the glider."[7] But the uneventful approach evaporated when the pathfinders discovered fog blanketing the drop zones and landing zones. Quick thinking became the order of the day as confusion crept into the mission. The nine C-47s filled with pathfinders circled high over the drop zones, circled again, and then again. Finally, the order came for the pathfinders to jump, only about fifteen minutes ahead of the inbound paratroopers.

Mayhem had seeped into Operation *Dragoon*. The pathfinder team for one paratrooper DZ landed at least ten miles away. Another team, destined for LZ-A, landed three-and-a-half miles away. Only the team for LZ-O was successful, landing within a football field of its objective.

Not far behind the paratroopers, the two serials of gliders in the morning's glider Mission *Bluebird* had taken off in Italy shortly after 0600 hours. As the first serial passed Corsica, a coded message chilled the tow planes' radio operators. Fog still blanketed the landing zones. The larger Horsas in one serial that required larger landing areas and at least reasonable visibility were ordered back to Italy.

Maybe the CG-4As could get in, but only if the fog cleared as daybreak warmed the ground. Could the second serial buy a little time? "China Boy LZ covered with ground fog return gliders land in Corsica if necessary, Williams China Boy." C-47 radio operator Martin Wolfe was shocked by the radio transmission. "China Boy" was code for recalling the CG-4As. "Williams" told him the message came from General Paul Williams who commanded the IX Troop Carrier Command in Italy. The entire serial started a broad turn back toward Corsica. Fog had become the frontline enemy of Operation *Dragoon*'s glider corps.

Then several minutes later, another message: "China Boy proceed to destination return gliders only if, repeat, if fuel insufficient." The C-47s reversed course a second time. But turning twenty C-47s took time. Flight Officers Robert Gilman and David Haggard, both on their first combat mission, didn't remember detours as part of their briefing's flight plan. But Flight Officers Jay Kattelman and Oscar Rains, both Normandy veterans, knew that a combat flight plan could become a suggestion in a matter of minutes. An hour's flight time had been lost and the gliders would be landing much closer to amphibious assault than planned, but at least they were back on course.

At about 0900 hours, the tow planes at last descended into the Argen Valley and released their gliders. Flight Officer Earl Sanford and 2nd Lieutenant Raymond Schinkel had been towed past German antiaircraft block towers and pill boxes on their approach but had reached the landing zone without any of the antiaircraft flak they had endured approaching Normandy. British paratroopers had largely cleared the landing zone of enemy troops and the pathfinders had marked the LZ with a "T" panel in its center and had lit smudge pots to reveal wind direction.

But death had greeted the glider pilots long before they had crossed the beach. Although glider quality control issues had improved, each glider pilot could never be sure his glider would hold up, even after he had checked it just before takeoff. The glider pilots' checklist called for Flight Officer William Kern and 2nd Lieutenant Robert Hardin to inspect their glider on the tarmac before taking off in Italy. That would have included checking their controls and double-checking their load for balance and tight lashings. Structural integrity, though, was a matter of trust on the way to war.

Not far from Corsica, in an instant their glider's right wing fell away. As their CG-4A laid over on its side and snapped its tow line, the crew sat helpless. It disintegrated as it plunged into the sea, killing everyone aboard. Bits of glider fabric and debris lingered in the sky, bobbing in the tow planes' prop wash turbulence, and then slowly drifted down toward the sea and the bodies.

Although an hour late, thirty-three of *Bluebird*'s thirty-seven gliders that reached the coast landed in LZ-O, perhaps the best success rate of any single serial in the war. Though many gliders were badly damaged when landing, their troops, weapons, and supplies were off-loaded to complete Operation *Dragoon*'s first glider mission. The Horsas that had turned back ultimately reversed course to join the battle later in the afternoon. By then, the paratroopers had been fighting for close to twelve hours and needed critical reinforcements, medical supplies, and more firepower.

Haze, dust, and smoke drifted across the late-afternoon shadows as the second major wave of gliders, Mission *Dove*, approached the French coast. Nothing in glider pilot James Ferrin's training had prepared him for the number of gliders in the air. Ten serials of gliders in troop carrier groups spaced only ten minutes apart comprised the afternoon's wave. He was part of the first serial of forty-seven CG–4s. Ferrin was "awestruck by the long lines of tow planes and gliders that stretched all along the coast [back] to Italy" as he crossed over the French shoreline, at the head of a tight parade on his way to his landing zone only ten minutes away.[8]

That wasn't exactly the plan. After passing Corsica, the tail of one glider in the lead serial's 442nd TCG had begun to vibrate badly. *Now what? Do I hang on and hope we make it across the Med to France? Nope.* The glider's pilot reported the problem to his tow pilot. An emergency landing might be in order. Rather than cut the glider loose, the tow pilot headed back to Corsica. The entire 442nd serial had turned with him, just as the tow pilots had been trained. *Always follow your leader.* Once the glider released over Corsica, its tow pilot realized his serial's pilots had followed him.

He began the slow turn to get his herd of C-47s and gliders headed back toward France. But Ferrin's 441st TCG had already overtaken the 442nd. The 442nd would have to squeeze into the other troop carrier groups bound for France.

Two other TCGs, all bound for LZ-O, now were much too close to his tail. Their ten minutes' separation had disappeared. Some tried to slow, but that risked the equivalent of midair chain collisions from behind. Others pulled their noses up to gain altitude and vertical separation from the others. Tow plane crews began freelancing their way toward land, trying to reassemble as they approached France. In only about thirty minutes, Mission *Dove*'s choreography had been destroyed.

Conditions worsened for Ferrin and others as they crossed the beach. Deep dust clouds 500 feet thick from earlier bombing runs obscured his tow plane. He steered by "following the rope" and its angle between his glider and his hidden C-47. The dust cleared enough for the tow plane to waggle its wings near the landing zone. *Time to release. There's the markers. Red T, green smoke. Maybe that field off my wing. Too many poles. There's a vineyard, go there.*

As soon as Ferrin's glider stopped in a rat's nest of vines, he, his copilot, and three infantrymen unloaded the jeep they had carried. He looked up. Gliders were inbound toward his field with few options nearby. One glider approached too high, too hot. The pilot overshot Ferrin's vineyard. The deep crackling sound of shattering tree trunks and perhaps the glider told Ferrin it was a hard landing. Now another glider held course for Ferrin's field. It clipped his glider's cockpit and then cartwheeled nearly 100 yards. The infantrymen climbed out once it stopped, shaken but unhurt.

Three of the four serials of gliders at LZ-O landed within nine minutes of each other in what one glider pilot called "a rodeo." It marked a mission that would be defined by freelancing and horror.

A few miles away at LZ-A, dozens of gliders were in free flight in broad descending circles, ever tightening as if they were over a drain, drawing closer to one another with each passing second. They were so close that some glider pilots could read the names written on passing gliders, until one glider pilot after another dove out of the converging pattern when he spotted a clearing off to the side.

Flight Officer Theodore Sampson had been told to expect release at 600 feet over a landing zone approximately 1,200 feet long with some bushes at one end. Instead, he was released five times higher, his zone's yellow T and blue smoke markers barely visible. There was no way he could settle on a field at that altitude, so he headed down, trusting fate, flying skill, and his copilot. Instead of calling out speed and altitude, his copilot turned spotter, alerting Sampson to the gliders on all sides of his descent, some perilously close, others veering away at the last second. As the terrain finally came into view at only 400 feet, Sampson was limited to a field with what at first looked like bushes but were mature trees and with a runout distance only half the length that he had been told to expect. *My God, there's a cliff at the far end!* Sampson made it, with precious few feet to spare.

As Jack Merrick approached LZ-A, a surreal mirage appeared up ahead. C-47s and their gliders were *approaching* Merrick. They were going the wrong way. *How could that be possible?* They were in the midst of circling an already hopelessly congested landing zone. Merrick could feel the downward pressure as his tow plane gained altitude, pulling Merrick's glider up to 3,000 feet to clear the incoming air traffic. At three times the height of the Eiffel Tower, Merrick had to release from his tow plane.

"Christ what a mess!" he recalled later.

> Everywhere I looked there were gliders in free flight or still tagging along [with their] tow planes taking evasive action, trying not to run into each other. I threaded my way down through diving and turning gliders as thick as flies around a dead road rabbit… I watched one glider come whistling in at about one hundred miles per hour, hook a wing, and go cartwheeling down the field like a cheerleader at a football game.[9]

Glider pilot Milton Dank might have envied others who later recalled that their tow toward France had been a milk run in the

absence of German resistance. Dank and his copilot, Flight Officer
Bud Klimek, had taken off in a dust storm in Italy. As they passed
over the Allied armada off the coast, Dank had spotted an American
cruiser, the USS *Tuscaloosa*, firing its guns. A second later, a blast
rocked his glider "as though a door had slammed against the tail
of the glider." Dank had lost his right horizontal stabilizer. Still
attached to the tow plane, his glider rolled over onto its right wing
and plunged 100 feet before the tow rope yanked the glider's nose
upward. Dank and Klimek hung on to the glider's controls, their
glider's nose high, the fuselage angled to the right as if it were sliding
through the air. They had lost two-way communication with their
tow plane pilot as they fought to keep the right wing from dipping
too low and flipping the glider onto its back.

*Only a few minutes more, just a few more miles to get the LZ. Watch
for the green light. There. And green smoke!* When Dank released as
he neared a field, he kept yelling at Klimek "who was as white-faced
as I'm sure I was" to fully engage the spoilers to force the glider to
descend fast and reduce speed as quickly as possible. Somehow, the
glider settled onto the LZ, coming to a rest with room to spare.[10]

Flight Officer Verne Ogden had watched part of Dank's glider
break apart over the ocean. Ogden engaged his spoilers to slow the
glider and increase its descent as his glider's pilot steered his way
through "the rat race to end all rat races" over the landing zone.
There, head for the grapes. They landed crossways to the grape field's
irrigation furrows, too fast at 100 miles per hour. Ogden pulled
his knees up to his chest to keep his legs from getting mangled as
the grapevines' posts and support wires tore through the floor of
the cockpit.

Had Mission *Dove* held to the plan, the tow planes would have
made a straight approach, released their gliders, then turned back
toward the south, and returned to Italy. No one expected an air
show of C-47s circling over landing zones, stacked as high as
3,000 feet as if each was waiting for a traffic control operator back
home to give him clearance to land in turn.

Major Bernard Parks and Flight Officer Warren Ward were
caught in the two-serial maelstrom over LZ-A. Like Merrick,

neither had expected to see tow planes with their gliders *coming at them.* As both serials released their gliders almost at the same time, they had to find a slot in the mish-mashed landing sequence. It soon became evident Parks and Ward would never clear a stand of trees on their final leg. They had only one option. "We stalled the glider over the vineyard and settled down on the vines and supporting wires and posts. Our glider never reached the ground." The Japanese American infantry medical personnel they carried helped both pilots out of their damaged cockpit before unloading their gear. "They were the best-armed passengers I ever carried," Parks reflected later.[11]

Splintered and shattered gliders littered fields, some on their sides, others belly up and pointing in every direction. *How the hell am I going to find a straight line to set down on?* First Lieutenant Richard Fort's assigned field resembled the aftermath of a demolition derby. So, too, were the others he could see. *Now what? A 180-turn, two 90-turns and maybe I can land on the far side between those gliders down there... I'm too low! Trees straight ahead!* Fort pulled hard on the controls and was surprised when his glider lifted just enough to clear the trees "like a gull in a strong sea breeze." Most of his right wing broke away when it hit another glider, sounding like "an implosion of a giant wooden match box," and then much of the other wing disappeared in a tangle of vines. The bottom of the glider disintegrated, plowing dirt into the fuselage. But it stopped before reaching the trees. "Nice landing lieutenant," yelled one of the soldiers whom Fort had delivered to the battlefield.[12]

Not far behind were 2nd Lieutenant Jerry Miller and his copilot, Flight Officer William Browne, who had graduated as classmates from SPAAF on the same day in December 1943. Eight months later to the day, Miller now cut off from their tow plane and turned away. As they joined Parks and the flock of gliders in a swirling, spring-shaped formation down toward the landing zone's fields, Browne watched for those on a possible collision course with their CG-4A. The most-heavily loaded gliders dropped faster than the others, breaking the sequence and nearly colliding. As gliders veered away from the near-misses, an aerial circus replaced the choreographed landing regimen Miller and Browne had rehearsed in Texas and then in Europe.[13]

As the last of Mission *Dove*'s serials turned toward fields that resembled a junkyard a few minutes before 1900 hours, Miller and Browne searched for any clearing that wasn't pockmarked with wrecks.

In only forty-nine minutes, Mission *Dove* was complete. Other than one serial in Mission *Bluebird* that had arrived that morning, in less than an hour more than 2,200 troops had been delivered to the two landing zones. The glider corps had delivered ninety percent of its glider infantry on or near its LZs, as well as more than 200 artillery pieces, more than 200 vehicles, and 500 tons of supplies and equipment.

The glider pilots had been lucky. Other than numerous broken legs and other injuries from landing in vineyards and orchards, casualties would have been profoundly higher if the glider pilots had encountered enemy fire after being released so high. Regardless, on their first night in battle many glider pilots faced gut-wrenching realities of how some had been luckier than others. A time, too, to briefly reflect. *Why him? How did I get here? Now what?*

Back in Italy, Flight Officer Leonard Stevens had bunked with Richard McFarland, the glider pilot who Arnold Wursten later had found dead at an aid station. Stevens had always been struck by McFarland's attitude. The man was convinced he was going to die and had spent most of his time getting his personal affairs in order. Unlike McFarland, Stevens had survived his landing but had been unable to climb out of his glider. The jeep he carried broke loose when he crashed, slamming into Stevens's back and pushing him out through the front of his glider. He suffered a compound fracture of his leg, a deep laceration, and broken shoulder. Once he was taken to an aid station at a farmhouse, it became clear that he would spend a week there before evacuation. Then months spent in a cast from shoulder to toe and several surgeries back in the States before he could hold his son for the first time.

Although he survived, death would haunt his rehabilitation. "There was a young sailor who just got out of his bed continually and walked around it, getting back in. He had fallen between ships and his insides [had been] crushed. Day after day he was slower, and finally he went to the dying room… There was nothing they could do for him."[14]

Most of the glider pilots who weren't injured would have to fend for themselves on their first night on the battlefield. Often their first task as dusk settled was to deduce their location and quickly scout for a place where they could get some rest. Reporting to a command post would come in the morning. For now, rest and maybe reflection.

"Jesus Christ, look at that bastard!"[15]

A glider had been headed directly at Flight Officer Harold "Goldie" Goldbrandsen earlier in the day. Only 200 feet off the ground, the two gliders had raced for a clearing. Goldbrandsen banked right toward a tree-topped hill, hoping there was clear space on the other side. He almost didn't make it as his glider plowed through the tree line, sheering off the right wing, and then part of the left wing. He had braked hard, putting the glider up on its skids and came to a stop. After evading the near head-on collision, grinding through the trees may have saved the lives of Goldbrandsen and his copilot. Only 100 yards ahead was the stately Chateau Valbourges estate.

That night they joined other glider pilots digging foxholes in the castle's lawn and lining them with parachutes or their gliders' inflatable rubber dinghies as beds. The sounds of ripping fabric awakened them throughout the night as troops cut the AAF emblem from wrecked gliders to cover their jeeps' hoods for the benefit of friendly aircraft. Survival ruled every thought, even after the firing had stopped.

First Lieutenant Joe Hesse had managed to land his glider between two rows of trees in an orchard, slicing both wings off while keeping his fuselage straight until he stopped. Not far away, a glider was obliterated in a crash seconds later. Hesse was shocked when the pilot, Flight Officer Jim Leach, climbed out. "Hi Joe, boy this is some stuff, isn't it?" he mused before walking away.[16]

Hesse had suffered a serious cut while landing that would require stitches. He had found an aid station close to where he landed. He was stunned at the mayhem. "Ye gods how that staff worked," he wrote. "Most of them were keeping awake by taking Benzadrine tablets, and every man was doing the job of three. Things wouldn't have been so rushed if there hadn't been so many German wounded." While he waited for someone to look at his leg, he and another glider pilot, 2nd Lieutenant Chester Erickson, found a quiet place where "[Erickson] brought out a little 'I. W.' [Harper whiskey], and we sat down for a smoke."[17]

Although glider pilots looked for soft dirt in the vineyards and fields to dig in for the night, comfort took a back seat to practicality. *Are we sure the Germans have been cleared out of here? Some of the guys have talked about watching for a counterattack. Where would it come from? And what about any Germans who might try to retreat from the beach tonight? Where should I hunker down? Probably better to stay close to some of the other guys.*

Few had slept well the night before D-Day and now they faced a second night of nerves, this time laced with danger. "Gunfire and other explosions ebbed and flowed all around us. We could identify the spatter and crackle of small arms fire and the heavier boom of artillery… We also listened to the whine of missile launchers and to men shouting at each other. The worst of all … was the horrible din … the sound of voices calling for medics." The first rays of the sun brought reflection. "We puny humans had not changed the course of nature one iota … as I think back … I could cry over the futility of war," recalled glider pilot Ben Ward.[18]

Toward dark, James Ferrin and other glider pilots climbed a hill to bed down, posting sentries along a nearby road. Sleep was impossible. About midnight, a large German truck approached. Ferrin and others blocked it with their weapons drawn. When they inspected its canvas-covered cargo bed, they discovered thirty German troops who appeared eager to be taken prisoner. Suddenly, Ferrin was responsible for making sure German prisoners of war did not change their minds, a fate many glider pilots would meet in the coming months.

The next day, the glider pilots' mission became hiking or hitching a ride back to the beach for evacuation to Corsica and then a flight back to their base. But the route to the coast was pockmarked with enemy snipers and pockets of resistance. Where the enemy had been cleared, cheering French farmers, bakers, storekeepers, and their families lined the road toward the beach.

For some glider pilots, collecting German prisoners of war became the order of the day as they made their way back to the beach. But first they had to identify enemy sniper positions and where other German troops might be hiding as they approached a town or hamlet. *Get down, look around first. There!* Many French residents had hung sheets or tablecloths from their open windows to indicate locals' presence to Allied troops. But a barren, open window might be an omen of a sniper's firefight. While there were enemy snipers ready to die, many German soldiers cautiously stepped out of hiding and were lined up against walls and searched before being herded to the beach.

As soon as he could, Ferrin handed his prisoners off to a British officer, and began walking with others toward the coast. It was a path through the horror of war's butchery. Bodies lying at impossible angles among smoldering trucks that smelled of fuel and rubber. The blackened skeleton of a French family's burned-out home, a gaping hole near the front door where their children once went off to school. War's litter of pistols, rifles, and ammunition on the roadbed and in adjacent ditches as retreating Germans had lightened their loads. The glider pilots kept walking, though some paused to search for souvenirs among the litter.

"A stench of death hung over the area as some of the bodies of German soldiers were decomposing. They may have been killed a few days earlier by bombs or strafing, and no one had removed them. The soldiers picking up the bodies wore gas masks," Ferrin later wrote.[19]

After his group found a command post and reported in, he would spend two days guarding prisoners before transferring to Corsica. While many German soldiers had been quick to surrender once their plight had become hopeless, the career SS troops proved to be imperious and stubborn.

Flight Officer Mel Pliner had been a laundry truck driver for his father when he volunteered for military service, with assignments in the motor pool and aircraft maintenance before volunteering for glider pilot training. After landing his glider in Mission *Bluebird*'s only successful morning mission with a sergeant in the copilot's seat in charge of the howitzer he was carrying, he had spent a surprisingly cold midsummer night in the field.

The next day, Pliner noticed a Fiat in a roadside ditch with a trunk full of wine. Once the car was pulled back onto the road, Pliner "requisitioned" it. As his group approached a church, he used his borrowed car to draw enemy fire to reveal the Germans' positions. He then took cover in a ditch until paratroopers advanced on the church's steeple and captured a sniper. When Pliner reached the beach, he offered his Fiat to the beachmaster as a bribe to be evacuated to Corsica ahead of others. He didn't know that other glider pilots also had commandeered locals' cars and already had swapped them for quick departures. There wasn't much of a market for the Fiat, Pliner discovered. He and other glider pilots were on their own for another night.[20]

Perhaps Sainte-Maxime had been a popular seaside resort town before the war. Maybe it had maintained some semblance of normalcy until the Allied naval bombardment the previous day. But now the seaside hotel with magnificent views of the ocean sat vacant, its windows blown out. Glider pilot Milton Dank and others commandeered a second-floor room, pulling mattresses onto the floor to avoid being spotted by snipers. After another restless night, they reported once again to the beach and successfully made it back to Italy.

Perhaps surviving Operation *Dragoon* was enough for some rapscallion glider pilots to take the long way back through the midsummer Riviera to their bases in Italy. "For the next month, MPs were rounding up cocky young glider pilots claiming to have become hopelessly lost on their way back to the beach," wrote Goldbrandsen in his diary. Perhaps grateful French residents had led to some pilots getting "lost" on what was a straightforward route to evacuation.

After three missions in World War II, combat gliders remained a painting only partially sketched. This time, the glider pilots had been lucky. Operation *Dragoon* in general was marked by feeble German resistance. General Wiese lacked the manpower, the equipment, and supplies necessary to cripple the airborne assault inland or stop the amphibious assault on the sand. Otherwise, the glider pilots may have faced a shooting gallery from 3,000 feet.

Spacing glider serials only ten minutes apart proved naive. The leading 442nd TCG's detour inadvertently had led dozens of following tow planes to overfly each other, climb to thousands of feet to avoid collisions, slow down if they got too close to one another, or race ahead at 150 miles per hour to catch up. By the time they reached the landing zones, the approach plan had deteriorated into a swarm of every glider pilot for himself.

Once released, many had no way of reaching their assigned field as they swerved around or dove below each other. *Find a field and get down!* became their mission. If one pilot was carrying a trailer, maybe another pilot in a companion glider with the jeep would land nearby, maybe not. Regardless, most fields looked nothing like what had been described in the final briefing.

One TCG's after-action report noted "the briefing for this mission was considered grossly inadequate and all but valueless as regards the landing zone." "Interpretation of the photographs was inadequate." "Wine poles were actually four-by-four anti-glider poles." "A high-tension wire in the LZ was missed." In a few places where vineyards had been noted in recon photos, they turned out to be orchards. Incredibly, the glider pilots had been told "there were no obstacles" in their assigned fields.[21]

Recommendations followed. If the pre-mission briefers had minimized the hazards to boost pilots' morale, "this should never be done." Glider pilots also needed to know the ground troops' objectives if the pilots were to be of any use once they were on the ground. Perhaps most critically, tow planes had to stay at their assigned release altitudes. The glider pilots would gladly contend with greater prop wash on their approach in return for much quicker descents through potential enemy fire. That, too, would have improved the glider pilots' ability to land in their assigned fields rather than fill fields assigned to others.

Yet for all the chaos that marked glider operations, Operation *Dragoon* was an overwhelming success. By the end of the first day, every combat unit of the VI Corps was ashore, there had been no large-scale counterattacks by the Germans, and enemy reinforcements had not proved to be a factor. Within hours, Allied advancements inland were ahead of schedule. In some quarters, it became known as the "Champagne Campaign."

Meanwhile, not a single glider that had landed inland would be recovered for later use. None had been outfitted with the reinforced Griswold nose that would have reduced damage and casualties. Instead, gliders littered the countryside, shattered, broken, and sometimes still containing glider pilots' equipment and supplies. Yet somehow, only eleven glider pilots were killed and just thirty-two wounded, a remarkably low casualty rate among the 675 glider pilots. But that didn't lessen the nightmares of some glider pilots who had witnessed how deadly a vineyard, pocket of trees, or peach orchard could be.

Second Lieutenant Harry Loftis, the Texas boy who "had never been anywhere in [his] life" and who had ditched school with another future glider pilot, "Goldie" Goldman, had been among the first glider pilots to land in Mission *Dove*. Dozens had followed him to the ground within minutes. Horror accompanied them. "I saw this big crash right up beside me and I ran up and I heard screaming and the anguish of a boy inside. He was praying to 'Blessed Mary, mother of Jesus…' and I crawled in, and it was a dear boy I had trained with in the States, and he died there in my arms, just crushed."[22] Eight months later, Flight Officer Lawrence Alto's Air Medal was presented posthumously to his father, Elmer, at a Traverse City, Michigan, ceremony.

By nightfall of Operation *Dragoon*, many injured glider pilots were being treated in wineries, farmhouses, and makeshift aid stations. Second Lieutenant Joseph Andrews had almost graduated as a pre-med student at The Citadel when he had enlisted. Late on D-Day he lay alongside other wounded men in a field hospital in southern France. Having avoided midair collisions with other gliders, he had slid into his field at a reported 100 miles per hour, striking an unspecified obstacle. He had been carried to the hospital with internal injuries and cerebral hemorrhaging. He died alone, before the sunrise lit a clear sky above a smoldering battlefield.

Glider pilots largely remained the guinea pigs of war planners after three missions. Sicily had proven the folly of nighttime missions following rushed training. Landing zone accuracy was more hope than reality in Normandy. And in southern France, advance briefing again was replete with misinformation that cost lives. Glider combat operations, planning, and tactics were being invented one mission at a time. Had enough been learned as the largest glider mission of the war approached?

As *Dragoon*'s glider pilots settled their nerves in Italy, Operation *Market Garden* in Holland would commence in less than a month, on September 17, 1944. It would be the largest glider mission of World War II. More than 1,900 gliders would need pilots from every corner of America. Young men like Flight Officer Lawrence Kubale who had hated his posting in Puerto Rico. Noel Addy who had been towed to Arizona instead of California by mistake while in training. Samuel Fine, one of the few survivors of the Sicily debacle. Pete Buckley, likely the youngest glider pilot to go into combat. And James Ferrin who had ridden his favorite horse, Old Red, to a friend's house so they could enlist together.

Each would play an important role in a massive mission that could either strike a crippling blow to Hitler's armies or exact a horrific toll on the Allies. Or both.

Like Hornets at a Church Cookout

Artillery rumbled across a nearly moonless night sky as Major Hugh Nevins stood before almost 400 glider pilots near Groesbeek, Holland. Nearly all of them were strangers.

There were men who had landed up to two days earlier on September 17, 1944, at the start of Operation *Market Garden*, a daring Allied airborne assault that could bring Allied troops to the German border; men from various squadrons who had braved antiartillery fire on their approach, crash-landed, unloaded their men and cargo, and then had reported to their command posts for orders. Some had seen friends die while strapped in their gliders, and many had stood long watches or had guarded German soldiers.

Now Nevins needed 295 of them to volunteer for frontline duty with little more than a pistol or a rifle and perhaps a couple of grenades.

Brigadier General James Gavin of the 82nd Airborne needed combat troops for an assault against a nearby bridge. Glider pilots would have to take their place along a defensive perimeter opposite enemy troops. The darkness prevented Nevins from seeing how many pilots volunteered to man foxholes following his announcement. With tears in his eyes he later acknowledged, he approached the group and began touching and counting each man in line. He soon had the number he needed. He never learned how many more had stepped forward to become infantrymen.

Together, they moved to the front line, two glider pilots replacing two infantrymen in each foxhole as they climbed out. By midnight, the glider pilots were in place and on alert.

Months earlier, it had become clear that the Allies were tightening their grip around the Third Reich's throat. Germany had lost France faster than expected. Soviet tank divisions were crushing German forces on the Eastern Front. The Allied assault through southern France had nearly reached the German border in only a month. Advances were being made in Italy. General Eisenhower now had forty-eight divisions advancing toward the Rhine River. How best to press his advantage?

Should the commander of Allied troops in Europe continue a broad frontal assault spanning hundreds of miles or forge a concentrated knockout blow that could bring an end to the war by Christmas? Was that possible with a force that now required one million gallons of fuel daily and whose supply lines were already dangerously stretched and vulnerable?

In early August, Eisenhower had created the 1st Allied Airborne Army under the command of Lieutenant General Lewis Brereton, for the first time consolidating the Americans' IX Troop Carrier Command, the 17th, 82nd, and 101st Airborne Divisions, as well as the British 1st and 6th Airborne Divisions. Brereton, a Naval Academy graduate, had resigned from the Navy shortly thereafter, joined the Army, and had flown combat missions in World War I. Only five feet six inches tall, he wore glasses that gave him a studious look and presence more likely found in a board room than on a battlefield.

The 1st Allied Airborne could be used to support American General Omar Bradley's proposal to take advantage of General George Patton's fast-moving tanks by launching a massive thrust toward Germany south of Frankfurt. Another option on Eisenhower's desk was Field Marshal Bernard Montgomery's "back door" proposal to lead an invasion from Belgium up through eastern Holland near the German border and seize the town of Arnhem and its strategic bridge. If he could accomplish that, the Allies could flank the northern end of the Germans' defensive Siegfried

Line, and drive into the heart of the Ruhr industrial region while Allied bombers pounded the gun and tank factories there.

The linchpin of Montgomery's proposal was to seize a massive bridge across the Lower Rhine at Arnhem. If the Allies could establish a bridgehead on the northern side, it would open a direct route into Germany. To accomplish that, Montgomery proposed the largest airborne operation to date and the first daytime airborne assault since the Germans' disaster three years earlier over Crete.

His concept depended on British airborne troops taking Arnhem and its bridge. American airborne troops would simultaneously seize about fifty miles of Highway 69 in two sectors near Eindhoven and Nijmegen to the south. That would enable the British 2nd Army's XXX Corps under the command of Lieutenant General Brian Horrocks to drive from the Belgian border north through Eindhoven and Nijmegen and link up with the British at Arnhem.

The southernmost airborne sector would start about ten miles north of the Belgian border and stretch between the towns of Eindhoven and Uden. Major General Maxwell Taylor's 101st Airborne Division would secure about fifteen miles of Highway 69. After graduating fourth in his class at West Point twenty-two years earlier, his postings reflected part soldier, part diplomat. Languages came easily and for a time he had taught French and Spanish at his alma mater. Taylor was known as a risk taker and had jumped at Normandy. Square jawed and quietly confident, Taylor was a cerebral combat leader.

This sector's glider landing zone would be designated LZ-W near the towns of Son and Veghel. Seizing the bridges at Eindhoven and Son was critical to the 101st's mission.

A few miles to the north of Taylor in the middle sector, Brigadier General James Gavin's 82nd Airborne's mission was to capture a ten-mile stretch of highway surrounding the city of Nijmegen. Gavin commanded respect without asking, in part by virtue of having led assaults in Sicily, Italy, and Normandy. He had become the Army's youngest brigadier general and was known as "the jumping general" for his penchant of joining his paratroopers in their assaults. The son of an unwed Irishwoman, he had been adopted and had grown up in the Pennsylvania coal fields. Thinning hair and narrow, piercing eyes gave him a driven look that fitted with his philosophy of always moving toward the sounds of enemy guns.

His gliders would land at LZ-N and LZ-T near Grave and Groesbeek. His troops would first seize the Groesbeek Heights southeast of Nijmegen. The 300-foot-tall ridge was the only high ground in the area. It offered flank protection against German tank units thought to be hidden in *Reichswald*, a sprawling forest of pines, oaks, and beech on the German border a short distance to the east. Once secured, the 82nd was to seize the bridges at Nijmegen and Grave.[1]

The northernmost drop and landing zones would be in the Arnhem area and were assigned to the British 1st Airborne Division. The 1st Airborne would seize the Arnhem bridge over the Lower Rhine and then hold on until the British ground assault from Belgium arrived from the south. The 1st Airborne was commanded by Major General Robert Urquhart, said to be prone to airsickness and an officer with no airborne experience. He would lead the division into combat for the first time since the Sicily disaster. A burly Scot, he was the kind of general who would do a sergeant's job if the situation called for it. His unassuming confidence had won over most of the airborne troops in his division who at first had resented an "outsider" being appointed as their commanding officer. The crux of the operation rested with the British 2nd Parachute Battalion under the command of Lieutenant Colonel John Frost. His battalion would capture the bridge with support from the rest of 1st Airborne and then hold out long enough for the ground troops to advance up Highway 69 to Arnhem.

Highway 69 was only two lanes wide and slightly elevated over a soft, boggy countryside. The British tanks would have limited maneuverability. Worse, six major water crossings along Highway 69 would have to be secured: the Wilhelmina Canal at Son, the Zuid-Willems Canal near Veghel, the Maas River at Grave, the Maas-Waal Canal, the Waal River at Nijmegen, and the Nederrijn (also referred to as the Lower Rhine) at Arnhem. An alert enemy could destroy any number of those bridges and bring the assault to a halt. Allied speed, coordination, and good weather would be critical to Montgomery's vision.

Montgomery suggested the assault from Belgium to Arnhem could take as little as two days. The British 1st Airborne Army's deputy commander, Lieutenant General Frederick Browning, thought four days for the ground assault to reach Arnhem was possible but added, "We may be going a bridge too far."[2]

Eisenhower had a choice: push ahead to the east or flank the enemy to the north. He opted for Montgomery's plan, made more feasible when the British 2nd Army captured Antwerp west of the assault route, the second largest port in Europe, on September 4. The operation would be called Operation *Market* (air assault) *Garden* (ground troops). It was a plan riddled with risk.

Disastrous airborne congestion over Sicily, Normandy, and southern France had not been forgotten. This time, the mission to deliver 35,000 troops and their supplies would be divided between two corridors from England. Each would contain three flight lanes, each one-and-a-half miles wide, with a fourth 1,000 feet above the other three.

The northerly route would be used by aircraft from bases about 100 miles north of London. The aircraft would fly southeast across the North Sea, cross Holland south of Rotterdam, and then turn northeast toward two landing areas. They would traverse eighty miles of German-held territory in Holland thought to have modest antiaircraft defenses. The southerly route from air bases about sixty miles west of London would loop around the northern edge of the city, turn southeast, then east to cross Belgium before turning north into Holland. Glider and paratrooper plane pilots would face flak batteries over the final thirty miles to their landing and drop zones.

A massive glider operation was hardly a secret in some British quarters. Between July 1 and mid-September, the assembled glider inventory had doubled from 1,045 to approximately 2,160. As much as ninety percent of those gliders would take off in Operation *Market Garden*, flown by nearly all of the 2,060 glider pilots available. That meant there would be no trained copilots on this mission. A glider infantryman, medic, radio operator, or frontline officer would sit in the copilot's seat amidst unfathomable glider controls. Ten minutes' instruction while sitting in a plastic bubble fully exposed on three sides usually brought a ghostly pallor on the man sitting in the copilot's seat and a private oath by the glider pilot that he would not relinquish his control short of imminent death.

To complicate matters further, the inventory of available C-47s forced glider missions to be stretched over three days.

The final planning for Operation *Market Garden* didn't begin until September 10, with the "go decision" coming four days later when the forecast indicated three days of good weather beginning on Sunday, September 17. That meant the operation would be the first major American airborne mission of World War II without specific training, preparatory exercises, or rehearsals.

No trained copilots. Daylight arrivals. No element of surprise. British weather in September. All were enemies of Operation *Market Garden* long before the glider pilots would be within range of the enemy that had been building its defenses for more than four years.

SEPTEMBER 17, D-DAY

One of the biggest variables in airborne warfare – the weather – threatened the start of Operation *Market Garden* when daybreak fog dampened English farm fields, villages, barracks, aircraft, and runways. But as the sun brightened at mid-morning, more than 1,000 Allied bombers took off from bases across southern England.

Dutch breakfasts, church services, and farm chores abruptly stopped a few hours later when bombs began cratering German positions in towns, pockets of trees, and alongside bridges and fields where haystacks hid enemy artillery. More than 800 American B-17s dropped more than 3,100 tons of bombs on 117 antiaircraft targets.[3]

Meanwhile, a deep growl fractured the Sunday morning serenity of the English countryside as the largest troop carrier fleet the world had known took off from air bases, carrying three-and-a-half divisions of troops. One by one, formations took shape near the airfields in a thin layer of stratus clouds, V-shaped clusters of planes and gliders aligning in precisely timed sequence.

More than 400 troop planes and two serials of gliders were bound for Arnhem, more than 500 would carry General Gavin and his men to the Nijmegen area, and another 500 aircraft would deliver the 101st Airborne Division's nearly 6,700 troops to the battlefield's southern sector. About ninety minutes passed before the last of the aircraft was in the air and in position before the fixed-wing flocks headed south over farmers and townspeople below. The 101st's armada alone stretched across eighty miles as it approached the English Channel.

The battle for survival for the seventy glider pilots supporting the 101st Airborne began shortly after their takeoff in England, hours before they would reach LZ-W near the town of Son. Like previous combat missions at takeoff, two gliders broke away from their tow planes almost immediately. Another glider's tail collapsed, sending the glider and fourteen men to their deaths at sea.

As the remainder reached Belgium on the southern route and then flew north, townspeople in dollhouse hamlets and farmers working their late-summer crops stopped and gazed at the river of aircraft overhead. Some civilians waved and others raised a fist with their fingers held as a "V" for victory as paratroopers and then the gliders passed overhead. Perhaps this would become a Sunday of liberation when the low-flying armada began to disgorge thousands of blossoming, colored parachutes followed by the gliders laden with critical payloads of officers, communications gear, and medical teams.

While the paratroopers' aircraft met little resistance, the CG-4As that followed faced an eruption of small arms and artillery fire once the Germans awakened from their Sunday lethargy. Several glider pilots cut away when their tow planes were shot down and one reportedly followed its tow plane to the ground and exploded.

The glider pilots had become a bruised bunch as they approached the 101st's landing zone in Holland. Some were released too soon over Belgium and six of the remaining sixty-four tow planes were shot down by the enemy. The gliders' losses on the daylight mission began to mount and could proportionately become more severe than what the glider pilots had suffered on daylight landings in Normandy and in southern France.

The remaining glider pilots reached the 101st's LZ-W by 1400 hours. Then coordination crumbled into heart-stopping chaos for the glider pilots, the infantry they carried, and war correspondent Walter Cronkite who was assigned to cover the start of *Market Garden*. None of his previous war experiences had prepared him for what he thought would be a quieter ride than inside a bomber. He was wrong. "Riding in one of those [CG-4A] gliders was like attending a rock concert while locked in the bass drum at a Grateful Dead concert," he later reflected. No bomber ride approached a glider's release when "we dropped like a stone, plunged straight down, it seemed to me. 'I knew it, I knew it, I knew it,' I kept saying to myself. 'I knew these things couldn't fly on their own.'"[4]

Then it got worse once he landed.

> … gliders were landing around us. But others came tumbling out of the sky. Two collided almost above us and a jeep, a howitzer, and soldiers, came crashing down. A C-47 came low overhead, streaming smoke, and exploded in the woods just beyond. Another glider came straight down and plowed into the soft earth like an artillery shell. The field was scattered with gliders on their noses, on their sides, on their backs. It was a scene from hell, but the 101st seemed pleased that it was a "successful glider mission."[5]

Flight Officer Thornton Schofield had flown over the flooded fields of Normandy in search of dry ground and had looked for a way to drop his glider into a vineyard in southern France. Those combat experiences had spawned a perspective that rookie glider pilots and Cronkite would have welcomed. But even veteran glider pilots could be rattled in combat, with lives hanging in the balance. "Tracer bullets hit my tow plane, and when the tow plane was out of firing range, I could hear the bullets hitting the glider… I tried to minimize the glider as a target by constantly moving right or left, or up and down … [others were] not as lucky as we were… I saw several C-47s on the ground burning," he recalled.[6]

Yet as he neared LZ-W, Schofield figured he was in good shape. *Get ready to turn off the downwind leg, there's a good field. Boy, I've got it made.* An American glider at that moment slammed into the left side of his tail. Schofield's glider shuddered, seemed to lose its breath as if it had taken a left hook to its ribs, and dropped its nose down toward the ground. A one-two combination followed when his glider slammed into the dirt from 150 feet and a second later when the jeep he was carrying crashed into his back. It drove Schofield partially out the front of his glider.

Knocked unconscious, Schofield suffered a dislocated pelvis and ankle, and a broken leg. It took several hours to extricate him and the others from the wreckage. The pilot of the other glider, Flight Officer Lloyd Shufelberger, perhaps wounded by artillery fire before colliding with Schofield, died from his injuries the following day.[7]

Over a landing area a few fields away, Captain Albert Waldon was one of the most experienced glider pilots in the air and carried particularly strategic passengers. He and some friends had built and then flew a glider before they had graduated Georgia Tech University in 1938. They had learned to fly it by towing the glider behind a Model A Ford with a 500-foot tow rope. Now he was on final approach, carrying the commanding officer of the 101st's 327th Glider Infantry Regiment and watching tracers approach his cockpit.

Like hunters leading ducks from behind a blind, enemy gunners first aimed about ten feet behind his tow plane and then "walked" their aim along the tow rope toward Waldon's cockpit. When the glowing tracers were only ten feet away, he released and banked hard to one side. Minutes after landing, Waldon saw how deadly small arms fire could be. As the twin-engine C-47s passed overhead, enemy gunners riddled two of the Skytrains that had been trailing Waldon's tow plane. Enemy fire hitting an engine that was only about ten feet from either side of the fuselage was always a near-miss of the crew.

One turned away, smoking badly, while the other looped over Waldon's field before heading toward the ground. With only

When learning to fly in biplanes early in his career, General Henry "Hap" Arnold developed a fear of flying that lasted several years. (Silent Wings Museum)

Glider pilots were a rapscallion bunch who volunteered for one-way missions behind enemy lines in defenseless aircraft; some of them would take a sightseeing week or two in getting back to their air base. (Holland Collection, Silent Wings Museum)

The combat glider: fabric covered, a hinged cockpit, cramped seating for infantry, and totally defenseless. Glider warfare largely was invented from one invasion to the next. (Silent Wings Museum)

Glider pilots took military aviation's tradition of nose art to a creative level, often drawing caricatures and adding their hometown, the name of their girlfriend or wife, or a special message for Hitler. (Silent Wings Museum)

Minutes before takeoff, some glider pilots and the infantry they carried affected a nonchalance that masked their fear of flying into combat in an aircraft whose nicknames included the Purple Heart Box, Plywood Hearse, and Flying Box Kite. (National Archives)

Glider pilots learned to be skeptical of some of the intelligence presented in their briefings. Aerial photographs tended to be days old and often were taken at a time of day when the lack of shadows prevented analysis of vegetation height and density. (Kammen Collection, Silent Wings Museum)

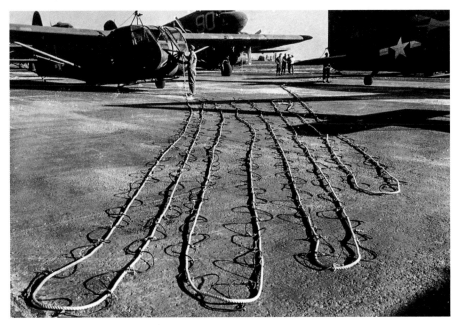

A glider's communication cable wrapped around the tow rope was vulnerable to damage when it was stretched taut along the ground at the start of takeoff. (Silent Wings Museum)

Glider pilots were in full view of enemy gunners on three sides, sometimes sliding to a stop only a few yards from German machine gun nests. Injuries suffered in hard landings were common. (Silent Wings Museum)

Glider infantry sat shoulder to shoulder in the forward portion of a glider sometimes in turbulence for hours on their way to the landing zone. Airsickness was common at times. (Silent Wings Museum)

Before takeoff, glider pilots and other personnel often checked how a howitzer or jeep was tied down. A hard landing could send it straight into their backs on its way out through the cockpit. (Silent Wings Museum)

Hundreds of C-47s and their gliders taking off on time and in sequence required the practiced choreography typically found on an aircraft carrier. (National Archives)

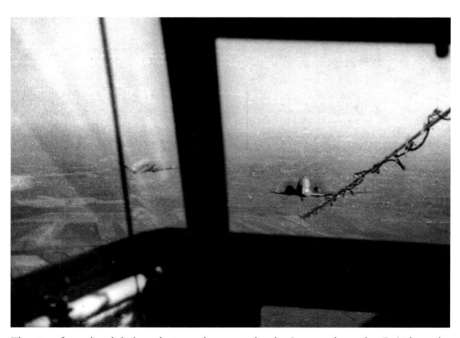

The view from the glider's cockpit on the way to battle. Staying above the C-47 kept the glider out of its turbulent prop wash. (Silent Wings Museum)

The glider program nearly was scrapped following its first mission over Sicily.
It had become a deadly debacle where most of the gliders landed in the ocean.
(Silent Wings Museum)

"Hedgerows" in Normandy actually were mounded embankments topped with dense
undergrowth and mature trees up to eighty feet tall, making each field largely an
independent battlefield. (National Archives)

On most missions, glider pilots relied on 101st or 82nd Airborne Division paratroopers to clear their landing zones of the enemy, sometimes only minutes before the gliders arrived. (National Archives)

When fields were filled with wrecked gliders, late-arriving glider pilots often were forced to land in stands of trees, into hills, woodlots, stone fences, and orchards. Extensive casualties usually resulted. (National Archives)

A glider could become a firetrap in seconds. Its fabric was flammable and cargo sometimes explosive. Burned-out skeletons were an unnerving sight following a glider mission. (Silent Wings Museum)

Gliders became the theme of several national product advertising campaigns during the war, often touting the glider pilots' bravery and "American know-how." (Silent Wings Museum)

Glider pilots not only contended with enemy fire; collisions on their final approach and in the fields were common. In an attempt to avoid this, some flew through tree lines, hoping tree trunks breaking off their wings would reduce their speed. (National Archives)

Glider pilot Thornton Schofield survived this crash after he was hit by another glider 150 feet above his landing zone. Once he hit the ground, the jeep he was carrying broke free and struck him in his back. It took several hours to extricate him from the wreckage. (Silent Wings Museum)

Elden Mueller was among the glider pilots who completed combat missions only to die far from the battlefield during routine training flights. A tow rope wrapped around Mueller's tail, forcing him to crash nose first. (Silent Wings Museum)

Propping up the tail of a glider after a successful landing enabled heavy equipment to be offloaded "downhill" out the front once the cockpit was pulled up and out of the way. (Silent Wings Museum)

It was nearly impossible to identify the snow-covered landing zones near Bastogne. As enemy fire intensified, glider pilots freelanced their way to any likely looking open space. (National Archives)

Flight Officer Richard Mercer was released just 300 feet over his landing zone. Seconds later, his Horsa crashed, killing him and fourteen of the men he carried. His copilot somehow survived to fly in Operations *Market Garden* and *Varsity*. This became one of the iconic photographs of World War II. (National Archives)

Once the fighting stopped, glider pilots and others sometimes returned to the battlefield to take a close look at the carnage and perhaps marvel at the glider pilots' survival. (Silent Wings Museum)

Standing a glider up on its nose or catching a wingtip in a landing zone could flip it uncontrollably into a somersault or cartwheel. (Silent Wings Museum)

Glider grates were a valuable commodity during the war. Here, one is converted into a barbershop (left), the other a post office (right). A single CG-4A glider required five of these shipping crates. (Silent Wings Museum)

Above Even after weeks of repair, relatively few gliders such as these following Operation *Market Garden* were airworthy enough for a second mission. Most were abandoned and left to scavengers. (National Archives)

Below Many glider pilots were married, and some had children back home. Letters, sometimes daily, revealed love and loss, purpose and passion for the day when the family would be together again. (Libbey Collection, Silent Wings Museum)

Bottom The fuselage of the larger British Horsa glider was designed to be separated just behind the wing to enable its combat payload to be offloaded. (Silent Wings Museum)

about 100 feet remaining, a crewman jumped from the plane. His parachute didn't open before he hit. The C-47 disappeared in a ball of fire.

A few miles to the north, paratroopers were watching for the scheduled force of fifty gliders to appear over or near LZ-N near Groesbeek to reinforce the 82nd Airborne in the middle sector.[8] Confusion had begun at takeoff when aircraft from another troop carrier group had flown across their airfield. Evasive action caused some glider tow ropes to break. Additional gliders were lost later when more tow ropes broke. For some reason, most of the remainder were released at least a mile short of LZ-N. Only a handful reached the landing zone.

It wasn't long before the aid stations near the landing zones began to fill with wounded paratroopers, glider pilots, and the enemy. Hate and perhaps fear seeped out of fresh wounds on the first day of battle, one whose outcome was uncertain, but would surely include buddies dying on the battlefield and medics working to staunch the bleeding of others. For some, seeing a wounded Nazi soldier arriving at one aid station broke an unwritten rule. Wounded Americans leaped onto him, intent on beating him to death before medics pulled them off the wounded man. Later, 82nd Airborne glider pilot Captain Elgin Andross checked on the glider pilots at the aid station. Andross saw one glider pilot who had not joined in the melee. He eased a bloody bandage off the man's chest. Andross could see through his body. He lit a cigarette for the glider pilot. Sometimes in war there was nothing left to do, other than to strike a match for a man.

The 82nd Airborne's Major Hugh Nevins had taken the long way to Holland on September 17. He had enlisted in the Army Horse Cavalry in 1935, had trained with the 10th Mountain Division to invade Norway, and now was responsible for the fifty glider pilots arriving in the Groesbeek area and more than 250 who would be touching down the following day. Some D-Day glider pilots landed only a few hundred yards from the *Reichswald* forest in the middle sector. Like the others, their duties would include escorting prisoners, military police functions, road guides, and helping recover supply pods dropped from C-47s. Hardly glamorous, but always within range of enemy fire.

As the shadows spread across eastern Holland, Operation *Market Garden* had become a mixed bag on D-Day.

Most of the British Horsa gliders had successfully reached their landing zone near Arnhem to support the 1st Airborne Division's paratroopers who had arrived earlier. But several British gliders carrying vital transport vehicles had been lost on the flight from England. A particularly devastating loss because the 1st Airborne's General Urquhart had chosen landing areas several miles from his objective, the bridge at Arnhem. Glider tactics had always been to leverage surprise by landing as close to the infantry's objectives as possible.

The British 2nd Battalion had managed to take control of the northern end of the key bridge that crossed the Lower Rhine. But the 700 men were badly outnumbered by two German panzer divisions and already were in trouble. The panzer divisions had arrived recently for retrofitting. The Dutch resistance had informed Allies of their presence, but the British had discounted their battle worthiness. That had been folly, given the number of guns and tanks the two divisions added to the German forces in the region that now amounted to 15,000 to 20,000 men.

In the middle assault sector below Arnhem, the 82nd Airborne had advanced close to Nijmegen but its critical bridge – nearly a half-mile long – remained in German hands.

Despite the early losses among the gliders bound for the 101st at Eindhoven, the bulk of glider pilots had held their course, delivering an estimated eighty percent of their infantry, vehicles, and equipment accurately enough that they had been able to mobilize almost immediately. But the 101st had not been able to capture Eindhoven and a key bridge near Son had been destroyed by the Germans. That would create a critical delay until a temporary bridge arrived from the rear and was assembled.

Meanwhile, the British tank assault vanguard from Belgium had advanced only about four miles up Highway 69.

The multiple bridge-crossing vulnerability of an "airborne carpet" along a single road was exposed in less than a day. It had started with a modest number of gliders in anticipation that the American paratroopers would seize their objectives quickly and that the British would rapidly advance into Holland. Waves of glider pilots would deliver the artillery, supplies, and support personnel on D+1 that the infantry would need to consolidate its position and defend its lengthy perimeters. But Operation *Market Garden* had got off to a stumbling start on September 17.

Reports from the aircrews of wounded C-47s returning from Holland carried stark evidence that the next day's mission – the largest of its kind to date in World War II – would be met by a dug-in enemy expecting its arrival, aware of its battle plan, and prepared to die to keep the Allies from reaching their families on German soil.

SEPTEMBER 18, D+1

The most relentless and unbeatable foe facing the Allies – fog and rain – greeted more than 1,000 glider pilots as they headed for breakfast before making their way out to the runways in England on September 18. Heavy clouds and rain also awaited them over the North Sea while the troops already in Holland prepared to renew their assault. But their airborne reinforcements, artillery, and supplies would not arrive when they expected.

Lieutenant General Lewis Brereton turned to his "weather guessers" with a simple question. *When will it clear?* By 1100 hours. He pushed back the massive armada's England departure to 1120 hours, putting its arrival over landing zones at about 1400 hours. But the weather pattern on the southern route did not look promising as rain and low clouds were drifting from Belgium toward the battlefield. The entire airborne assault would take the northern route. More than 2,000 aircraft would be forced onto the four northern-route lanes for nearly three hours before reaching the battlefield.

The 101st and 82nd troops on the ground would simply have to fight, suffer casualties, and potentially conserve their ammunition until reinforcements and supplies arrived hours after they had renewed their bridge assaults. Early-morning progress was mixed as the 101st took Eindhoven but the 82nd faced renewed German attacks. In both sectors, time was growing short on clearing the enemy from the glider landing zones by mid-afternoon.

More than 400 glider pilots were inbound with about 1,900 infantry to the 101st. Another 400 glider pilots were headed for the 82nd Airborne in the middle sector, primarily with artillery personnel. In both sectors, the glider serials would be arriving over the landing zones nearly at the same time. Veterans of Normandy and southern France knew how that could become a melee as deadly as an artillery shell.

The glider pilots would face a gauntlet of antiaircraft fire by a fully prepared enemy. The troops on the ground would have little time to roust the Germans from pockets of trees near the landing zone shortly before the equivalent of "rush hour," when dozens of glider pilots would be descending, weaving, and diving from nearly every direction. It would remind one glider pilot of "hornets at a church cookout."[9]

Some pilots would land and somehow survive but would never reach their assembly areas. Flight Officers Chester Ritter and Philip Jacobson took off within minutes of each other from different airfields in England, bound for the 101st in the southern sector. Ritter had arrived in England only two months earlier, after spending six months recovering from a glider accident in the States.

After crossing flooded fields and then terrain "as flat as a pancake," their LZ was only minutes away. The enemy's antiaircraft fire greeted them with concentrated bursts of flak "like crows over a tree," according to another glider pilot. When Ritter saw his tow plane take hard hits and begin to lose altitude, he released early. On his first combat mission, Ritter scanned the countryside, looking for a place to land the infantrymen he carried. Not far away, enemy flak caught Jacobson's glider, shredding his elevator controls. He, too, released quickly, and dove toward a field. Both landed in enemy territory, far from their landing zones and anticipated assembly points. They were on their own.

They would share a fate common to dozens of men who failed to reach their landing zones on September 18 and the following days. They would be rescued by the Dutch resistance, a *sub rosa* network of civilians determined to sabotage the Germans and rescue downed Allied airmen. Most rescue missions started similarly, in Jacobson's case a limping priest approaching him and his glider's troops and quickly leading them to a nature reserve hideout. An eighteen-year-old Dutch boy, Wim Coppens, saw Ritter crash, approached on his bicycle, and led Ritter and his troops to friends whose bravery and nerve would likely determine if the Americans would survive.

Their new friends hid the Americans in barn lofts, attics, hospitals, churches, and forests. They arranged for emergency medical care and devised devilish methods to deliver food and water while evading German positions and patrols. Within a few days, more than 100 downed Americans and British troops were gathered and shepherded to the *Kampina* forest near Boxtel north of Eindhoven. There, a large hole had been dug in the forest floor and covered with camouflage netting. Ritter, Jacobson, and the others subsisted on loaves of fresh bread, butter, and meat hidden in milk cans that were delivered by resistance fighters disguised as farmers.

Glider pilots who were seriously wounded posed unique challenges that required daring creativity by the Dutch. First Lieutenant George Brennan's approach over Holland had been nothing like the "cake walk" he had experienced in southern France. Near Eindhoven, it seemed as if everyone on the ground who had a weapon was locked onto his glider. The *vvvvppt* of bullets passing through his glider was dwarfed by a 20mm flak shell when it pierced the floor, mauled his foot, and exited the roof. More rounds pounded the glider, one hitting his hand. Another shell hit, its shrapnel striking Brennan in his thigh, chest, buttocks, and elbow. Up ahead, Brennan's C-47 trailed smoke from the direct hits it was taking.

Soon the smell of a ruptured can's fuel soaking into the glider's wood floor mixed with the metallic, rusty scent of fresh blood that was drenching uniforms.

Then, with uncanny precision, an enemy tracer shell ignited the glider's leaking gas can fuel briefly, singeing Brennan and setting the pants of the man sitting in the copilot's seat on fire. They had to get onto the ground. *Now.* Despite another direct hit, Brennan somehow landed the glider with only one functioning hand and one foot. A firefight drove Brennan and his wounded copilot toward a ditch filled with sewage and then to a barn about a mile away where they collapsed on blood-soaked straw. They didn't know that the farm wife – perhaps out of fear of German reprisals for harboring Allied troops – sent her thirteen-year-old son to find German soldiers to tell them about the growing number of glider pilots in the family's barn. When they arrived, they beat the bloodied Brennan and another glider pilot. But when they fell asleep the two escaped and would again trust strangers.

Hours later that night, members of the Dutch resistance laid them in a cart under a tarp topped with wet cow manure. It was a rough ride for the wounded men to the Saint Lidwina Maternity Hospital in the town of Schijndel, a daring feat since the town was in German hands. Sewing and splinting Brennan back together would require weeks of recovery. *Where do we hide him that long?* In plain sight. The staff disguised Brennan as a pregnant farm wife and covered him in a bed alongside other pregnant patients. At one point, he was moved to a private room with a "TB" sign on the door to discourage curious Germans.

In another room, 2nd Lieutenant James Swanson hid, weeks after the Dutch had shuffled him from one hideout to another. A Dutch farmer named van der Linden had hidden him in the woods for four days, and then in a wood shed. When Germans approached, he was taken to another patch of woods, joining several Americans. After they were given civilian clothes, a Dutch guide took groups of three at a time to the hospital. His hopscotch journey was typical of how the Dutch resistance saved Americans' lives.[10]

"Hang on, I see a field straight ahead." Those were the best words over a functional C-47 intercom that 1st Lieutenant Herb Bollum and other glider pilots could hear on D+1 when their tow planes bound for Eindhoven were hit by artillery fire. For the past twenty-eight miles, Bollum had watched smoke pouring out of tow pilot William McCormick's left engine. For hours across the sea and then enemy territory, every glider pilot had trusted his fate to the dedication of his tow pilot and the skill of his aircrew. In some cases, that trust was misplaced. But often it saved a glider pilot's life.

He might not make it to LZ-W, but McCormick stayed his course, his mission still his priority. The final few miles seemed an endless nightmare. Once Bollum released, McCormick turned back toward the coast as rubbery, oily smoke filled his aircraft. His radio operator spotted flames under the plane's floor as an engine quit and McCormick lost his hydraulic pressure. His plane had died. They would have to ditch in the ocean with his landing gear down. Fast. He put the Skytrain into a nearly vertical dive from 4,000 feet at more than 200 miles per hour, leveled at 1,000 feet, slowed the plane as much as he dared, and managed to set down onto the water without breaking apart. The entire aircrew survived and was rescued. Bollum's tow plane pilot later received the Distinguished Flying Cross for McCormick's "remarkable display of technical proficiency ... devotion to duty ... leadership." For the rest of his life, Bollum called McCormick "my life saver."[11]

Other glider pilots, like 2nd Lieutenant Bill Lane, witnessed firsthand the price some C-47 pilots paid in a single moment when approaching the 101st's landing zone. Still attached, Lane saw his tow plane take a direct hit in the right wing. Fire erupted there, and spread along the back half of the fuselage, reaching the tow rope assembly and then the tow rope. *Is the prop wash gonna push the flames along the tow rope to my glider?* They were short of the landing zone. *Now what?* Lane stayed with his burning tow plane as the pilot ordered his crew to jump. He climbed to 1,300 feet to give Lane more gliding distance when released. Maybe Lane could reach the LZ from that altitude. Once he released Lane, the pilot jumped. His parachute never opened. Lane watched as the pilot gained speed toward the earth, his collapsed parachute overhead fluttering like a kite's tail. He "streamered," as the pilots called it, to the ground and bounced once.[12]

As glider pilot casualties mounted on September 18, some became more personal than others. Second Lieutenant Noel McCann was a family man from Cincinnati. At twenty-six years of age, he and his wife, Clara, had a daughter, Marilyn. He named his glider "Queen City," his hometown's nickname, and wrote "Clara" under his cockpit window before checking his load of infantry and a jeep. Enemy fire surrounded his glider about nine miles from the landing zone. Not far away a good friend, 2nd Lieutenant George Anderson, carried infantry and a load of grenades and landmines. His glider infantry had laid their flak jackets on the floor of the glider, especially near Anderson, because "anything that happens to you, we're gone," said one.

The enemy found McCann. A burst near his glider sliced off his left wing. Anderson watched as his good friend's glider turned nose down. Bits of glider skin danced in its wake as it turned vertical in its plunge from 500 feet. Perhaps clarity broke through the terror, giving McCann a second to say goodbye to Clara and Marilyn as he stared at the ballooning ground in front of him. The glider slammed nose first into a ditch, crushing everyone and everything inside.

Meanwhile, Anderson pressed ahead toward the 101st's landing zone with his men and explosives, looking for the T-shaped landing signal and the smoke that would reveal wind direction. Coping with visions of a crushed friend and a devastated wife and little girl would come later.

> I'll never forget it, [seeing] his glider going down into the ground… You can't live together two or three years … [training at the same bases] … when you're in the middle of it, things happen so fast that you're detached from the moral aspects of it … you went out on a mission, came back to a bottle of vodka and clean sheets and everything would start over the next day.[13]

Six trooper carrier groups towing gliders approached one of the 82nd's landing zones and four more approached the other. A mash-up of glider squadrons already littered fields as more pilots descended, some of them intent on following their companion glider all the way down. A familiar face perhaps was what many glider pilots most needed to see once they had come to a stop, had checked for casualties, unloaded their men and cargo, spotted the companion glider across the field, and then tried to make sense of battlefield mayhem.

First Lieutenant Fred Lunde had tried to exude confidence back in England three hours earlier. He wondered if the troops he was about to carry had seen his hands shaking as he lit a cigar. No matter. He had to get them to the 82nd Airborne, along with a trailer, mines, and weapons. Maybe his glider's name, "MISSIFFY," named after his girlfriend, Ida Frances, would bring him luck over Holland. Despite his pilot's window coming apart in mid-flight, he reached his landing zone in good shape and spotted the glider that carried the jeep for his trailer. He followed that glider pilot to the ground, even though he was headed downwind.[14] He plowed to a stop in the soft Dutch farm soil, unloaded, and got clear of the glider while under fire.

Once away from his glider, he spotted another glider pilot, 2nd Lieutenant John van Sicklen, sitting under a tree. "Fred, you'll get cold. Better go back and get your jacket." In the middle of battle, a buddy was concerned about Lunde getting cold in a few hours. Later, Lunde approached a church near the tree. Van Sicklen lay dead, killed by a mortar's shrapnel tearing into his back. Perhaps telling a friend to retrieve his jacket from his glider before it got dark had been his last words.[15]

As glider pilot "Goldie" Goldman neared his LZ, he recalled how there had been muffled chuckles among his squadron's pilots as intelligence officers had laid out the assault. Veteran glider pilots who had survived Normandy's D-Day remembered how poorly those briefings had prepared them. Descriptions of landing zones, hedgerows, and the area's terrain had been simplified to the point of becoming deadly inaccurate. Now they were being told that the Germans' antiaircraft guns would pose no serious threats because scores of British aircraft would be strafing their positions as the gliders passed.

Everyone then quieted when Colonel Theodore Kershaw stood up. The commanding officer of the 441st Troop Carrier Group was a Southerner who had graduated law school as a reservist and had flown for United Airlines in the 1930s. He had flown missions over Normandy and southern France. He told his men the 441st soon would be transferred from England to the continent but wasn't sure where or when. Once his glider pilots landed in Holland, just get back to their base as best they could, they were told. Inbound, they would fly straight and true to stay in formation and then become freelancers to get home.

As Goldman and his overloaded cargo comprising a jeep, communications equipment, driver, and radio operator crossed the Dutch coast, up ahead an airborne rodeo appeared as fighter planes prowled, dove, and strafed enemy artillery positions. Explosions in forests and plumes of smoke marked success, yet the way ahead did not look promising. "The sky just ahead of us seemed to be pitted with little black clouds where antiaircraft shells had exploded, and at eight hundred feet altitude, we were headed straight for them," he recalled later. Tethered to their tow planes, the glider pilots were as vulnerable as a roped calf.

When he approached his landing zone, Goldman had little choice. A steep dive toward what appeared to be a farm field was necessary to keep the overloaded glider from stalling. He turned the wheel hard, trying to line up with the field's furrows. He didn't make it. "I had the wheel all the way back in my gut when we hit the ground, and it was ten thousand miracles that the glider did not cartwheel" as it thumped across the soft furrows.

Once the glider's jeep was unloaded, Goldman raced to a stand of trees and spotted glider pilots from another unit. "Have you guys seen my buddy, Elden Mueller?" he asked, hoping to find his best friend from the States. "Hey Goldie." It was Flight Officer Mueller.

About forty miles into enemy territory, the two flight-school friends had landed within a few hundred yards of each other. They would spend the next few weeks guarding German prisoners, exploring the town of Groesbeek, being hosted by a grateful Dutch pastor and his family, collecting overcoats from dead Germans, and joining a group of 82nd paratroopers in combat before reaching Brussels.

They each found transportation back to their squadrons in England and reported in. "Take care of yourself, you big lug," Mueller told Goldman.[16]

As the 101st and 82nd dug in for the night of the 18th, and the British 1st Airborne hunkered down near Arnhem after the first full day of fighting, Operation *Market Garden* was behind schedule.

In the southern sector, the British XXX Corps had reached Eindhoven but had stalled when the Germans blew up the bridge at Son. A 101st assault at the town of Best to capture its bridge as an alternative had failed. As a result, the XXX Corps would have to wait until engineers installed a temporary bridge across the Wilhelmina Canal. The glider pilots, though, had delivered about ninety-five percent of their men and cargo to date, a remarkable achievement. Though they were scattered outside the landing zone more than General Taylor would have liked, nonetheless he had received the critical troops he needed.

In the middle sector, the 82nd had been forced out of Nijmegen and had encountered heavy fighting at Grave and in the Groesbeek Heights. Less than half the gliders had reached the 82nd's two landing zones as others touched down anywhere from a half mile to several miles from their LZ. Overall, the glider pilots had delivered about eighty-five percent of their payload for practical use, even though many had landed in fields that had been only marginally cleared of the enemy.

Farther north, however, the day had been a disaster for the British. Two battalions trying to reach the 2nd Battalion at the Arnhem bridge had suffered brutal losses. Though they were now less than two miles from the bridge, they had lost more than half their men. Polish paratrooper reinforcements the next day would be critically needed.

There now were about 900 American glider pilots on the ground, not all of them in friendly territory. Gavin had helplessly watched as twenty-five gliders carrying field artillery were towed past the LZ and landed five miles into Germany. "They were not given the green light ... [and] thought it more proper to wait until the tug gave them an indication to release," he wrote later.[17]

On the far side of the *Reichswald*, their fate rested on a deadly game of hide and seek on the way back to friendly territory; of watching the enemy loot and burn their gliders as they crawled away in ditches; seeing other glider pilots nearby with their hands raised and already prisoners of war; finding a dike where they could hide in tall grass until dark as Germans passed by; skirting pockets of gunfire up ahead; jumping the Germany–Holland border fence; and always listening in the chilled dark. And of again hunkering down in a pocket of trees as the sun rose, scanning, considering options, and finally spotting a hint of a path that led to Groesbeek and their command post.

Some pilots and crews, though, were never seen again.

Other glider pilots who found themselves too isolated to reach their assembly points and in the absence of a specific duty assignment were eager to explore a nearby town. A few, like Goldman and Mueller, decided to take the night off and head into Groesbeek in search of "pubs or can-can girls."[18] Like hundreds of others that day, they had fulfilled their mission but in doing so had become orphans in the crosscurrents of battle.

"Less than ten percent of the glider pilots who went into Holland gave all of them the reputation of 'wanton unruliness,'" wrote one historian. "To their credit, others performed well but not without conflict among other ranking glider officers."[19]

While a few went exploring, the rest would stand a watch in a foxhole, spray a field with gunfire, pour sulfa on a buddy's open wound, guard prisoners, or assist medics. Others would not leave the battlefield for weeks. Some, like Ritter, Jacobson, and Brennan, fought a more personal war of survival by hiding with the Dutch resistance for as long as a month until a town or forest was liberated. Some were released so far from their landing zones that they missed Holland all together. Others climbed out of waterlogged gliders floating in the North Sea.

Clearly most glider pilots proved themselves worthy on the biggest airborne day to date. The list of those missing had grown throughout the day, and it would be more than a month before reliable casualty and prisoner-of-war tallies could be compiled.

Although the setbacks in American sectors had not been fatal to the operation, the unfolding British disaster at the Arnhem bridge had made the airborne missions the next day on September 19 critical.

Another 400 glider pilots in England prepared for that mission, the third major lift in Operation *Market Garden*. The reinforcements, artillery, and firepower they carried might determine whether the British ground troops near Son could reach the Arnhem bridge thirty-seven miles away before their comrades were overrun.

9

They Were Invisible

Flight Officers Kenneth Hinkel and Adolf Riscky had watched C-47s limp back to the airfield at Membury, west of London, riddled with holes, smoking, leaking, pockmarked by sweeps of machine gun holes, and looking as if piranhas had bitten giant chunks of metal out of their wings and tails. They stood aside as medical crews had gently carried blood-covered airmen, some of them burned or missing limbs, to waiting ambulances.

The two Normandy veterans finally would be taking off on *Market Garden*'s third day. Playing cards and drinking would pass the last night before it was their turn on September 19. As the gin level lowered, their Texas accents thickened, and tempers erupted. The fight became inevitable. As they were pulled apart, "I'll kill you!" threats were exchanged. *Just pre-mission jitters*, some of their buddies thought. *Let's get them to bed.*

Meanwhile, Lieutenant General Lewis Brereton faced a critical decision on the night of September 18 as the weather gods conspired against the British at Arnhem. Rain mixed with dense morning fog over the airfields, heavy clouds over the southern route, and fewer clouds over the northern route were expected the next morning. He had planned to send fifty glider planes to reinforce and supply the British at Arnhem. More than 200 gliders were scheduled for the 82nd Airborne, and nearly 400 for the 101st. Would the critical needs on the battlefield trump the weather forecast?

General Brereton decided the day's glider missions would fly the southern route on D+2 despite the weather, fearing a third consecutive day on the northern route could produce unacceptable airborne casualties from flak. The departure time for the mission was set for 1130 hours. The troops on the ground would have to fight for hours before their anticipated reinforcements and resupply would arrive.

But Brereton also gutted the third day's mission plan. He called off the Arnhem mission to reinforce General Urquhart's force with a Polish Parachute Brigade, as well as the troop carriers and gliders bound for the 82nd. For the second day, the critically needed 325th Glider Infantry Regiment would not arrive. General Gavin now was faced with defending a twenty-five-mile oval-shaped perimeter in his sector that measured approximately seven-and-a-half miles north to south and ten miles east to west, while mustering an attack to capture the Nijmegen bridge. At best, a paradrop resupply mission in the afternoon might help, but when only thirty-six of sixty resupply planes made it to Gavin's location, he would remain short of men and materiel.

Only the 101st expected to receive its 385 glider lift of men, equipment, and supplies. More than 2,300 troops would depart England along with nearly 150 jeeps, seventy-seven trailers filled with ammunition, and 500 cans of gasoline.

As critical as the glider missions were to reversing the setbacks of the day before, the day began on a promising note. While James Di Pietro, Darlyle Watters, Pete Buckley, and other glider pilots prepared for their departures later in the morning, the British ground breakthrough finally came at dawn when British troops crossed the new Son bridge north of Eindhoven that had been cobbled together by American combat engineers. More than thirty hours behind schedule, in the next two hours they rumbled across enemy territory in the 101st's sector and connected with elements of the 82nd near the town of Grave south of Nijmegen. The 101st now had to keep about ten miles of Highway 69 open for the

British Second Army's push northward. The dashing attack that Montgomery had envisioned finally was building a head of steam.

Meanwhile, as the British ground assault reached his sector, General Gavin had orders to capture the Waal Canal bridge near Nijmegen by the end of the day. Like Taylor and Urquhart, he badly needed what was supposed to be the third consecutive lift of *Market Garden*. He would need his glider pilots to stay on the front line facing the *Reichswald* forest to protect his eastern flank if he were to take the Nijmegen bridge ahead of the approaching British ground troops.

The cloud cover over Greenham Common west of London shrouded the C-47 pilots after they had taken off and began to finesse their way into a precisely choreographed formation. But the route to the sea was even worse. Visibility disappeared, forcing ten serials of glider pilots to "fly the rope." Dropping down to 200 feet over the English Channel helped, but visibility remained at one-half mile or less. Towing gliders nearly within skimming height across the sea posed too great a threat to the entire lift. *Return to base.* Hinkel, Riscky, and the others in the last serial were recalled. Instead of continuing to the battlefield, they turned and headed back to Membury.

Fighting the Germans no longer was on their horizon. But perhaps battle was. A copilot trailing them watched as they released from their tow planes over their home airfield. He expected both to follow procedure by turning left as their C-47s headed away. But for some reason, one of the gliders turned right, directly into the other under the gray English sky.

> For a split second, the two intermingled gliders seemed to hang in the air and then broke apart. A jeep, its driver still sitting rigid at the wheel and his passenger slumped beside him, tore out of the front of one of the gliders and tumbled to the ground. Bodies spilled out from the wreckage like toy soldiers out of a great box, turning over and over, arms and legs outspread as they fell. The two gliders crashed a short distance apart, and one of them burst into a brilliant white flame from the phosphorous shells it had been carrying.[1]

Hinkel and Riscky had killed each other and had taken six glider-borne troopers with them into the British soil.

Mission casualties on the approach to Belgium, meanwhile, were already mounting. Seventeen gliders ditched into the sea, some the victim of armada turbulence. About midway across the English Channel, the smell of vomit reached some gliders' cockpits. Sitting back in the dim fuselage, rocking and rolling from side to side, and lurching up, then plunging down in the turbulence with no visual points of reference brought airsickness to many. But the glider infantry had a plan. *Throw up into your helmet and then pass it from one soldier to the next to the last man in the back of the glider. He'll empty it into a bucket and pass your still-wet helmet back. When the bucket's nearly full, he'll open the glider's door and empty the bucket at arm's length, hopefully without the contents blowing back inside. Meanwhile, put your helmet back on. You don't want to crack your head open when the glider suddenly drops again.*

With almost no visual cues as he crossed the water, James Di Petro's glider had swerved left and right far more than usual in the soupy fog. As he had been trained in the States, he struggled to stay centered and just above the C-47's prop wash. In clear weather, he could judge his speed by the arc in the tow rope between his glider and tow plane. But like many others, he was judging his position by his rope's angle from the nose of his glider a few feet into the clouds ahead.[2]

At some point, the intercom line had gone dead. When the clouds thinned briefly, he spotted a C-47 to his right and below. *How'd he get over there?* A hard turn to the right and Di Pietro's tow rope snapped. Only then did he realize that it wasn't his C-47. With the tow line hanging from his nose, Di Pietro now was in free flight at sea and dropping fast.

Silence swept into the glider as the C-47 pulled away and the glider slowed. If all went well, the glider would hit the water with its tail, perhaps bounce a little, and then bellyflop hard with its nose digging into the sea. It would be a bone-jarring stop. Di Pietro began reciting the ditching procedure. *Keep your seatbelt fastened and wait for the second hit. We'll stop fast. Forget the exit door.*

Ram your fist or the butt of your weapon through the top of the fuselage. Then climb out onto the top of the glider. We'll wait until an aircraft drops us a dinghy or a rescue ship comes up alongside. No matter what, stay together!

Di Pietro didn't tell his passengers that he wasn't entirely sure the glider would float as he watched the altimeter spin down to 500 feet, still with no water in sight. His speed at 150 miles per hour was much too fast. Lower and lower to 100 feet when the sea surface finally appeared, remarkably smooth, Di Pietro thought. *Full spoilers and hang on!* The glider hit hard the first time, its nose lifting like a breeching whale, and then slammed back down, the nose biting into the water, its tail popping up, and then settling. The glider stopped almost instantly.

Unlike when his glider had crashed in Normandy and the Greek soldier he carried who was bent on revenge had been thrown out of the glider and killed, this time Di Pietro and everyone aboard scrambled out onto the glider's wing. Within fifteen minutes, they were picked up by a rescue ship. When they reached their base in England, their pals were shocked to see them walk through the door. A C-47 pilot had watched the glider crash into the ocean so violently that he was sure there would be no survivors.

"To this day, I don't know how I avoided colliding with another airplane. The sky was full of them and they were invisible," Di Pietro reflected later.[3]

For some glider pilots, training had shown the Germans would not be their only enemy as their gliders caromed through the C-47s' turbulence. Flight Officer Ed Walters never forgot what the sand bags used as glider ballast had inflicted on his friend Albert Wyatt when Wyatt had crashed in the States. Half his face had been torn away, the remainder a bloody pulp. Arms and legs splayed at impossible angles, white bones protruding from uncounted breaks. Broken bodies on the battlefield soon would be added to the haunting memories of glider pilots who already knew what their cargo's jeep, trailer, or howitzer could inflict if they lost control.

Another thirty-one gliders were released over Belgium or broke free as tow planes abruptly changed course to avoid collisions.

Perhaps worse, many were off course, too far west to find the highway that would lead them to their LZ. They encountered some of the most brutal enemy artillery fire of *Market Garden* as the cloud cover forced them to fly at lower-than-normal altitudes which made small arms fire more deadly. Twenty-six CG-4As were lost. Another fifteen gliders were released fifteen miles from their landing zone.

A sports axiom holds that every boxer has a plan until he gets hit on the chin. Dozens of C-47 aircrews took it on the chin as the enemy's antiaircraft fire shredded their wings, tails, and engines with shrapnel on the run from Belgium up to the 101st's landing zone. Snap decisions by tow plane and glider pilots overruled flight plans that had been carefully laid out in the final briefings.

Second Lieutenant Darlyle Watters's tow pilot and squadron commanding officer, Captain David Brack, had flown a remarkably steady course through the clouds over the ocean. Brack had been a civilian pilot before the war, was highly respected, demanding, quick to wash out those who did not measure up, and didn't like to be saluted. As the sky brightened on the approach to the 101st, Watters watched Brack's plane take direct hits, straight down the fuselage. But, like the other glider pilots, he kept an eye on his plane's engines. They looked good, right up to the moment the tow rope came flying back onto Watters's cockpit. Too soon. *An abort? Did it snap? Maybe hit by flak?* It didn't matter. Watters was over German territory and had to get down.

With the man sitting in the copilot's seat dead from enemy fire, Watters managed to set down with the infantry he carried next to a ditch. It was a good place to hide, regroup, and improvise.

"Surrender!"

Within minutes, several German soldiers stood at the edge of the ditch, their Luger pistols pointed down at Watters and the others. They were lined up, searched for weapons and souvenirs, and later became prisoners of war in Germany's Stalag Luft I. Brack, meanwhile, had turned back to the south and landed in Brussels.

Pete Buckley emerged from a fog bank, towed by Captain Bill Miller's C-47. They were alone. Several formations had dissolved in the fog bank before crossing Belgium on the way to the landing zone. Miller circled over enemy territory waiting for the others to catch up, in tight circles that made it difficult for Buckley to hold the proper towing position after three hours in the air.

The others never arrived. It didn't seem possible that they would be up ahead, though. As Miller returned to his course toward LZ-W, Buckley wondered just how a solitary C-47 and its glider could survive an onslaught of enemy fire so close to the ground that he figured they would be within the range of a shotgun.

Handfuls of splintered sheet metal peppered Buckley's cockpit when shrapnel from an enemy flak wagon ripped through the tow plane's left wing, part of its fuselage, and the radio compartment. Miller held his course until Buckley found a field that resembled a country dump. Wreckage was strewn everywhere, some of it on fire. Craters marked points of impact and death. Less than a minute after he released, Buckley plowed his glider into the middle of what had been a potato field, partially burying his nose in the soft dirt. Like many glider pilots, Buckley and the men he carried had to clear mounded soil from the front of the hinged nose so they could lift it and unload their combat cargo.

A short time later, he stopped by a medical tent to see if any glider pilots were being treated. Not far away a C-47 burned. Inside, he saw "some of the crew members of the C-47 that [sic] had been terribly burned on the faces, head, and hands before they had bailed out ... and [outside] in the wreckage were what was left of the crew members that [sic] were unable to get out in time." Buckley later dug in for the night, figuring he would try to determine his location in the morning.[4]

For many glider pilots, the approach to a landing zone became a movie in fast forward. Flashing images, no time to think. Look, react. Ignore the *kha-boomps* of artillery shells narrowly missing and exploding outside the glider, the bullets splitting the air as they ripped through the fuselage. Stay focused despite gagging on grisly smells of torn bodies filling the fuselage until the movie ended with a glider belly down in a field.

Second Lieutenant Kenny Coffman's landing zone approach was ghostly, just blurred brown and green tones below in a gray mist. *Pop-pop-pop.* Bullets probably hitting the fabric, like a clean wound, penetrating one side of the fuselage and exiting the other. Up ahead, green tracers were disappearing into his C-47's wings and fuselage. Pieces of aluminum skin flying past his cockpit. Sweeps of enemy fire through the glider now. He could feel the impact of 20mm shells through his controls. *Not good.*

"Somebody get up here!" An infantry squad leader, sitting in the copilot's seat, leaned over in a death slump against his seat belt. A corporal crawled forward, smelling of vomit and blood, and pulled the man back onto the floor of the fuselage now slick with bodily fluids.

"I'm working on getting down, guys," he shouted back to his passengers.

"We're okay, sir."

He got down fast, nearly too fast. The glider hit the ground and porpoised perhaps twenty feet up and then turned nose down. *Keep her straight, get her down on the main gear. Good. Keep the tail up. Skidding, nose low, good. Not too much. Please don't flip. Don't flip. Don't flip. Drop the tail … now! BAM!* As the glider stopped, dust boiled into the cockpit. They were down. "Get out, get out, get out!" Coffman shouted as he pulled his feet out of the rudder pedal straps.

Holding onto the CG-4A's framework to steady himself, he made his way back through the fuselage to check on the troops he was carrying. *No, no, no, no. The other side … all dead.* Coffman gazed at the corporal who now had a hole the size of a softball in his chest. Not far away, it looked like three others might have been shot through with a single slug, probably a 20mm that hadn't exploded before exiting obliquely under the wing, he later reflected. Almost everyone had taken bullets to legs, feet, chests, guts, and their heads. Several had bled out as Coffman had landed. *Which one had said, "We're okay, sir,"* he wondered?[5]

The first wounds that some glider pilots suffered that day were to their gliders. Ironically though, fire may have saved glider pilot Lawrence Kubale's life. On his way to delivering supplies to troops near Son more than six miles away, the aim of a German artilleryman had been perfectly timed, his shell penetrating Kubale's glider directly between his feet. It had exploded when it hit his steering column. Shrapnel shredded portions of Kubale's head and arms, his flak jacket probably saving his life.

Despite the rudimentary flight instruction he had given the infantryman sitting in the copilot's seat, he wasn't about to hand over the battered controls. Stunned at first, he figured his arm soon would be numb from shrapnel buried in his shoulder. Kubale had to get the glider and the troops he was carrying down in a hurry, despite the blood flowing into one eye from a temple wound.

His survival depended on more than a successful landing. Barren ground resembled a cratered lunar landscape and offered sparse cover and little hope. Some fields were waiting for winter, their harvest stubble offering no nearby refuge as a glider was unloaded. Fallowed fields with tall grass could conceal enemy positions and could be set afire by artillery. If a glider pilot dug in near his glider, he might face the prospect of fistfuls of incoming enemy artillery methodically "walking" across the LZ toward his position. A parade of explosions, spewing shrapnel, steadily approaching him where he lay flat on his belly, face down. Sprinting toward vegetation at the edge of LZs – and out of the way of incoming gliders – often was a glider pilot's best bet on survival. But first he had to get down.

Kubale spotted a burning field. "I figured no one else would be there so that would be the safest place to land." Somehow, he landed to one side of the field, avoiding the flames. He was taken to an aid station in a basement in Son. Nuns took care of him for several days, changing bandages on his raw arms and face.

Ultimately, he would be shipped back to England for extended rehabilitation. "What are these holes and scars in the middle of your back? Where did they come from?" asked a doctor. "I don't know." X-rays revealed shrapnel near his spine. Kubale later received the Distinguished Flying Cross for delivering his troops to the battlefield.[6]

The glider pilots knew their mission was to deliver the infantry and their supplies under enemy fire, likely by crashing their gliders, then to get back to their base hundreds of miles away as quickly as possible, and to be ready for their next assignment.

That could be flying as a copilot on subsequent C-47 supply missions, helping evacuate the wounded, retrieving gliders that somehow had survived, or preparing for the next airborne assault. Combat training had always been secondary. Yet hundreds of glider pilots endured tremendous enemy mortar fire and remained on the battlefield for days within sight of Germany.

At twenty-nine years of age, Captain Elgin Andross was an "old man" in the glider corps and was pure Army. He had enlisted in 1931 when he was sixteen years old and had received his glider rating eleven years later. Now he was a glider officer in charge of the 313th Troop Carrier Group's glider pilots.

Late on September 19, he and about 100 of his pilots were part of Major Nevins's frontline deployment. Many of Andross's men already had been in the field for two days. They had survived an enemy aircraft attack and had scavenged the countryside in search of food. Now their foxholes were flanked by American infantry and mortar units.

Nevins's men were opposite a crack German parachute regiment supported by a German armored unit. Nearby, the *Reichswald* forest surely held unseen artillery emplacements, tanks, and infantry. Once infantry reinforcements arrived by glider the next day, Nevins expected he would pull his glider pilots out of their foxholes. But not before they endured artillery attacks, and at one point called for antitank support after Nevins spotted eight German tanks "looking like enormous, crawling, prehistoric monsters" attempting to flank his position. Within one half-hour, antitank bazooka teams destroyed the first three, forcing the remainder to retreat.

The day had deteriorated into disaster for the glider corps in an alien world of ground combat. Men reported that enemy sniper fire passing by a man's cheek felt like a June bug flying unnaturally close. Tightening every muscle throughout one artillery barrage after another sapped a man's strength. Surprise at the loneliness that followed a firefight when there was no one nearby to resume a conversation or share a cigarette. The cries of wounded men out in the open, their resigned sobs, howling pain, bawling, and "help me, help me" echoing over and over haunted those powerless to help.

And shock at seeing some wounds emptying blood as fast as an overturned canteen.

Fourteen glider pilots had been killed, nearly half of all those who would perish in Operation *Market Garden*. A like number of C-47s had been shot down as well. Fluid front lines made finding safe landing zones even more difficult. By one analysis, only about two-thirds of the gliders reached the 101st's LZ, while ninety-seven were listed as lost or missing, and the balance as "abortive."[7] Meanwhile, dozens of glider pilots were recalled to base in mid-flight, the 82nd and 1st Airborne never received reinforcements and supplies, and tow plane pilots drifted off course in foul weather over enemy territory.

September 19 saw the single largest one-day loss of gliders to date in World War II. By one account, 172 glider flights of the scheduled 385 were ruled ineffective, an attrition rate approaching fifty percent.[8]

SEPTEMBER 20, D+3

Command anger rose as the predawn fog descended onto the British airfields the next day. *Market Garden*'s premise of three clear days of airborne operations had long disappeared in the mist. General Brereton again postponed an airborne mission to drop the desperately needed Polish infantry reinforcements for Lieutenant Colonel Frost at Arnhem. General Gavin to the south would have to fight a second critical day without glider infantry reinforcements.

The delays proved deadly. The British troops holding the northern end of the Arnhem bridge had nearly run out of ammunition after most of the supplies dropped the day before had landed in enemy territory. Casualties mounted as German tanks pounded their position. Frost was wounded and ordered his men to disengage at about 1200 hours. The battle for the Arnhem bridge was lost. The heroic battalion had stood its ground while the rest of the 1st Airborne remained about two miles away, squeezed into an area that measured one mile by one-and-a-half miles, a target-rich expanse for German artillery.

A German counterattack against the 82nd finally emerged from the *Reichswald* forest. The enemy advanced 1,000 yards before being turned back. While the glider pilots remained on the front line, Gavin's troops finally seized the Nijmegen bridge. But to their shock and disgust, the advancing British tanks had stopped short of the bridge, waiting for the British infantry to catch up. Morale among American glider pilots and ground troops took a hit when reports began to circulate that the British troops were quick to halt or at least pause at tea time.

Bad weather remained the Germans' ally on September 21. The Polish infantry finally were sent to Arnhem but only about half the transports made it to Holland. Too little, far too late for the British who were down to one ration for every three men. Meanwhile, some of Nevins's glider pilots were pulled off the line at 1200 hours after 36 hours' combat duty and "fell asleep on the nearest level ground" while Andross and his men remained at their posts.[9]

SEPTEMBER 23, D+6

A late-summer morning sun finally greeted 2nd Lieutenant Vincent Boyer and the other glider pilots in England on D+6. Only a few clouds and passing showers, but nothing like the fog that had shrouded everything for days. About 400 gliders that had sat on runways, some for as long as four days in bad weather, finally could take off on September 23. All of them on the southern route, eighty-four would break away to land in the 101st's southern sector while the remainder would press ahead to the 82nd. The 325th Glider Infantry Regiment would deliver the long-overdue 3,400 troops, more than 100 jeeps, two dozen howitzers, and nearly sixty trailers filled with ammunition.

It became a mission of two tales. The approach to the battlefield had been routine, although the leading serial wandered outside the prescribed route. Regardless, the landings at LZ-W were successful. Seventy-seven of the 101st's eighty-four gliders reached their landing zone near Son. But a few miles north near Veghel, German artillery raked the glider force inbound for the 82nd's middle sector.

More than 100 C-47s were damaged, nine of them crashing. Lead tow planes plowing through the barrage cut their gliders loose early, twenty-one of them landing far from their landing zone. Sixteen other gliders released six miles early when they saw their lead glider release from a wounded C-47. The rest pressed ahead to the 82nd and began their landing sequence at about 1600 hours. Although the 82nd lost seventy-four of its 400 inbound gliders, seventy-five percent of the glider regiment they delivered was able to assemble within two hours and head toward its defensive sector near Groesbeek Heights.

In some areas, infantry along the edges of large farm fields paused to watch swarming gliders at various altitudes, all drifting downward in circles. Off in the distance, their silent final approach looked almost as if it was in slow motion. Sometimes they disappeared behind the crown of a field, their presence visible only by the rooster tail of dirt their skids kicked up as they slowed to a stop. Sometimes a wing appeared from below the field's horizon, as a glider pilot lost all semblance of control and began cartwheeling sideways, tail over wing over cockpit. One, sometimes two, revolutions before a wing collapsed in the dirt or a cockpit slammed into an unseen stump, house or stand of trees.

Higher in the sky, a C-47 broke away from several others, nosed downward at a forty-five-degree angle and began trailing smoke. Perhaps the pilot tried to level, but the descent became an even sharper nose dive as if the plane had decided to rush toward its death. As the ground approached, white specks appeared at quick intervals up and behind the C-47's downward course. Parachutes. Somehow a few crewmembers had reached a hatch despite the incredibly steep pitch of the fuselage. As they floated above the plummeting aircraft, it appeared as though the pilot was still struggling to pull it out of its dive. It turned a little, but then settled into a course straight into the ground.

Seconds later a ball of flame near the tail blossomed and the trailing smoke darkened. The fireball boiled up above the tree line, where the horror had unfolded in less than two minutes. The infantry turned its attention back to the enemy. Others would have to search for personal effects among corpses once they cooled. And it would be up to the C-47's crew – if any had survived their low-altitude parachute jumps – to find Allied troops or the Dutch resistance before the Germans found them.

The last glider mission of Operation *Market Garden* had met its objectives. But there would be no bridgehead on the far side of the Lower Rhine. Field Marshal Montgomery's vision of plunging a dagger into the heart of Germany's industrial region had disappeared in the smoke of enemy artillery, burning aircraft, and gunfire in a week's battle. And more glider pilots had been killed or had disappeared.

Second Lieutenant Vincent Boyer and six other glider pilots from the same squadron had been released over unfamiliar territory. Was it another landing zone? An odd farm field, but large enough for landing? Had the enemy been cleared out? Boyer couldn't be sure. He had circled, perhaps one time too many. His glider lost its speed, stalled, and plunged 100 feet into the ground, killing Boyer. Two weeks later, the other glider pilots who also had been released, 2nd Lieutenant Hester Barfield and Flight Officers Roy Bailey, John Kirlin, Frank Taflewitz, Eugene Meyer, and Robert Palmer, would still be listed as missing in action. Bailey was captured by the enemy and Meyer later was listed as killed in action.

On September 24, the glider pilots received orders to disengage and head back to their bases in England. Some would have to fight their way toward Brussels. That included Captain Andross and his 100 glider pilots who were finally relieved and taken off the front line. Andross and his cadre hitched a ride on a convoy of twenty-five trucks. It would not be a smooth ride. The glider pilots dove to the floor of their open trucks, piling on top of each other, when unseen German troops opened fire as the trucks passed. Wood and metal slivers pierced the air as they bailed out, took cover, and listened for orders. "Pretty soon I had my guys fighting back with everything they had, and most of them had Thompson submachine guns," Andross recalled later after his men had turned back the German counterattack.[10]

After the convoy reached the town of Veghel in its seventeen remaining trucks, the 101st later reported Andross and his glider pilots had killed 125 enemy soldiers while suffering only a handful of losses. Andross later received the Silver Star for his battlefield bravery and leadership.

As the glider pilots headed back to England, the British mission in Arnhem had become one of saving those who remained. On the blustery, rainy night of September 25, General Urquhart evacuated the 1st Airborne from its positions to the south side of the Lower Rhine, leaving the most seriously wounded behind. British glider pilots were posted as guides along the route for those heading to the river. Most piled into barges, rafts, and assault boats while some opted to swim 150 yards across the river. The remainder, many of them wounded, awaited capture after firing their weapons and simulating headquarter radio traffic to disguise the retreat.

The remaining British troops near the bridge crossed the river in driving rain, wicked wind, and relentless British artillery fire covering their retreat. Their chilling loses echoed the bloodletting Urquhart's 1st Airborne Division had suffered. It had lost more than seventy percent of its 10,000-man force.

In the meantime, 2nd Lieutenant William Reidlinger and others were handed a variety of mop-up duties as the Allied assault moved up through Holland, consolidating its hold on the southern half of the country. The glider pilot first joined a group picking up abandoned parachutes, released tow ropes, and bundles of supplies dropped by aircraft. Later, a truck needed to be loaded with ammunition and driven to an abandoned German camp. All the while, he and some other pilots looked for a way to get to Brussels about 100 miles to the south to catch a flight back to England. Glider pilots learned to become the best hitchhikers in the Army.

Perhaps no other unit in World War II carried such haphazard orders as hitching rides to get back to base. Reidlinger managed a ride on a British reconnaissance vehicle heading south and reached Eindhoven across what had become the backstage of the battle. The blackened skeletons of trucks and tanks, still smoldering, lay tilted in roadside ditches. Weedless patches of churned dirt marked freshly dug graves. Smoke drifted up from a charred C-47 amid mangled gliders in a field, as if a father and his children had died a horrible death together.

Both hope and horror framed Dutch villages as the glider pilots passed through. In some, nearly every building had been pulverized. A town's culture crushed into unrecognizable rubble. Yet many residents lined the roads as the Allies passed, yelling "Yanks!" at the sight of the American flag patch on the pilots' shoulders, and tossed some of the summer's apple crop in their direction.

Upon reaching Brussels, Reidlinger and the others hoped for a flight the same day, but no luck. A night's stay in a hotel (authorized by the town mayor for returning troops), and then onto a C-47 to one airfield in England, and then another to his base, nearly six days after he had begun evacuation.

But other glider pilots, including Flight Officer Guy Anderson, were headed east as prisoners of war. He had been a coal miner, auto-mechanic, and had played a little professional baseball before registering for the draft and looking "for some way to keep out of the walking Army."[11] The glider program had been his ticket. He had received his glider pilot wings only four months earlier and had been rushed to England.

A new kind of uncertainty gripped the pilots-turned-prisoners. Some were marched to the Dutch town of Utrecht and loaded onto a prisoner train. Allied aircraft attacked it as the train headed east, knocking out its engine. They sat on the track for two days, crowded, hungry, and thirsty while waiting for a replacement. After Anderson finally reached Oberursel, Germany, by truck, eleven days of solitary confinement ended with interrogation. He reached Stalag Luft I on another train where "the guards were armed, the dogs looked vicious, the guard towers surrounded the prison, the high fences, [and] the desolation drove home how almost helpless and hopeless our situation was."[12]

On his first combat mission, a three-hour flight from England to Holland had ended days later in a prison camp where it was clear that rumors of the war perhaps ending by Christmas had become fantasy.

Operation *Market Garden* had failed.

Many military analysts and historians have argued that Operation *Market Garden* had little chance of succeeding. Field Marshal Montgomery had attempted to take too much territory too fast along an extremely narrow corridor in a grand plan that could not be properly supported in a timely manner by the airborne forces. Further, stretching airborne operations over several days required too many paratroopers to guard landing and drop zones for future arrivals rather than take the fight to the enemy. All of this was further complicated by the Arnhem decision to land troops and gliders too far from the strategic prize and ultimate objective: the Arnhem bridge. It proved to be a house of cards blown asunder by underestimating enemy strength and Britain's weather.

Yet the 101st and 82nd had achieved all the objectives in their sectors within a day or two of the original schedule. Nearly 1,900 glider pilots had climbed into their CG-4As (with no trained copilots), had flown three hours through sometimes life-threatening weather, and had completed their missions. More than 100 glider pilots had been wounded or injured, others had been taken prisoner, and an alarming number simply had disappeared without a trace after landing in enemy-held territory or on the far side of the Rhine in Germany. While hundreds of their gliders had been retrofitted with the Griswold nose reinforcement and deceleration parachutes, less than 300 were salvageable even after weeks of repair.

Within days of the battle, the 1st Allied Airborne Army headquarters glowed in its self-assessment, noting the glider pilots delivered 8,500 men to the battle, along with nearly 900 tons of supplies. It claimed all the airborne troops "dominated" their sectors, even in Arnhem. "Hence the airborne troops accomplished what was expected of them" and claimed the "almost perfect accuracy in the drops and landings."[13]

Yet combat glider doctrine still had not yet been fully invented, much less refined. Glider pilots were perhaps the only unit in the Army that did not have a defined chain of command once they were on the battlefield. Their fundamental squadron command structure remained in England. Orders given them on the battlefield by strangers often were haphazard and based on immediate circumstance. Given their priority to return to their home airfields as quickly as possible, the wily glider pilot usually could find an officer willing to give him permission to find any way back to England "on the double."

Even Major Nevins encountered resentment when he marshaled nearly 300 glider pilots from several units for frontline duty that stretched to several days for some men. To many, he was a stranger who didn't carry the credibility that the glider pilots' direct superiors had earned earlier during training back in England. First Lieutenant Hugh Farler referred to being "pushed to the front lines" by Nevins. Second Lieutenant George Daugherty resented what he saw as no real effort to plan the glider pilots' evacuation for a week, while 2nd Lieutenant Ray Welty later wrote that Nevins acted "with utter disregard of the danger ahead, formed combat companies, and marched us to what was called the front lines."[14]

When glider pilots remained as a unit under the direction of another glider pilot on the ground, even evacuation could become chaotic. After one group of glider pilots had come off the front line and was headed toward the rear, their truck convoy encountered a road block near the town of Grave. The senior officer in the group "turned them loose and told them to make their way back any way possible."[15]

Frustration among some glider pilots was palpable by the conclusion of Operation *Market Garden*. Flight Officer Jack Rice wrote in his interrogation checksheet:

> After being released from [command post], we were shuffled around from one place to the other and kept in a state of confusion, not due to airborne but due to lack of air corps organization on the ground. It appears to me we could have been handled much better and better evacuation arranged for since we were kept in this area six days and then had to make our own way out via Brussels which necessitated an overnight stop. We needed money. A kit of currency for this region should be included in our equipment.[16]

The majority of glider pilots had served admirably, standing posts on the front line, enduring foul weather, and sometimes subsisting on little more than gritty, unharvested turnips and potatoes. They performed their duty despite inadequate combat training, a shortage of compasses and useful maps, sketchy briefings, and no way to communicate with ground personnel. Perhaps not surprisingly, many officers, including General Gavin, considered them a liability and distraction once they were on the ground.

In fact, Gavin, one of the most experienced officers in the Army, wrote to Major General Paul Williams who headed the IX Troop Carrier Command on September 25, a day when most of the glider pilots were still on their way back to England. Excerpts painted a dire picture.

> I do not believe there is anyone in the combat area more eager and anxious to do the correct thing and yet so completely, individually, and collectively incapable of doing it than our glider pilots. Despite their willingness to help, I feel that they were definitely a liability to me. Many of them arrived without blankets, some without rations and water, and a few improperly armed and equipped ... they frequently became involved in small unit actions to the extent that satisfied their passing curiosity, or simply left to visit nearby towns... In an airborne operation ... the first few hours are the quietest ... this [conduct] can be very harmful since all units tend to lose control because of the many [glider pilots] wandering about aimlessly, improperly equipped, out of uniform, and without individual or unit responsibilities... I feel very keenly that the glider pilot problem at the moment is one of our greatest unsolved problems...[17]

Gavin argued that, like the British system, glider pilots should be assigned to combat units and receive proper ground training. The 442nd Troop Carrier Group's summary report echoed many of Gavin's concerns.

> Paramount among them was the need for some system of communication between forces already landed on the ground

and incoming serials ... [glider pilots] were obliged to stand helplessly by and watch our incoming formations ... fly over patches of wood held by the enemy. Had some sort of radio communication been available, with a competent flying officer in charge, the formations could have been notified to make their approach over ground in friendly hands, thus avoiding losses. Because of the extremely short time [of] interval[s] involved, it is unlikely that the enemy could make any use of intercepted information. Speedier and more accurate intelligence on the overall ground situation was a secondary need... For example, the route was charted to the west of Eindhoven based on information that the British had moved into that area, when actually their main forces had driven past Eindhoven to the east. A third need indicated by the results of the mission was escape materials for glider pilots. More glider pilots found themselves down in enemy territory than power crew members, and the fact that they were without escape [kits] was an unwarranted handicap. The necessity of providing chest chutes for glider pilots and glider passengers also was emphasized, for in several instances bail outs were possible, but could not be made owing to the absence of chutes.[18]

A month later, General Brereton was angry enough about the lack of military organization that, in a letter to General Arnold, he threatened to take his concerns to General Eisenhower. He complained about a lack of support and communication between his First Allied Airborne Army and the generals running the ground attack. A turf war loomed when he wrote, "The direct command of the air and ground forces in an airborne operation must be in a single commander and he should be the air force commander." A "complete failure of communication" between the fluid conditions on the ground and air command led to unnecessary losses, he added.[19]

Few changes, however, would be instituted. General Matthew Ridgway, commanding officer of the airborne XVIII Corps, disagreed with Gavin's perspective. Glider pilots would remain with the troop-carrier squadrons, and it would be up to ground combat officers to make the most of them or send them on their way back to their bases. And the airborne and ground commands would have to find ways to work more effectively together.

Nearly five percent of the men on the ground in Operation *Market Garden* were glider pilots; the equivalent of a regiment. Had they received more rigorous infantry training, they may have significantly influenced combat decisions made by Generals Taylor and Gavin. Regardless, the Germans' defensive front had been pushed back to the Lower Rhine and the glider pilots would play key roles in landmark missions throughout the winter of 1944–45. Some would be flying their third or fourth mission of the war, ultimately reaching Germany's heartland.

Some glider pilots, however, would not return to their units until the end of October when Dutch towns were liberated, and pockets of enemy troops were cleared. Many had been hidden in and near the town of Boxtel that was liberated on October 24. Not far away, the Allies liberated Schijndel before glider pilot George Brennan "was due" and pilot James Swanson was discovered.

Still other glider pilots, such as James Ferrin, would join Anderson at Stalag Luft I for the winter. Some were destined for the infamous Stalag Luft III and a midwinter death march to Moosburg.

Like Severson and other glider pilot POWs, in only two months the glider corps also would face temperatures near zero degrees and fields covered with ice and snow. And like Normandy and Holland, glider pilots again would immediately be surrounded, this time by an estimated 250,000 enemy troops in what became known as the Battle of the Bulge.

The Hole in the Donut

The odor of the garage stabbed at us… Low moans from the
wounded sounded as [though] we had literally stepped into
hell… Inside, the light was poor, and it took a while for our eyes
to get used to the semi-darkness, but our noses told us what was
going on. We groped our way through straw piles and litters
which were serving as beds.[1]

Minutes earlier, Captain Edward Zinschlag, a surgeon, had climbed
out of 2nd Lieutenant Corky Corwin and Flight Officer Benjamin
Constantino's glider and had shimmied under a blackout tarpaulin
to enter a garage in Bastogne, Belgium, on the day after Christmas,
1944. An invisible, fused fog of rancid almond, ammonia, and the
unique sweetness of dying flesh greeted Zinschlag and the rest of the
nine-man medical team that had been delivered in the one-glider
mission. Infection had become the lethal enemy of hundreds of
wounded men ten days into the Battle of the Bulge.

The harshest winter in two decades seemingly had iced the war in
December 1944 along a seventy-five-mile stretch in the Ardennes
Forest that spanned the southeastern third of Belgium. Winter's
biting winds, temperatures approaching zero degrees, and heavy
snows had already reached the Ardennes.

Almost the size of Connecticut, the wrinkled plateau of dense
timber, farm fields, rivers in deep ravines below rocky bluffs, and

peat bogs had been Germany's thoroughfare into France four years earlier. Seven of the relatively few all-weather roads in the region and three railroad lines converged on Bastogne, a town of 4,500 residents.

General Eisenhower had moved some of his Allied units out of the region, as his intelligence officers believed the Germans had lost so many troops and equipment since Normandy that there was almost no threat of an attack before spring. Less than four mostly green or undermanned divisions remained in the region, about one-third the manpower that normally would be required for an area that size.

December in the Ardennes was a time to dig in, hunker down, and replenish as the weather allowed. The area was considered safe enough that a USO show featuring Hollywood star Marlene Dietrich had been held in Bastogne on December 14. The next day, New York Giant Mel Ott and other big leaguers had visited the troops in the Belgian town of Spa. Both were within thirty miles of the front line.

But Hitler had other plans. Increasingly unstable as the Allies had neared the German border, he had been rebuilding his forces. Though poorly equipped and less than full strength at 10,000 men each, forty-four skeletal divisions had been created since July. They were replete with the underaged, the too old, and the broken down from the Eastern Front.[2]

Without consulting some of his most experienced field commanders, Hitler also had conceived an all-or-nothing plan to somehow stymie the Allied tidal wave approaching Germany. German troops would invade southern Belgium at the start of winter with twenty divisions (plus five in reserve), advance west through the Ardennes, cross the Meuse River forty miles southeast of Brussels, turn north, and recapture the port of Antwerp. On paper, Hitler's troops would deny the Allies a critical supply port and potentially cut off as many as twenty Allied divisions.

Perhaps a lost cause could be gilded as a war won through a negotiated peace. But advancing about 120 miles under such conditions was considered lunacy by some of Hitler's most battle-hardened officers.

Josef "Sepp" Dietrich, commanding officer of the 6th Panzer Army that would lead the offensive and a member of Hitler's inner circle, was a highly decorated SS general and one of Germany's most respected field commanders who was widely regarded as fearless. He groused:

> All Hitler wants me to do is cross a river, capture Brussels, and then go on and take Antwerp. All this in the worst time of the year through the Ardennes where the snow is waist deep and there isn't room to deploy four tanks abreast, let alone armored divisions. Where it doesn't get light until eight and it's dark again at four and with re-formed divisions made up chiefly of kids and sick old men ... and get the job done by Christmas![3]

The snow had crackled under thousands of German soldiers' boots two hours before sunrise on December 16, ten days before Zinschlag arrived in Bastogne. Trees alongside the roads leading from Germany into the Ardennes shrugged snow as the vanguard of approximately 1,000 tanks headed west. Vehicle exhaust and soldiers' breaths billowed in the sixteen-degree darkness, as three German armies comprising thirteen infantry and seven armored divisions engaged American positions in the forest. Outnumbered by more than two to one, the Americans' defensive line buckled with shock and then broke, creating a three-mile gap on the Western Front. As the enemy pushed ahead, the attack that could not take place quickly had created a bulge toward the west.

The following day, tactical troop movement plans had been made to halt the Germans before they crossed the Meuse River in central Belgium. Then on the afternoon of the 18th, a battered 101st Airborne Division mobilized aboard almost 400 trucks from its base in France where it had been resting and refitting, only a few weeks after having spent seventy-two days on the line in Holland.

The "Screaming Eagles" had arrived in Bastogne only about eight hours ahead of the Germans. The 10th Armored Division also arrived, along with stragglers from other units, and were placed under the command of the 101st's Brigadier General Anthony

McAuliffe. Additional reinforcements were planned for Bastogne, but severe fighting elsewhere forced the 82nd Airborne and others to be diverted.[4]

By December 20, telephone and teletype communications between the 101st and its headquarters seventeen miles away had been established. The incoming messages carried a note of creeping desperation. The 101st had drawn only two days' rations before climbing onto the trucks bound for Bastogne. One hundred supply trucks were loaded and ready to move, but the Germans had cut off the last road to the town.

The 101st was surrounded.

"Urgently need supplies as follows…." Messages on the 21st and 22nd painted an increasingly dire scene in Bastogne. One artillery battalion had only 200 rounds remaining for its estimated eighteen guns. Other units had only ten rounds of long-range ammunition each. Armored vehicles were so short of fuel that drivers no longer had the luxury of warming their engines before heading into battle.

The 101st also had lost its division field hospital one night when six enemy armored vehicles and 100 infantry had ambushed a truck convoy of wounded. Machine gun fire ripped across the trucks and nearby hospital tents. In only about two hours, the hospital had disappeared. More than 140 medical officers, medical enlisted men, and twelve medical personnel from other units had been captured. Meanwhile, a maintenance garage in Bastogne that had been converted into a primitive hospital held 120 soldiers who urgently needed surgery, another 250 litter cases, and about 400 walking wounded.[5]

Food also had become critically short after a quartermaster unit had been captured. Within a few days of its arrival, foraging by soldiers among Bastogne's residents had become part of the 101st's battle plan. When queried by headquarters by radio for a situation report in Bastogne, the reply had been succinct.

"We're the hole in the donut."

There were approximately 18,000 American troops in the Bastogne area, surrounded by an estimated 45,000 Germans. The town had been cut off when two enemy panzer divisions had bypassed it on the north and another on the south. In only four days, the Germans had penetrated nearly sixty miles into Belgian territory. General George Patton had turned his Third Army north toward the 101st in Bastogne but was still several days away.

Pathfinders, airborne drops, and gliders were being mobilized in France and England for what would become known as Operation *Repulse*, but bad weather forcing delays had become an ally of the Germans. The 101st now needed hundreds of tons of supplies delivered by C-47s in air-dropped parapacks and bundles, as well as fuel for armored vehicles, artillery ordnance, and medical personnel aboard gliders.

But McAuliffe remained undaunted despite his twelve artillery battalions starving for ammunition. When German General Heinrich von Luttwitz sent two men to McAuliffe carrying a surrender ultimatum on December 22, his "Nuts!" reply became the shortest and perhaps most iconic battle cry of World War II.

Bravado notwithstanding, if the 101st could somehow hold Bastogne, it would force the Germans' advance columns and supply trucks onto the secondary roads that were becoming impassable due to the weather and heavy traffic. Stopping the German breakout that had been planned for months would come down to whether ordnance, food, medical supplies, and fuel could somehow be delivered to the surrounded troops.

For the first time in World War II, glider pilots would not lead an amphibious invasion in Europe. They would not deliver glider infantry and supplies to paratroopers behind enemy lines. This time, a rescue mission was critical to stopping an enemy's advance. To destroying Hitler's dream of carving the Low Countries' Allied forces off from the juggernaut squeezing Germany into inevitable defeat in late 1944.

Thousands of American troops had spent December 25 cold and hungry as a plague of Christmas Day gloom blanketed England, France, and the Ardennes. In places the snow was so deep it could only be cleared to frozen soil to serve as an above-ground foxhole. Men huddled in the kind of cold that glued snow to the leeward side of spindly brush, pines, leafless trees and to a soldier's uniform; where steam followed every breath and vehicles' tires or armored tread spun on frozen country lanes.

A drop of parapacks had taken place on the 24th with 160 tons of rations, fuel, and batteries. But the "want list" the 101st radioed to headquarters the same day remained voluminous, far too much for solely jettisoned bundles in the absence of a secure airfield near Bastogne. Medical personnel, thousands of gallons of gasoline, and artillery shells that weighed as much as ninety-five pounds each had to be brought in by glider. After nine days' battle in cruel weather, glider pilots in the 439th Troop Carrier Group prepared to report to gliders coated with frost and snow at Chateaudun while others in the 440th TCG at Orleans also mobilized.

But relentless bad weather again grounded resupply flights from England. The troop carrier groups in France lacked adequate numbers of parapacks and enough men trained to pack them.

For the third time, the 101st asked that gliders be considered for resupply on the 26th. Surgeons were the top priority. There were reports from the Bastogne area of only one surgeon and three medics per battalion. In the converted maintenance garage, surgeons relieved one another on a schedule that ensured two were always working, twenty-four hours a day. Surgeries were taking place in a tool room while the wounded lay side by side on a floor covered with sawdust.

Morphine, litters, plasma, surgical dressings, and blankets were critically low. A headquarters operations report noted "There are one thousand casualties which cannot be evacuated… There is no reserve of rations and the men are living from hand to mouth on food that can be obtained from civilians… If an attack is launched, [they] would be in a position to hold out only for a few hours."[6]

Lead German elements now were within five miles of the Meuse River, but their supply lines were stretched dangerously thin. The region's network of roads converging on Bastogne had become more critical than ever. The 101st had to be resupplied the following day, nearly at any cost. Bastogne could not fall to the enemy and waiting any longer for Patton's rescue column to reach the town from the south could not continue.

There's the smudge pot, lots of smoke! And the T panel. But that's not right, I can see Bastogne up ahead. This isn't our LZ. Hang on. Glider pilot Corwin wasn't about to come up short with the nine-man medical team he and Benjamin Constantino, his copilot, were carrying. Constantino had spotted the same smoke and panel and yelled at Corwin, telling him to cut off, the tow plane's green light was on, the LZ markers were below, and they were passing their destination. When Corwin heard Constantino's confirmation of the landing panel, he cut off and banked hard into a U-turn back toward the open field.

Corwin and Constantino had volunteered before breakfast on December 26 for an unknown combat mission. Many of the others in their squadron were on holiday leave or sleeping off holiday hangovers. They then hustled to a briefing to learn they would fly an empty glider at 0800 hours 200 miles from their base at Orleans to another base at Etain and load nine passengers and cargo for a ninety-minute flight to Bastogne. Their passengers would be five surgeons and four medical technicians with crates of medical supplies tied to the glider's floor between them.

The glider pilots didn't know that the mission had been put together so quickly that their tow plane's navigator had been handed only a photo of the LZ at the last minute. He would have to recognize it through the haze of ground fog hugging a snow-covered field on a random checkerboard of snowy fields and patches of forest. When they had reported to the glider, someone had written "FireTrap" in chalk on its fuselage.

The medical team was convinced the sole glider inevitably would be flying through heavy flak on the way to Bastogne. Few had flown before, and several had been under the impression they were going to parachute into Bastogne. Instead, they sat on benches whose seat belts were missing, their feet crammed against the supply crates.[7]

Corwin and Constantino landed close to a 101st unit at 1510 hours after a surprisingly uneventful run, perhaps catching the

Germans by surprise. Once the glider pilots and medical team had taken cover, an infantryman told Corwin the markers in the field were to show American bombers and fighters the front line so that they would not blast or strafe American troop positions. Corwin and Constantino had landed about 1,000 yards from enemy troops. Their C-47's aircrew had turned on the release signal light one minute early, about two miles short of their glider's landing zone.

Within an hour, though, the medical team had been driven to the makeshift hospital in the Bastogne garage. Like Zinschlag, the smell of torn flesh struck surgeon Henry Mills when he entered the primitive hospital. "Some of the wounded had been in there for days. It looked like the Atlanta station scene in *Gone with the Wind*," he recalled later.[8]

Once the glider had cut loose, the pilot of their tow plane had banked over Bastogne, dropped the tow rope, and climbed to 3,000 feet for the flight back to France. He soon faced ten inbound C-47s with gliders in tow. The second glider mission of Operation *Repulse* was underway in a race against the setting winter sun.

Second Lieutenant Charles Sutton had been lying in his bunk earlier that morning when his squadron's glider operations officer, Captain Wallace Hammargren, walked in.

"Who needs flying time?"

"I do."

"Get your combat gear. Draw ammo and three days' ration and report to the briefing room at 10 a.m."

Sutton and other glider pilots learned it would be a resupply mission to Bastogne, although it wasn't clear whether the Americans or Germans would be in control of their landing zone upon arrival. The intel report for the mission was two days old. Crews, meanwhile, were loading gliders with fuel, medical supplies, and ammunition.[9]

Six hours later, Hammargren and Sutton were in the back half of a ten-glider serial headed toward Bastogne, only a few minutes behind Corwin's solo glider mission. When they had reported to their gliders, they had discovered nearly 3,000 gallons of gasoline in five-gallon jerricans had been lashed to the floors. Each glider would be carrying about fifty-five gasoline cans.

The Belgian countryside below looked almost idyllic to the passing glider pilots as smoke wafted above farmhouse and village chimneys. But as the late-afternoon light flattened, enemy flak over the final seventeen miles to the LZ appeared, "looking like Fourth of July Roman candles in the dusk," thought Hammargren. Corwin's earlier "milk run" had roused enemy gunners. Below, burning houses and barns marked the battlefield.

Each glider's pilot and copilot fought a private battle on his way to the landing zone. Flight Officer William Burnett's tow pilot took evasive action early, approaching at "tree top level," then quickly climbing to 600 feet to release Burnett. It seemed to him that the enemy artillery had been set to detonate at an altitude higher than Burnett's approach. But it found 2nd Lieutenant Richard Baly's glider. An artillery shell ripped a four-foot hole in his left wing and exploded. Shrapnel damaged his left elevator, grazed his steering column, and knocked out a panel cover above his head. Seconds later, shrapnel cut Hammargren's tow rope twelve inches in front of his nose. Gunfire passing through Sutton's fuselage reminded him of a popcorn machine. It punctured two cans of gasoline, draining ten gallons' worth onto the floor of Flight Officer Joseph Dubbe's glider.

Yet all ten gliders landed in the designated LZ, a short portion of his tow rope still attached to the nose of Hammargren's glider. A delayed departure had led them to land at about 1710 hours, thirty minutes past sunset but before moonrise.

Soldiers hustled up to Hammargren's glider. In the dim light he hoped they were American.

"What are you carrying?"

"Gasoline."

"And the other gliders?"

"Gasoline."

"Thank God! We're at the bottom of the barrel!"[10]

Within a few minutes, hundreds of jerricans were loaded onto trucks and were on their way to some of the 101st's armored vehicles. Although the glider mission had been wholly successful, an intelligence report later that night recommended that future glider missions be routed more from the south along the route of General Patton's approaching relief column to avoid the heavy artillery fire that Hammargren, Corwin, and the others had endured.

In England, the day after Christmas also had begun with bad weather, initially grounding another planned resupply air drop. By late morning, the decision had been made to take off with the hope the cloud cover and visibility would improve during the five-hour flight to Belgium. If not, the armada would be recalled. But it did. More than 280 C-47s arriving from England had dropped nearly 170 tons of signal equipment, ammunition, fuel, and other supplies.

That same afternoon, 1st Lieutenant Charles Boggess couldn't make out the spots of color in a distant field as he stood in his tank's open turret about two miles south of Bastogne. The red, yellow, and blue supply parachutes looked like scattered confetti. *There!* He opened fire on a German pillbox. He had been pushing his lead Sherman tank as hard as he dared through the forest toward Bastogne, firing straight ahead while three tanks behind him blasted enemy positions left and right. He was leading the 4th Armored Division's relief column, trailblazing a path for the Third Army. Only an hour's worth of dim light remained as the temperature dropped.

The pillbox destroyed, he spotted foxholes scattered nearby.

"Come here, come on out!" he yelled. "This is the Fourth Armored!"

Silence. Then helmets slowly appeared over the rim of the foxholes. American helmets. He yelled again. A single soldier stood and approached the tank.

"I'm Lieutenant Webster of the 326th Engineers, 101st Airborne. Glad to see you."[11]

Boggess leaned over and shook Webster's hand.

In the course of only a few hours, air drops had resumed, glider pilots had begun delivering critical supplies, and Patton's troops had reached the outskirts of Bastogne. December 26 had become a day of hope as dozens of glider pilots prepared for the next day's mission over enemy artillery that had zeroed in on their route and altitude.

A grayish, hazy cold "where one scraped the frost off the outhouse seat with your trench knife if you were the first one in," greeted glider pilot Richard Fort and forty-nine other pilots early on December 27.[12] They had a fifty-glider mission to Bastogne scheduled for 0815 hours to deliver seventy-six tons of mostly artillery ammunition as well as four more surgeons (and in at least one case, sheet covers for the dead), the last of the Operation *Repulse* glider missions.

Originally scheduled for the day before, some glider pilots had learned of the mission while eating lunch and had scrambled to get to their briefing. The intel was out of date and of minimal value. Their route would be the same as that which the eleven glider pilots had flown. They would fly in low, at about 400 feet or less, to stay below the effective range of the German 88mm artillery. They should expect deteriorating visibility under 500 feet and were advised to land with the sun at their backs. They would be clay pigeons on a straight, predicable path, each filled with flammable fuel vulnerable to a single piece of red-hot shrapnel.

They also were told that so many glider pilots were on holiday leave that there would be no trained copilots on this run. But Colonel Charles Young, commanding officer of one of the two troop carrier groups assigned to the mission, had another reason. "Since the cargo was HE [high explosive] ammo, it was felt any direct hit would instantly destroy the glider along with its pilot ... there was little use in losing two [glider] pilots to a direct hit since there was little hope for survival by either."[13]

But the artillery shells had not arrived in time to load the gliders, take off, and reach Bastogne before dark. The mission had been rescheduled for the morning of the 27th. And then delayed two hours as attempts to de-ice the aircraft and gliders proved no match for the cold. By the time they took off at about 1000 hours, Young had made another fateful decision. He had learned nearly at the last minute that Patton's men had opened a corridor from the south to the 101st Airborne. A glider route over the new corridor likely would be safer than the approach flown the day before. That intel had been sent the night before, but by the time it was routed through the IX Troop Carrier Command it had reached Young shortly before takeoff. He felt it was too late to notify fifty pilots and aircrews. They would fly the same "milk run" route flown the day before.

There could be no hope of surprise on this mission for the fifty glider pilots from the 439th Troop Carrier Group's 91st, 92nd, 93rd, and 94th squadrons. They were all bound for a patchwork of rolling fields, some blown clear of snow, others nearly thigh deep, and some freshly churned by tank warfare. Fields separated by pockets of trees or rickety barbed-wire fences. A collage of grays, dirty whites, and earthen tones.

The milk run became a carnival shooting gallery. The enemy's 88mm and 20mm guns locked onto the lead squadron's gliders' and tow planes' altitude and route, each glider essentially a flying armory filled with explosive ordnance behind its tow plane's non-sealing gas tanks so vulnerable to fire. "Ahead there was a solid wall of flak bursting. They had our altitude cold," recalled one glider pilot.[14] The LZ was about nine miles away, on the far side of the flak.

When Richard Fort, the mission's lead glider pilot, came to a stop in the LZ, he turned to watch dozens of gliders approaching the landing zone. "The sky ... was black from air bursts. The concentration of fire must have been tremendous. It reminded me of a black summer storm cloud."[15] Yet the thirteen pilots in the leading 91st Squadron managed to land mostly in sequence near 101st troops standing by to unload their cargo.

Flight Officer Chuck Berry, flying in the fourth position, had been shocked at the amount of antiaircraft fire in the last ten miles to the LZ, about a mile northwest of the 101st's headquarters. "You could see so much heavy flak ahead of us that I thought we could land on it." But as he was descending toward the LZ and passing over tank hulks on fire, the flak remained overhead. "I sat there, fat, dumb, and happy watching the tracers go past the nose of the glider and thumping into the wings." Overloaded by several hundred pounds, Berry had to somehow come to a stop on snow and ice at a faster-than-normal speed. Once he touched down, he put his glider "up on its nose" and plowed through farm fences before coming to a rest near a 101st welcoming party desperate for artillery shells. "We've been firing our artillery for four days, using only our charges [propellant without the artillery shell attached]. We fired the charges to make [the Germans] think we were firing at them," one soldier told Berry.[16]

As 2nd Lieutenant John Hill approached his landing zone, the small arms fire ricocheting off the 105mm artillery shells behind his seat became unnerving. He hoped none would find his box of detonators. But a fire erupting in his tow plane became terrifying as it spread from its belly to the back of the plane. It grew over the next three miles as the C-47 pilot held his course.

Then as the flames blew halfway back on his tow rope, two parachutes emerged from the fire. The radio operator and crew chief made it out. A little later as the C-47's cargo compartment burned, smoke filled the plane. After setting the plane on autopilot, the copilot ran through the flames and jumped. The pilot, Bill Fry, soon followed. The parachutes barely had time to fill and swing once, maybe twice, before the crewmen hit the icy snow. Still short of his LZ, Hill cut loose from the fireball and landed. He later learned that his tow plane crew had survived, but at least one member spent a month in a hospital recovering from his burns.

Enemy fire became so deadly that some tow planes in the remaining three squadrons abandoned the flight plan and flew higher than planned toward the LZ. That forced their glider pilots to circle over Bastogne after they released to bleed off altitude and look for fields close to the LZ. Other C-47s released their gliders so prematurely that the glider pilots had to fly nearly straight ahead, stretching their descent to reach the LZ. Bastogne had become a target-rich environment for enemy gunners.

An eerie sight stretched out in front of Flight Officer Herbert Ballinger on his approach in the thirty-fifth glider. "It looked like a big cumulonimbus cloud starting at the ground and [extending] way up above the formation … [aircraft] and gliders kept flying right into it… [I] saw ships go down and gliders blow up." As he flew the final gauntlet to the LZ, his tow ship took a direct hit in its left elevator, leaving a large hole. As the flak approached his glider from one direction, Ballinger pushed it away, as far right as he could manage. *There's the green light, get ready to release. But where's Bastogne?* Ballinger hung on to his wounded tow plane. Its red light told him that in sixty seconds the tow ship's pilot was going to release his glider.

Ballinger started counting. *One, two, three, four…* When he reached forty, he reached up to the release lever and turned away from his tow plane. *There!* He leveled toward a field, dropped down onto it while keeping his wheels up so they would not catch and flip the glider. He landed 250 yards inside the 101st's position with a load of 155mm shells.

Immediately behind him, Flight Officer Albert Barton carried four surgeons squeezed next to a load of 155mm shells. He, too, watched his tow plane take direct hits, smoke trailing first from one engine and then the other before the flames erupted in both. His C-47 dying, Captain Ernest Turner faced critical decisions. He ordered his crew to bail out, gave Barton's glider another ten seconds, and then cut him loose with no warning. Those ten seconds likely enabled Barton's glider to barely reach a field just inside the 101st's perimeter. Turner belly landed the C-47 in another field alongside a stream and stacks of baled hay.

Two gliders were still rolling to a stop when enemy artillery blew both pilots out of their gliders. Somehow Flight Officers George Juneau and Frank Hobart – classmates in training earlier – survived but became prisoners of war. Others were captured as they climbed out of their gliders in enemy territory or after they had taken cover in ditches, stands of trees or behind haystacks and returned fire until it became hopeless.

The last twelve glider pilots of Operation *Repulse* found themselves on a suicide mission. Almost fifty gliders had already flown their route that day and the day before, at a nearly identical speed, almost at the same altitude, and bound for the same destination. The only way they could survive and join the others on the ground was if the Germans ran out of ammunition. They didn't.

Wallace Hammargren, who had landed the day before, recalled:

We saw several gliders and tow planes hit in the air. One flaming C-47 continued on its course until the glider pilot cut loose directly over the LZ. Then the pilot jumped. When he landed, he was badly burned. Pieces of molten metal still clung to his jacket... We saw two gliders overshoot the LZ and watched helplessly while green-clad figures rushed out and captured the pilots.[17]

"You can't imagine what it was like. You know how a goose feels when he flies over a bunch of hunters and they start shooting?" asked Flight Officer Verbon Houck, in the next-to-last of the day's fifty gliders, years later.[18] Those who had landed earlier were powerless to help their buddies.

The extent of carnage among the glider pilots on December 27 was not only catastrophic, but it may also have been more deadly than necessary. Throughout the previous night, Third Army tanks, artillery, and troops had arrived in Bastogne after the corridor from the south had been opened. Had the officers planning the gliders' mission on the 27th known that in time, changing their route to an approach along that corridor may have saved lives, and months spent in German prisoner-of-war camps.

While only three of the first twenty-five gliders failed to reach the landing zone on December 27, eighteen of the next twenty-five glider pilots either did not reach the landing zone, were killed, or were taken prisoner. Of the last twelve glider pilots in Operation *Repulse*, eight became prisoners of war. Three others were killed. The twelfth, Henry Nowell, had put his glider into a steep dive to simulate being hit by enemy fire, landed at nearly twice the recommended speed, and had crashed into a concrete telephone pole in a field. With the help of a local family, he was able to find a 101st outpost the following day. Nowell was the only man from his squadron that day to return to his base.

For some who were taken prisoner, their horror would last until the following May. Flight Officer Pershing Carlson hid for five days and nights in the snow after he crashed when the bottom of his cockpit had been blown away. When a meager supply of fruitcake and candy bars ran out, he attempted to reach Allied territory but was captured by a German solider. With others under German guard, Carlson walked more than 150 miles into Germany, surviving on frozen potatoes and turnips. Once he arrived at Stalag Luft I north of Berlin, he suffered from malnutrition until liberated on May 2, 1945.

Flight Officer Mike Sheff, flying the last glider on December 27, was captured as soon as he landed. He, too, was marched into Germany. When his guards were distracted at one point, he ripped off his dog tags that showed he was Jewish. He ultimately trekked and rode in filthy boxcars crammed with prisoners more than 500 miles to a POW camp in Poland. He then endured another two-week march in April to Moosburg's Stalag VII-A POW camp, near Berlin and almost 400 miles from Bastogne.

Other glider pilots who had been marched through the snow and crammed into cattle cars bound for Moosburg included Flight Officers Velton Brewer, Kenneth Avery, Francis Carroll, and Clifton Kizer, 2nd Lieutenant George Freeman, and perhaps others. By the time they were liberated on April 29, starvation had become their enemy. Barley soup, boiled potatoes, and bread containing sawdust sometimes was augmented by periodic Red Cross food parcels. But each parcel had to be divided among six men. The canned food in the parcels was punctured by German guards so prisoners had to eat it right away before the food spoiled instead of saving it for an escape attempt.

By percentage, December 27 became the costliest glider and tow plane day of the war for some units. Twenty-six percent of the gliders' tow planes were shot down. Nearly one in five C-47 crewmen did not return. Thirty-two percent of the glider pilots that day were killed or captured. In comparison, historian Rex Shama notes that of the 2,933 glider pilots in Operations *Neptune* and *Market Garden*, 114 were listed as killed or missing, a loss of less than four percent.[19]

Losses on December 27 proportionately were eight times greater than World War II's two largest glider missions to date.

Yet the glider pilots delivered 100,000 pounds of cargo that final day and the surgeons and medical supplies they brought on both days likely saved untold lives at the makeshift hospital in Bastogne.[20] On the final day of Operation *Repulse*, seventy ambulances evacuated 150 of the most seriously wounded soldiers in the corridor opened by Patton's troops.[21]

Within a day or two of landing, most of the glider pilots began their journey back to their bases in trucks transporting German prisoners. Richard Fort rode in a convoy that drove through villages and past smoldering farmhouses, many of them a passing snapshot that became haunting. He later recalled,

> Near the barn was a stack of German bodies, like cordwood, with an odd body or so scattered about the barnyard, all sprinkled with an inch or so of new snow. Across the road, the house had no windows, the roof was partly gone, the front door ajar, a dead cow and broken fruit trees [littering] the area. In the middle of it stood an old man and old woman with blank gray eyes, the old man holding up a chair that had only two legs left. All set in the cold gray of a winter dusk. I'll probably always remember that.[22]

Not long after they had returned to their bases, a new battle emerged for the glider pilots, one of recognition. On January 12, 1945, a letter written by Brigadier General McAuliffe appeared in *Stars and Stripes*. He rebutted published references that the 101st had been in a "desperate" situation in Bastogne. The siege had been "rough at times but we were hurting badly only for medical attention and a little bit of ammunition," he wrote. Perhaps fueled by bravado, his version of being surrounded for nearly a week bore little resemblance to the urgent messages his officers had sent, characterizing their supply shortages as "urgent" and deliveries by paradrops or glider pilots as "imperative."

His attitude enraged some of the men who had flown the relief missions, especially since McAuliffe's letter appeared only sixteen days after the deadly fifty-glider mission on December 27.[23] Colonel Young, whose 439th Troop Carrier Group aircrews and glider pilots had suffered so horribly that day, publicly responded only three days later:

> What am I to give as an answer now to those of my men who survived the terrible flak and machine gun fire and to the families of those who did not, when they ask why they were sent in on a task which the general now, in effect, says was not necessary? The word "Nuts" does not seem appropriate.[24]

The skirmish among those senior officers reached General Eisenhower's Supreme Headquarters Allied Expeditionary Forces command. Soon thereafter, McAuliffe's reply to Young's letter carried none of the cockiness of his previous public statements. "Had it not been for air resupply, the situation would have become worse than desperate. It would have been untenable… Air resupply at Bastogne was superior. We recovered more than ninety-five percent [of] ammunition, medical supplies, rations, gasoline, and other items," he wrote the following month.[25] His conciliatory letter ultimately was forwarded to each squadron in the 439th TCG.

It is unclear whether the glider pilots who spent the rest of the war in POW camps received a copy when they came home.

The Americans held Bastogne and other key towns, denying the Germans much of the road network in the region. The arrival of Patton's Third Army and other units was faster than the Germans had anticipated in midwinter. Effective attacks on the flanks of the German salient ultimately forced a withdrawal beginning in mid-January. By the end of the month, the Americans had regained the territory they had lost in December at a cost of 75,000 casualties.

Hitler's gamble had failed. He had lost the reserve divisions (approximately 120,000 men) that he desperately needed against the Soviets who had advanced to within fifty miles of Berlin. The Battle of the Bulge became the last German offensive of World War II. The defeat of Germany had become inevitable.

Meanwhile, a dozen glider pilot families would not know for nearly six months whether the bodies of missing sons, brothers, or husbands would be found when the snow melted and when farmers returned to their fields, or if they had been captured and might have survived POW camps deep inside Germany.

For the glider pilots who survived Operation *Repulse*, scars ran deep as evidenced in their post-mission reports where few pulled their punches. "Not enough enemy position information furnished." "Need timely and accurate information on enemy positions and AA." "No flak suits or parachutes and we were carrying gasoline." "Glider operations very poor, no flak suits in glider. Briefing very poor, news 48 hours old." "Lieutenant Colonel Barnes said that as he saw us flying in, he knew we would pass over intense flak, because he had known for some time that the Germans had flak positions on the course we flew." "An Airborne 1st Lieutenant at the radar station told me that a much better route had been sent to Paris. The route should have been some miles to the right of the one we followed." "Operations for glider lift unexcusable [sic] for unprepared."[26]

Their sacrifice became even more painful in the days following Operation *Repulse*. "When one of the [glider pilots] returned to his hut at Chateaudun, he was astonished to find the beds occupied by replacements. Furious, he drove them out in the snow threatening them with a pistol. Then he sat down on his cot and cried for his friends."[27]

To some extent, the grief would subside on a current of devotion to duty and glider pilots' preparation for the next mission, the last airborne operation of the war.

It likely would become their most dangerous, landing on German soil for the first time.

11

Beyond Commendation

They sat mute, shoulder to shoulder. Stiff as the back row on a chessboard. Conversation was impossible between Frank O'Rourke and the other glider infantrymen sitting on facing benches in the glider's fuselage as it crossed the Rhine River. Six on a side, several sat hunched forward, the fronts of their helmets resting on the barrels of their upright rifles held steady by clenched knees. Awash in the airborne armada's roar, some glanced at the man on the other side, others fixated on a memory. Or perhaps a fear.

"Five minutes!" the glider pilot yelled over his shoulder, just as flak appeared ahead.

"Get ready!" a few minutes later. Time to hug rifles against bellies and chests; as a mother would to protect her child.

The instant the glider pilot released from the tow plane, the glider almost unnaturally rose sharply for a moment, then banked hard left and seemed to stall, its left wing perpendicular to the ground. *Are we flipping over?* But then the glider pilot straightened it into a dive at a terrifying speed until he pulled out as he neared a field. *Only a few more seconds...*

O'Rourke pulled the release on the exit door shortly before touching down. He couldn't risk it being jammed if he and his buddies survived the landing. The rear of the glider pitched up when its nose dug into the ground, then dropped hard. They were down. A good landing. Seat belts were unsnapped, and the passengers hustled out and into enemy fire. Thirteen more infantrymen had been delivered to the far side of the Rhine in Operation *Varsity*.

The Allied plan to cross the Rhine River had simmered at headquarters since early November 1944, before the Battle of the Bulge in December had placed it on a back burner. But in the first few months of 1945, Allied armies had pushed east across a broad front to the western bank of the Rhine. The Western Front now stretched 450 miles from Holland to the Swiss Alps.

General Eisenhower decided the primary assault across the Rhine would take place along the front's northern flank, a few miles northwest of the German city of Wesel, and only about forty miles southeast of Nijmegen, Holland, the central point of Operation *Market Garden*. Field Marshal Montgomery's 21st Army Group's three armies, the Canadian First (eight divisions), British Second (eleven divisions), and American Ninth (eleven divisions) would establish a bridgehead on the eastern bank of the Rhine extending six miles farther into Germany that would reach the west bank of the Issel River.

Simultaneously, the American 17th Airborne and British 6th Airborne Divisions would fly over the German east-bank defensive line along the Rhine and cross flat farming country dotted with crossroads, hamlets, farmhouses, and woodlots to drop troops, supplies, and release gliders north of Wesel.

Ten British and American landing and drop zones were within an area approximately six miles long and five miles wide. Some were within 200 yards of each other. They bordered mostly the south, north, and east sides of the *Diersfordter Forst*, tree-covered high ground 100 feet above the river (prime territory for observation that also provided cover for artillery). If the airborne forces could capture the bridge crossings on the Issel River a short distance to the east, they would trap the German troops between the Rhine and Issel and be positioned for the charge toward Berlin, about 300 miles away.

Although 80,000 men comprised the amphibious assault, Montgomery commanded more than 1.25 million men in

Operations *Plunder* (river crossing) and *Varsity* (airborne). It would be the largest ground and airborne assault since Normandy.

The airborne lessons and scars of Operations *Neptune*, *Dragoon*, *Market Garden*, and *Repulse* remained fresh in the minds of Operation *Varsity* planners. Glider pilots Sven Berg, James Larkin, and Edwin Blanche would not be flying at night as they had in Normandy. They would be landing late morning. Unlike in the Holland operation, Tom McGrath, Milton Dank, and "Goldie" Goldman would not fly a fragmented, multi-day mission against a well-prepared enemy after days of crippling weather.

On March 24, 1945, Operation *Varsity* instead would be the largest single-day airborne attack in the history of warfare, including 17,000 airborne troops, seven million pounds of equipment, 130 pieces of artillery, and more than 1,200 vehicles and tanks. The airborne armada would include more than 1,800 powered aircraft, more than 900 American gliders, and nearly 450 British gliders. They would converge from twenty-three French and English bases over Wavre, Belgium, and then fly northeast in a straight line across the Rhine to the Wesel area.

"Gentlemen, this mission is the beginning of the end. Tomorrow we land gliders in Germany."

Somber faces had looked up at Colonel Frank Krebs standing on Orleans' town theater stage, the commanding officer of the 440th Troop Carrier Group who would send his men on the next day's airborne mission. Glider pilots Dick Redfern and Tom McGrath – veterans of Operation *Market Garden* six months earlier – knew what lay ahead; the chaos of glider warfare and the uncertainty of survival. It was Krebs's job to put that in perspective for both the veterans and the newcomers who were sometimes called "virgins."

Not far away, Colonel Charles Young of the 439th TCG had stood before his pilots and crews who would tow Flight Officer "Boots" King, 2nd Lieutenant Edwin Blanche, and others. More the technician, he reviewed the airborne game plan, sounding like a football coach reviewing the team's playbook only minutes before leaving the locker room. "I'd be very pleased if we can do the job without any cutoffs… I'll pay particular attention to the gunfire… Study the … maps until you know the approach by heart."[1]

Glider pilots in the last serial slated to arrive at either of two landing zones, LZ-S or LZ-N, would be following hundreds of others ahead of them. Discipline and perhaps luck could dictate whether they would find space to land.

The glider pilots had listened to their briefings in theaters, TCG "war rooms," Quonset huts, or any available location that could hold a hundred or more men. Alongside them were approximately 350 power pilots like Lee Whitmire who had been cross-trained to be flight officer glider copilots. Whitmire had dropped supplies at Bastogne as a C-47 copilot. Beginning in late 1944, more than 700 power pilots had completed two weeks' cross-training to offset glider pilot shortages. It wasn't a popular assignment among many power pilots, but more than 900 glider pilots were being held in reserve for a possible assault farther south near the city of Worms.

They learned they would be taking off between 0730 and 0945 hours. About every ten seconds for nearly three hours, a glider would be lifting off. Part of the briefing was routine: flying at about 1,000 feet before dropping down to 600 feet for release. Red dots on an oversized map marked enemy artillery locations. They were told they should expect early-morning haze that would dissipate by the time they reached the landing zones. The paratrooper aircraft would lead the way, followed by the gliders, and then bombers dropping supplies from the air. It would be the first time in the war that paratroopers and gliders would be arriving nearly at the same time.

There were presentations that grabbed everyone's attention. More than 900 gliders would be pulled mostly in pairs by C-47s. "Double tows" had been flown in training, but everyone recognized the inherent danger of two gliders, nearly side by side, each wrestling with their tow plane's prop wash.[2] Now they would be double-towed for the first time in battle. Unlike previous missions, there would be no pathfinders on this run since the landing zones were only about six miles east of the Rhine River.

The gliders would arrive over their two landing zones within a two-hour window from 1030 to 1231 hours. They would be landing almost on top of some paratroopers whose drop zone was between the glider pilots' LZ-S and LZ-N. There would be no French or Dutch underground if a glider pilot landed far from his designated LZ. Every German civilian should be considered the enemy. Some spoke English and it might be impossible to tell if a German soldier had shed his uniform for civilian clothes.

One group of 288 glider pilots attended a unique briefing. They would become the first combat team in World War II to be comprised solely of officers (435th Provisional Glider Pilot Infantry Company). They also would be the first group of glider pilots to be assigned a specific frontline combat mission, roadblock duty in support of the 194th Infantry Regiment. Unique within the glider-pilot corps, they had received additional ground combat training with particular emphasis on handling M1 rifles and carbines, weapon-firing techniques in the field, scouting, patrolling, and tactical defense techniques. Others received additional infantry training, a shortcoming in previous missions, and for the first time most were issued trenching tools, compasses, canteens, maps, and light sleeping bags. But nearly all would be committed to battle only in an emergency and in defensive roles.

Sven Berg, Max Hunt, Bernard Smith, and others had both glider and specific ground combat orders for the first time. For some, it also was their first glider mission of the war.

Not only was a surprise assault impossible, but this time the Germans bragged that they knew the Americans were coming. German spies had watched the massive buildup, leading "Axis Sally" on March 23 to warn the American troops on her propagandist radio show, *Home Sweet Home*, that "We know you are coming 17th Airborne Division, you will not need parachutes, you can walk down on the flak."[3] And on this mission, Flight Officers Max Hunt, Roger Krey, 2nd Lieutenant Bill Lane, and the other glider pilots would wear chartreuse scarves – which seemed like great sniper targets to many of the pilots – and a first aid kit strapped to their helmets for identification purposes.

A few pilots wrapped the scarves around their arms while many stuffed them into a pocket.

The Allies faced an estimated 85,000 German soldiers along a 22-mile stretch of the Rhine. But it was a staggering, punch-drunk enemy. Boys, old men, prisoners of war, suffering from inexperience, critical shortages, exhaustion, plummeting morale, and constant turnover in the highest military commands that now defined the German army. Divisions were undermanned, reserves were in training, two divisions had only thirty-five tanks, and the entire German Army Group H commanded by General Johannes Blaskowitz held only about 200 tanks and assault guns. The only good news for the Germans was a concentration of 330 heavy and light antiaircraft guns. Every available artillery gun had been moved to the area where the Germans expected the Allied assault, between Wesel and Emmerich to the north. Artillery crews were on constant alert against the Allies who owned the air.

Veteran glider pilots had seen changes, and in some cases improvements, leading up to Operation *Varsity*. Second Lieutenants Frank Slane, Tom McGrath, James Larkin, and dozens of others had flown in Operation *Market Garden* six months earlier without any rehearsal exercises. This time, tens of thousands of flight hours had been logged earlier in the year. The 50th Air Wing, one of three to participate in *Varsity*, logged more than 4,000 glider tows in the first eighteen days of March.[4]

Most gliders now featured reinforced noses to lessen damage and facilitate efficient handling of cargo. They also had deceleration chutes that more quickly reduced their gliders' speed before landing.[5]

The *Market Garden* veterans also recognized the familiar multi-lane Holland approach plan and orders spawned by friendly-fire lessons from Operation *Ladbroke* over Sicily. There would be three lanes of airborne traffic with the British 6th Airborne in the left lane, gliders followed by Allied resupply bombers in the middle lane, and the American 17th Airborne in the right lane. Antiaircraft fire over England, naval fire along the Thames River and over the English Channel, and groundfire along a thirty-mile-wide flight path over the continent would be suspended between 0700 and 1500 hours.

Poor communication between the ground and the airborne had plagued previous missions. Untold lives could have been saved if tow plane and glider pilots had learned at the last minute that a landing zone had fallen into enemy hands. Operation *Varsity* would include four combat control teams – two for each division – to provide real-time communication from the LZs. Each team comprised five men with a jeep and trailer carrying a power unit and two powerful radios, one for communicating with headquarters, the other for conversations with aircraft.

For many glider pilots, Operation *Varsity* began the minute a chaplain's prayer ended their briefing. For some, a battle of nerves was fueled by self-doubt. Each sought a tonic to soothe the hours that would stretch through the night. Some obsessed over details: sharpening their knives one more time or cleaning their weapon for the third time. Perhaps heading to the airstrip in the dark to recheck their load. First-timers' speculation raged while the carnage of earlier missions haunted some battle veterans. Some, like Flight Officer Les Judd, Jr, wrote letters home to their wives and parents. A few favored music, others solitude, but all were alone as the hours passed.

For some glider pilots, the invasion day started with a Catholic Mass at 0400 hours. Then a steak-and-eggs breakfast accompanied by the usual macabre "prisoner's last meal" humor by veteran glider pilots, in part to rattle the newcomers.

Glider pilot Goldman awoke that morning convinced he would not survive the day. He silently repeated the Lord's Prayer, the only prayer he knew and one that he had not recited since boyhood. But on a morning when the enemy was waiting it seemed appropriate, even necessary when no man could predict his fate. Only a month earlier, his best friend in the army had met his fate beyond the reach of the enemy.

"It's too bad about that glider pilot, Mueller of the 439th," a glider pilot had mused while dealing a blackjack hand.

"What did you say?" asked Goldman, suddenly chilled.

Mueller and Flight Officer Walter Lindberg had been practicing ninety-degree turns and approaches in unsettled weather while preparing for *Varsity*. After cutting loose, as Mueller gained altitude in making his turn, the tow rope of a trailing C-47 had wrapped around his glider's tail. The rope strangled the tail assembly, grinding and screeching, as it cut through the glider's frame. Mueller had lost control of his glider.

Eight hundred feet above the ground, the glider nosed over as nearly two tons of ballast rock (simulating troops or cargo) slammed into the back of the cockpit and glider debris flew out the high end of the amputated fuselage. Plummeting straight toward the ground, the nose hit first, crushing both Mueller and Lindberg instantly.

Goldman and his best friend, dating back to flight school, had celebrated each other's birthdays at a base in Dreaux, France, only about two weeks earlier. They had shared a host of memories, from pranks to landing in vineyards in southern France to the *Market Garden* disaster.

Mueller had written a letter to his family the day before, asking for soap and pipe tobacco that were "worth more than money here," and asked for only one Coke per parcel so his buddies would not drink too much at once. He wanted deposit slips, too, so he could balance his checkbook. A man tending to his business affairs with the help of mom and dad. A short time later, they received his personal effects. No need to send deposit slips.[6]

Goldman left the card game and walked for miles until he spotted a culvert. He crawled inside and cried until only exhaustion remained. After a long walk back to his quarters, he climbed into his bunk without saying a word. Mueller had turned twenty-two years of age nine days earlier. Now, a month later, Goldman would cross the Rhine River in a few hours with hundreds of other glider pilots, this time without his best friend.

Operation *Plunder*'s amphibious crossing began at 0200 hours, one hour after a massive artillery barrage – as much as 65,000 pounds of shells an hour – had erupted and as bombers had pummeled twelve German airfields and reduced the city of Wesel to smoking rubble.

By about 0630 hours, glider infantry were meeting their glider pilots near their aircraft prior to takeoff. Glider infantryman Frank O'Rourke recalled:

> [My] pilot looked like a typical glider pilot. Wearing a wool knit cap, an old flight jacket and [what looked to be] dress shoes, he was not outfitted for combat. His appearance was so casual that it gave me a sense of security to be in his hands… A C-47 pilot had been pressed into service [as a glider copilot] because of the shortage of glider pilots. He looked nervous and he should have been.[7]

As the C-47s began warming their engines, roiling the already-tense morning, glider pilots and their passengers waited their turn. One after another, each C-47 pilot eased forward at the signal from a member of the ground crew clad in overalls and a ball cap standing a short distance ahead and facing the pilot. When he began pulling an oversized ping-pong paddle slowly toward his chest over and over … *easy … easy …* the C-47 slowly taxied forward to pull the tow rope taut. At that moment, he spun toward the far end of the runway swinging his paddle up, over his head, and then straight down the airstrip at arm's length, like an enthusiastic football referee signaling a first down. *Full power, now!* Goldman's glider jerked nose up and then settled, gaining speed behind his tow plane. Veteran pilots knew when to pull back on their sticks to lift their gliders off the runway above the tow planes' prop wash and how not to drift into their companion glider if they were on a double tow.

To avoid each other's turbulence, early departing C-47s flew at a lower altitude, with subsequent departures each leveling off at 500 feet higher, creating a stair-step effect, in search of smooth air as much as possible for the entire armada. No one wanted to fight unnecessary turbulence for hours before reaching the battlefield. Assembly into the formation to fly into Germany would come later, but casualties were immediate.

An unexpected tail wind posed an instant threat as aircraft takeoffs began. That complication was hardly needed by the C-47 pilots towing two gliders as they struggled to get both gliders off the ground. Shortly after one takeoff, Flight Officers William Heelas and Leonard Hyman's glider on the shorter rope began gyrating crazily and partially crossed the rope of their long-tow glider, flown by Flight Officers Dale Smith and Berkley Halstead. Both gliders released simultaneously, but the long-tow rope had become entangled around Heelas and Hyman's glider. Heelas and Hyman struggled to regain control as their glider dove toward the ground. But when a wing separated from the fuselage at 200 feet, the two glider pilots and their five passengers were doomed. They died on impact.

Once the converging British and American airborne armadas joined over Wavre and then approached the Rhine, the sky ahead darkened as the leading serials neared the landing and drop zones. Black and white flak popped around them, almost precisely at their prescribed 500–700-foot release and drop altitude. Axis Sally had not been kidding. The Germans were locked onto Operation *Varsity* almost from their first shot.

As in previous missions, maintaining preordained separation between the serials proved impossible. As one group of tow planes began to overtake the group ahead, the tow pilots again had the same two choices: slow without reaching stall speed or "stack up" by climbing above their prescribed altitude. Glider pilot Les Judd's tow plane pilot elected to decrease his speed: "we were wallowing just above stall speed. We would creep up on the tail of our tow ship, and to avoid running into it, I had to pull up and over ... then settle back in behind again ... the rope would tighten, and we'd begin another surge forward and repeat the process."[8]

As if a war movie were unfolding in slow motion, glider pilots could see the gliders ahead cut loose and bank to the left. "They wheel like eagles looking for prey, and then they disappear down into the smoke," reflected one glider pilot.[9] It was nearly impossible to know which were being flown by buddies they had known since training, and which were newcomers whose names had not yet stuck.

No one had expected the low-level smoke smothering the approach and landing zones. Field Marshal Montgomery had ordered chemical smoke machines along the Rhine to cover the amphibious crossing. But prevailing winds had carried the whitish-gray haze mixed with smoke from the Wesel bombing raids toward the gliders' landing zones. Visual landmarks on the approach had disappeared in the smog. Glider pilots would have to release on training, timing, and visual cues from their C-47 aircrews as shrapnel and bullets tore through the gliders.

They released one after another, turning, scanning, and diving toward open fields and countless firefights. If a glider pilot successfully landed, veterans like James Larkin knew a new danger lurked.

Exiting a glider potentially surrounded by the enemy that had watched it land unsettled many glider pilots. No one wanted to be at the mercy of a C-47 for hours, be released into a combat zone and look for a landing area, somehow survive a managed crash landing, spot snipers nearby, and then crawl over what might be damaged cargo or the bodies of glider infantry toward the exit doors. And then choose.

Which door? Which side is the lucky one away from the gunfire?

Some took steps to make sure that didn't happen. Larkin had graduated in one of the earliest classes of the glider program. He had been released so far off course on his first mission in Normandy that it had taken several days before he could reach friendly territory. He had carried Japanese American troops in southern France and troops, a jeep, supplies, and explosives in Holland. He had learned through experience to plan ahead for the moment his glider came to a stop.

> Before we took off, we always knocked out [the pilot's and copilot's side windows]. It made a lot of noise in the cockpit, but it worked okay. And then when we landed we didn't have to climb over [cargo], we could just go out that window, and it was big enough we could get out of there in one leap. And then, after things settled down, go back to our glider and get the stuff [we] needed out of it.[10]

First-time glider pilots had to overcome an overdose of alien sounds and smells. High-pitched screams of 88mm shells, mixed with bursts of American machine guns, the *eck-eck-eck-eck-eck* of the enemy's submachine "burp guns," and hollow *whumps* of mortars. Yells for "Medic!" Strange buzzing a few feet away, the telltale signs of gunfire narrowly missing a head or chest. All blended against the groaning rumble of C-47 pilots throttling to full power as they turned away from the battlefield, some trailing smoke. The acrid, gagging smell of gunpowder mixed with burning farmhouses, glider fabric, and supply crates. Fresh blood's thick sweetness. Sights and smells never experienced in training that had to be ignored if a glider pilot was to find cover, return fire, or reach a man helplessly wounded. Or simply to survive.

> *Hail, hail, the gang's all here,*
> *We're a bunch of live ones,*
> *Not a single dead one,*
> *Hail, hail, the gang's all here,*
> *Sure glad that I'm here, too!*

Glider pilots Roger Krey and Bill Lane didn't expect to hear the eleven soldiers they carried break into song seconds before they landed. Like Krey, perhaps it was their first combat mission. One of the first serials to reach their landing zone, they had just released from their tow plane. They could hear the crack of enemy fire as they descended through the smokey haze. Some of those able to look out the small fuselage windows were struck by gunfire that looked like "a junk yard [from] back home with hundreds of tin cans glistening back at you," as one soldier phrased it.[11]

The soldiers fell silent at the start of a second chorus when a 20mm shell exploded in front of their glider, shrapnel slicing through both glider pilots. Krey took hits in his head, face, and neck. The blood flowed but "both of us pilots were fully effective, not uptight, and fairly busy."[12]

As Montgomery's smoke screen finally thinned almost at ground level, a large transmission line loomed up ahead. Lane had one option. He told Krey to deploy the deceleration chute and added, "we'll go under it." A quick pull of the yellow chute-release handle

BROTHERHOOD OF THE FLYING COFFIN

a few seconds later as Lane leveled the glider and settled into a remarkably smooth landing.

Not far behind Krey and Lane, glider pilot Oliver Faris had smelled burned gunpowder as he crossed the Rhine toward LZ-S. Seconds later, artillery fire hit the tail of his tow plane, blasting away pieces that missed the glider and reminded him "of shooting quail back home and seeing the feathers fly out of the tail." Enemy fire from every direction followed, "looking like candles burning from a giant birthday cake" as he neared the landing zone. When he released, dropped, and made a turn into sunlit haze, he was flying blind.

Nearly on the ground, he saw one glider land too fast, stand up on its nose with the glider pilots inside, and stay there. Another disappeared in a stand of trees. Faris had only two options, landing between trees on a lane leading to a barn or setting down in the barn's adjoining feedlot. If he could make it.

"Get ready to crash. We're going into the woods."
"You're gonna make it! You're gonna make it!" yelled a soldier from behind.
Well, if he thinks I can get in this lot, maybe I'll try it.
He slowed the glider as much as he dared with a cargo of five men and a jeep.
"You're gonna make it!"

Faris almost cleared the last fence but caught his rear wheel, slammed down into the lot, put the glider up on its nose, and stopped ten feet short of a canal on the far side of his impromptu landing zone. In a split second, his passengers became a race car's pit crew. Some grabbed the 2x4s that were aboard and propped the glider's tail up to push the nose down. Another started the jeep inside and inched forward, pulling a cable that lifted the glider's nose into the air so that the jeep could roll forward and out of the glider. They had only seconds to unload and get clear, knowing enemy gunners would turn their attention to them as the C-47s turned away from the landing zone. Meanwhile, Faris hustled into a patch of trees, checked his map, and began a half-mile hike to his rendezvous point.[13]

Every clearing seemed surrounded by 88mm and 20mm artillery, and nearly every farmhouse held snipers or machine gun crews. By now they knew to hold the bulk of their fire until the gliders released, and for the first time in the war the 88s targeted the gliders on their descent and then intensified again when glider infantry and pilots were climbing out of their gliders.

The power pilots sitting in the gliders' copilot seats encountered some of the most vicious enemy antiaircraft fire of the gliders' war. More than one power pilot took the controls nearly at the last minute. "Bullets ripped through the nose of the glider, across the front of my stomach, and into the side of my pilot, 1st Lieutenant Frank Blood… He grunted, lifted his hands from the controls and said, 'It's all yours,'" reported power pilot Harry Dunhoft.

> That's when I got scared. The flak was coming up pretty thick, so I put down the nose and headed for the ground. An airborne boy sitting just behind me displayed the bravest set of guts I've ever seen. He had his kneecap shot away, but in spite of that he supported the pilot with one hand, puffed at a cigarette, called off the air speeds to me. His courage gave me courage. I landed the glider safely, considering… After we all got some sort of cover, the colonel, who had been one of my passengers, [later] offered me a shot of scotch. We got to talking and he congratulated me on the landing. I told him I hadn't thought it was wise to tell him before, but this was the first time I had ever landed a glider alone. The colonel did a doubletake at that, patted me on the back, and said, "You're alright for my money, kid."[14]

Some glider pilots tried to keep an eye on their buddies' gliders close by on the final approach. Hoping they, too, would survive. They could not be sure, though, until they reached their designated rendezvous point with the others. "Have you seen…?" A quick exchange with the friends or strangers there could be heartbreaking.

Second Lieutenant Dick Redfern reached his rendezvous point once the fighting had calmed. *Anybody seen Daugherty?* Flight Officer Harold Morgan had been flying close behind Flight Officers Fred Daugherty and Walter Chandler when their glider filled with TNT had taken a direct hit and had exploded, leaving little more than "just the two wingtips ... fluttering down." Reflection swamped Redfern.

He thought back to his training when Daugherty had somehow managed to get their wives into a secure area of the base. To a conversation about how he, Fred, and a couple of others had planned to take a Caribbean cruise after the war. And how Fred never wore dog tags on a mission so that if something happened to him, his wife "would get a year's worth of missing-in-action money."

Redfern walked away with tears in his eyes for his good friend who had been his best man at his wedding.[15]

Another pal, Flight Officer Delmar Switzer, had been shot as he approached his LZ. He had partly stood up in his seat briefly, sat down, landed his glider, and slumped over. His load of glider infantry charged into a firefight a short distance away. Before they could return, the glider was hit by an 88mm shell. The fire left little more than scorched metal ribs and charred fabric. "We only hope that he was dead before he burned," a glider pilot said.

Glider pilot Edwin Blanche and Flight Officer Leroy Brobst had seen the worst of glider warfare, flying missions together over Normandy and then over Holland. They knew enemy artillery was a far greater threat than German aircraft. But neither mission had compared to the artillery fire they met as they approached their landing zone. Hundreds of gliders approached or were making curved descents a few hundred feet above the ground, a few more steeply than others, in flickering clouds of flak, like bees in slow motion, some swerving to avoid collisions and some almost hovering in the distance, it seemed.

Carrying four airborne troops and a 75mm howitzer, Blanche's glider trailed smoke over the landing zone. Blanche and Brobst managed to land, though there were no witness reports of the impact. Blanche, Brobst, and all but one passenger were killed either by the crash or enemy fire. "As long as we have control of the air, I am not in a lot of danger, & you don't have much to worry about," Blanche had written his wife and three daughters less than a year earlier following his Normandy mission.[16]

What would be worse, some glider pilots had wondered, after seeing friends die in training, on missions, or simply disappear in the miasma of war. *Do I want to get hit by shrapnel or red-hot bullets 800 feet above the ground? Watch the ground expanding in an uncontrollable nose dive? Or burn alive before I can kick out the Plexiglass? Please, God...*

"Boots" King already had confronted those prospects on four glider missions. Along with Flight Officer Theodore Ring, they were in the next-to-last serial approaching their landing zone. By now, the enemy's artillery had zeroed in on the incoming gliders. Their glider took a hit in its belly just as they cut off, setting it on fire. As it spread from cockpit to tail, they managed to land, just before another artillery shell connected as it stopped. Despite burns on his right arm, right foot, ear, the top of his head, neck, and face, Ring kicked out the nose's center section, crawled out, and hit the dirt. A few feet away, King was on fire. He managed to exit and immediately had fallen to the ground, perhaps from enemy fire, perhaps from sucking in the flames' scalding heat. He died where he fell.[17]

"Boots" King would not return to the air base where he had been known for his oversized, comic complaints anytime stewed chicken was served after boiling it in open fifty-gallon drums. He would never start a family with the girl he had married three years earlier. He would never return to the Texas cotton country he had called home. He had celebrated his thirty-second birthday fifteen days earlier.

For some, seeing glider pilot corpses would haunt them for a lifetime.

Enemy fire on "Goldie" Goldman's approach slapped his glider's fabric. It was too late to evade the enemy fire. His target, a partially furrowed farm field, beckoned. He held his course even when it was too late to evade a paratrooper he spotted lying in the field.

The sound of a glider wheel crushing the paratrooper's torso sickened Goldman. But there was no time for remorse. He ripped his seat belt off, pulled a chin-up in the cockpit, flexed both knees and kicked out a Plexiglass window. He dove headfirst onto the ground and crawled on all fours as fast as he could for cover.

Later, when the firefight had settled, Goldman asked about the paratrooper. He learned "while he was still in the air a bullet [had] hit him. That bullet literally exploded his guts out of his body, causing him to bleed to death long before we ran over him on the ground," recalled Goldman. "That did relieve us somewhat, but neither of us will ever forget that awful moment when [he and his copilot] thought that we had killed one of our own."[18]

Morbid curiosity sometimes gripped surviving glider pilots in the aftermath of a firefight. Once his LZ was secured, one glider pilot took a quick look close to where he had landed. There was 1st Lieutenant Gene Attebury's body lying beside his glider. It looked like he had been shot and perhaps burned by a flamethrower, the stench of his burned flesh coating the nostrils and uniforms of anyone who approached. Not far away were 2nd Lieutenants Lee Secaur and Leonard Hulet. They were close friends and now lay dead within 100 feet of each other.[19]

Yet there were islands of mercy that saved lives.

Blood was everywhere in the fuselage of 1st Lieutenant Sven Berg's glider. Within seconds after he had landed, every man he carried, including his copilot, had been shot. After taking cover behind a water tank, Berg crawled back to the glider to patch the wounds of the men who were pinned down there. One of them was shot a second time as he pulled the man to a safer position. Enemy fire forced him to withdraw, but he returned a second time to give morphine to two of the wounded men. The men he saved were evacuated after snipers in a nearby farmhouse had been killed.[20]

Flight Officer Max Hunt and 2nd Lieutenant Arnold Holt looked for a place to land among burning gliders, others that had slid up onto the canal embankments, some that had been dismembered by transmission wires, and at least one that had landed in a canal. Holt and Hunt were met with machine gun fire and mortars as they climbed out of their glider. Hunt was shot in the head as he was yelling to Holt over the gunfire. Seconds later,

Holt was hit in the right hip by a mortar shell's shrapnel and then took a bullet in his right shoulder. He would be hit six more times. When one of his passengers, a British soldier, stood to surrender he was shot and killed.

Once the firing eased, three soldiers carried Holt to a farmhouse. While the elderly German couple whose yard had become a battlefield cared for the Kansas farm boy through the night, at one point the old man took his ID to Allied troops nearby. The next morning, they arrived, laid him on the hood of their jeep, and drove him to a field hospital. Recovery would take three months, made possible by a German family he never saw again.[21]

Shortly thereafter, a series of Army telegrams reflected the agony of uncertainty endured by many glider pilot families.

> ... YOUR SON 2LT ARNOLD L. HOLT HAS BEEN MISSING IN ACTION OVER GERMANY SINCE 24 MARCH
>
> [...]
>
> RETURNED TO MILITARY CONTROL ... HE IS HOSPITALIZED IN THE EUROPEAN AREA ... FURTHER INFORMATION FOLLOW DIRECT FROM HOSPITAL ...

And finally, a telegram from Arnold.

> ARRIVED IN STATES TODAY ... AM AT HALLORAN GENERAL HOSPITAL STATEN ISLAND NEW YORK ... HOPE YOU ARE FINE WILL LET YOU KNOW ADDRESS AS SOON AS POSSIBLE LOVE.

By nightfall on March 24, three squadrons of Captain Charles Gordon's 435th Provisional Glider Pilot Infantry Company had taken their position near the intersection of Holzweg and Hessenweg roads (with a fourth in reserve), a route German soldiers might take as they retreated north from the ruins of Wesel. The glider pilots had no communication between foxholes, although many were within yelling distance if they dared.

Just before midnight, a mechanical growl grew in the distance, unseen near the bottom of a wooded slope in front of the glider pilots' position. *That's a German tank!* A tank and an armored personnel carrier, each towing a 20mm gun, and an estimated 200 Germans headed for the glider pilots' position. Flight Officer Albert Jella waited, watching the enemy tank approaching his position. When it was only fifteen yards away, Jella fired his bazooka.

The night erupted in gunfire, red tracers' paths revealing positions and targets. Heavy machine guns pounded soldiers' positions. The distinct "burp" of German machine guns was unmistakable in the mayhem. Tank fire thundered. Unexpected yelling by German soldiers added an Old West flavor to what became an otherworldly firefight as the Germans repeatedly attempted to break through the glider pilots' position.

Its tread disabled by Jella's bazooka, the tank backed off. Glider pilot fire disabled the enemy's mobile artillery as they held their ground. Dead and wounded Germans littered the roadbed as a sole German medic knelt over one after another, doing what he could as the others withdrew. Silence returned to a battlefield flickering from wreckage fires.

Hours passed before a rising sun revealed at least fifteen dead German soldiers. More than twenty-five Germans were taken as wounded prisoners along with eighty others. The glider pilots had suffered one minor casualty in what became known as "The Battle of Burp Gun Corner." They were relieved from their frontline duty later in the day.[22]

The "virgins" had survived their first mission. Before they headed back to the Rhine, some returned to what had become graveyards of gliders. Some mangled, others smoldering, a few upright on their cockpits or at impossible angles against trees or along canal banks.

Second Lieutenant Frank Slane had enlisted with dreams of becoming a fighter pilot but had been sent to Texas as an instructor. It wasn't long before he "volunteered for anything to get out of south Texas." He had earned his glider pilot wings five months earlier. On his first mission, he had flown alongside another glider in double tow in what he called "a big box kite with wings," carrying nine glider infantry and 1,500 pounds of ammunition.

After landing and reporting to his CP, he returned to his glider the following day before he joined glider pilots on a long hike back to the Rhine. He spotted a hole in his glider's windshield. Had he been in his pilot's seat when that bullet had broken through, Slane would have been shot through the head. Flak had ripped holes in the fuselage and a wing strut. His first glider had become carrion for local scavengers.

But it was Operation *Varsity*'s human toll that stayed with Slane for a lifetime. "Death was everywhere. Paratroopers were hanging in trees. Some were draped across power lines. Bodies were in hedgerows, in ditches, and in the bunkers. It was a bloody mess," he recalled.[23]

For the first time, the Army was prepared to evacuate the glider pilots off the battlefield after some had collected souvenirs, had taken photos, or had spent a few minutes retracing their way through what had been a killing field the day before. When ground troops linked up with the airborne, many glider pilots began walking back to the Rhine where amphibious craft were standing by to transport them over to the west bank. There, trucks ferried them to a bivouac area where aircraft flew them back to their bases within a day or two.

Second Lieutenant Howard Schultz heard a lot of grumbling over the Army's newfound efficiency. Some veteran glider pilots preferred the previous autonomy of taking a few days off before returning to base, though he noted "the vast majority came back within a week or two while only a few of them stretched out their return to a few months or longer."[24]

Some *Varsity* glider pilots would not return to their units for weeks. Second Lieutenant Tom McGrath had flown through artillery fire on two previous missions. This time, part of his left wing had been shot away and some of his passengers hit before he found a small field and landed, only about 200 yards from a German command post. Injuries mounted when machine gun and small arms fire rocked the wrecked glider.

"Soon all but two of our guns jammed due mostly to blood from two airborne boys who were killed. Metoxen was hit in the right leg, [a] lieutenant who was hit by flak was again hit in the leg [and] I was hit in the left hip," recalled McGrath. Surrender had become the only course toward survival. The three wounded survivors were marched twelve days farther into Germany to the city of Fallingbostel, surviving on a few slices of bread and turnip soup. During another relocation, McGrath escaped, hid in the forest, and slowly worked his way west to friendly troops.[25]

It also would be weeks before some glider pilots managed to share a sanitized version of their experience to spare their loved ones a sliver of the worry they constantly carried. Flight Officer Bernard Smith's letter following his first mission was written a month after Operation *Varsity*.

I had too much speed and tried to get it between a couple of trees. Well, I misjudged, and I hit a tree on the left side of the glider. It instantly cut off my left foot about five inches below the knee… If I could have moved my foot [toward] my right one inch I'd have never been scratched, but God didn't have it planned that way. I still have good knee action which will make a big difference when I get my artificial foot and leg… Things are not too bad now so don't you be worrying, and I will endeavor to write you every day, letting you know just how things are going… All my love, Bern.[26]

Perhaps when he returned home, he would share the details of how he had completed the first of three ninety-degree turns toward the wind when his glider shuddered at the impact of a shell near his wing, three feet of it collapsing in a heartbeat. That had forced the glider into a downward spiral. Smith could control it only to the extent that he aimed for a trail through a stand of trees. Clipping trees with his wings might have slowed him enough to survive unscathed, but a stump crushed the nose of his glider, taking off part of his leg. When he reached for his machine gun under his seat, he saw that part of his leg had disappeared. Smith lowered himself down through a hole in the bottom of the glider and leaned up against one of the glider's tires.

Later, he was confronted by two approaching German soldiers. Weak from loss of blood and likely in shock, Smith shot first and killed both. He would always be haunted by his decision. *Was I too hasty in my action to fire first? Did I kill those two boys needlessly?* Ghosts not shared in letters from the battlefield.

"Mein Gott! Mein Gott!" (My God!)

Operation *Varsity* didn't end for the glider pilots when the battle-field quieted or when they returned to their bases a few days later.

Flight Officers Donald Martin and Ken Moore had shared a foxhole the night of March 24, sleeping in shifts in case of counterattack. "Shoot him!" Martin yelled, when Moore thought he had seen a German soldier approaching in the dark. Moore sprayed the man with his Tommy gun. He fell, mortally wounded, a few feet from their foxhole. He repeatedly called for God, slowly fading until he died with a grenade in his hand. The next morning, Moore had been so devastated looking at the man he had killed that he started giving his valuables – his wedding ring, money, and other items – to Martin for delivery to Moore's wife in case he was killed in battle later. Moore also told Martin that if he somehow made it through the war, he never wanted to see or hear from a glider pilot again. Operation *Varsity* was Moore's second mission.[27]

Some farm boys as well as teenagers from the city who had never killed an animal had become men callous to killing strangers, even in letters written to their mothers. "I had my rifle follow the second [German] … the other fellow waited till the first Jerry was about six or eight feet [away] and then shot him. The second one dropped to the ground, and I shot him twice. We shot the other two," wrote one glider pilot.

For others, Operation *Varsity* would extend into their tents long after they were evacuated from the battlefield. When Flight Officer Horace McLin got back to the tent he shared with Martin, he awoke at 0200 hours on the first night. Frantic, he rolled off his cot and ran outside with his Tommy gun to stop an imagined German attack. Despite a two-week leave, McLin changed from a quiet teetotaler to "drinking, smoking, and dating girls at every opportunity he had. He seemed to be searching for some kind of a release from the pressures of combat."[28]

For some, post-mission mood swings of depression, mourning, exhilaration at survival, survivor's guilt, pride in mission accomplished, and then waiting and wondering whether the next mission would have "a bullet with my name on it" marked the passage of time.

The families of other glider pilots would learn little more than what was contained in a "deep regret" telegram or a knock on the door by somber strangers.

"Boots" King's daughter would never see him at the dinner table or in the audience at a school play. She would never meet the man who had left for Europe as a widower, shortly after she had been born when her mother had died in childbirth. His dead wife's family would raise her in the memory of a mother and father the little girl never met.

Second Lieutenant Gordon Chamberlain, the go-getter at San Diego State University as a young actor and president of his Toastmasters Club, would never finish his college education. He had been knocked unconscious at Normandy in a crash so violent it twisted the cockpit around to face the glider's tail. "I won't worry once I can act on the ground but know how scared I'll be while in the air," he had written days before *Varsity* where he would be among the first to land. After he had taken cover in a stand of trees, a sniper killed him, five days short of his twenty-fourth birthday.

On the morning of March 24, General Eisenhower and Prime Minister Winston Churchill had stood on a hill west of the Rhine, marveling at the massive Allied armada as it passed overhead. "My dear General," Churchill kept repeating, "the German is whipped. We've got him. He is all through." Within a week, Operations

Plunder and *Varsity* became a signature success. Four Allied armies had crossed the Rhine and two more were about to establish bridgeheads as well.

Operation *Varsity* had played a vital role in the first twenty-four hours of the Allies' invasion into Germany. The IX Troop Carrier Command calculated that 97.5 percent of airborne sorties in *Varsity* were successful. More than 4,000 power and glider pilots delivered 4,810 soldiers, their equipment, and more than two million pounds of supplies to their assigned drop and landing zones despite horrific glider losses.[29]

The price they paid on their last combat mission was unprecedented. Eighty-six glider pilots were killed in about twelve hours on March 24, twice the proportionate losses suffered by the tow plane aircrews. Every nine minutes, a glider pilot on approach was killed by enemy fire or in a midair explosion, was crushed in a mangled glider, or died from shrapnel or gunfire. That amounted to nearly forty percent of all the glider pilots killed in World War II and more than the glider pilot deaths in Operations *Neptune* and *Market Garden* combined.

But now no significant barriers remained between the Allies and Berlin. From Sicily to Normandy; from southern France to Holland; from Belgium to Germany, America's glider pilots had flown at the tip of the Allied spear across the width and breadth of the European Theater of Operations.

In the final weeks of war in Europe, some glider pilots and tow plane pilots formed a unique alliance as Allied forces closed in on Berlin. Supply lines were stretched so severely and so many bridges had been destroyed that C-47s were used to deliver the most critical supplies, especially gasoline, to captured German runways and ferry the wounded and liberated prisoners of war back out of Germany. Some flew two or three missions daily, fighting exhaustion as much as enemy fire and cratered airstrips. They were classified as combat missions for the aircrews, but not for the glider pilots who volunteered to be copilots.

Power pilot Lee Whitmire had delivered supplies at Bastogne, had flown as a glider copilot crossing the Rhine, and had dug in near the battle at Burp Gun Corner. He returned to the C-47's pilot seat in an armada that included several glider pilots who had volunteered to become auxiliary navigators and copilots. One of them was Flight Officer Bob Swenson who had flown his first glider mission in *Varsity* and had fought at the Battle of Burp Gun Corner. On pipeline flights back from Germany, some of the liberated prisoners he carried died in their cots in the back of his C-47. The plane was fumigated for lice after it landed.

"The Flying Pipeline" became the glider pilots' last mission of combat service and sacrifice in Europe, one that began by crashing off the coast of Sicily and concluded twenty-one months later by helping emaciated POWs step onto French soil as free men.

Meanwhile, the invasion of Japan loomed.

Glider pilots had pioneered the use of the combat glider, an aircraft that had not existed only four years earlier. They had been the only pilots to fly one-way missions into battle. Unlike paratroopers and glider infantry, they had served on the battlefield as orphans with minimal command presence. Every one of them had volunteered for glider pilot duty.

In addition to the 218 glider pilots killed in combat during the war, 178 were killed in the line of duty outside of combat. Only days after their final combat mission, Lieutenant General Lewis Brereton, commanding officer of the First Allied Airborne Army, forever codified their contribution in a written report.

> The conduct of glider pilots, in general, is beyond written words of commendation. Not only did they deliver a magnificent and well-coordinated landing which in many cases was in the midst of hostile positions, but were immediately engaged with their airborne associates, in the hottest kind of hand-to-hand fighting… The discipline and combat efficiency of these glider pilot soldiers has called forth the highest praise of division and regimental officers.[30]

General William C. Westmoreland captured the legacy of those who volunteered to fly the "Purple Heart Boxes" into battle.

> Never before in history had any nation produced aviators whose duty it was to deliberately crash land, and then go on to fight as combat infantrymen. They were no ordinary fighters. Their battlefields were behind enemy lines. Every landing was a genuine do-or-die situation for the glider pilots. It was their awesome responsibility to repeatedly risk their lives by landing heavily laden aircraft containing combat soldiers and equipment in unfamiliar fields deep within enemy-held territory, often in total darkness. They were the only aviators during World War II who had no motors, no parachutes and no second chances.[31]

They were a motley crew of young Americans, as dedicated to serving and sacrificing for their country as the battle-hardened career officers fighting in their second world war. A slice of the Greatest Generation whose legacy stood apart from others, in audacity, accomplishment, and anonymity.

> *To the glider pilots. Conceived in error, suffering a long and painful period of gestation, and finally delivered at the wrong place at the wrong time.*
>
> Glider pilot Milton Dank
> *A toast of surviving World War II glider pilots*[32]

> *We were a bunch of wild Indians, I guess you might say. You had to be crazy to be [a glider pilot], I guess. Or a little bit on the nutty side, to get into something without an engine. But we were just doing our duty.*
>
> Glider pilot Guy Gunter[33]

World War II's Orphans

Captain Albert Waldon had watched C-47s drop out of the sky over Holland. James Larkin had flown a glider on four missions across Europe. Guy Gunter's glider had crashed into the sea off Sicily. Now that Germany had surrendered, surely it was time for America's glider pilots to come home.

Waldon would return to Alice, whom he had married more than three years earlier, while Larkin would marry Arshula, a girl he had known in high school. The day he got home, Gunter planned to ask a girl he had known since junior high school to marry him. But for some glider pilots in the summer of 1945, family life would have to wait. Waldon, Larkin, and others received new orders: prepare for the invasion of Japan.

Gliders were disassembled in France and crated for shipment back to the States. Many were missing radios, parachutes, compasses, and other equipment that had been scavenged. But they, too, would be needed for war in the Pacific. Planning, as well as training, was well underway for Operation *Downfall*.

One significant combat glider mission already had taken place in the Far Pacific on March 5, 1944. It had received little public notice, perhaps because Operation *Thursday* proved to be an ominous omen of what glider pilots would face in Europe in the coming months. Sixty gliders flew from India 165 miles into Japanese-held Burma. They carried British commandos as well as the men and equipment necessary to build an airstrip that could accommodate C-47s. The gliders would be at the forefront of British Brigadier General Orde Wingate's plan to insert a large force of men into Burma to break the Japanese hold on the country.

Many of the gliders were overloaded, in part because some commandos smuggled additional ammunition in the fuselages. Gliders broke loose almost immediately at takeoff, some released or turned back en route, and the remainder dragged heavily against their tow planes at 8,500 feet to clear mountains. Just thirty-seven gliders reached the designated landing zone.[1]

Photo reconnaissance had failed to reveal the stumps, deep ruts, buffalo wallows, and other obstacles hidden in the tall grass. Radios were not available to advise the glider pilots of the hidden dangers as landings became crashes. All but three of the thirty-seven gliders were heavily damaged. Glider pilot casualties mounted as the mission's loss rate approached eighty-five percent.

But the gliders that reached the landing zone carried enough equipment and men to enable a mile-long airstrip to be scraped out of the jungle and become operational within twenty-four hours. Wingate's men were able to operate behind enemy lines for two months.

Now a million casualties were expected in the two-phase Japan invasion plan that would become the largest amphibious landing in the history of war. An estimated 750,000 troops would invade the Japanese island of Kyushu in November, with a second massive assault near Tokyo on Honshu about four months later, both with airborne support. In the run-up to Operation *Downfall*, a deception plan called for a glider buildup on Okinawa, including dummy gliders as well as authentic glider pilot training missions.

But how could hundreds of gliders land in Japan's postage stamp-sized farm fields and rice paddies? By blowing each glider up after landing and then pulling the pieces aside to clear space for the next glider. At least that was the speculation among glider pilots during late spring exercises held at Laurinburg-Maxton Air Force Base in North Carolina.

Power glider pilot Walt Raby volunteered to land a glider rigged with explosive primer cord attached to its steel and wood joints. A timer was attached to an exit door. He landed after a smooth flight and was the last man to leave the glider, activating the timer as he left. He ran as fast as he could. At 300 yards, the glider exploded. Chunks of steel and wood peppered the area. Raby and others then ran back to the wreckage and pulled the larger pieces to the side to clear a path for the next glider. Maybe it would work in waterlogged rice paddies, too.

Meanwhile, as America rejoiced over Germany's defeat and the invasion of Japan approached, glider pilots still in Europe once again had time on their hands and not enough tow planes to accumulate their required four hours' monthly flying time. A number of light aircraft were made available. But what would glider pilots do with powered aircraft? Stunts. A "follow the leader" game took a group of pilots under a high-voltage transmission line. Another time, they simulated strafing runs at a civilian train, surely horrifying its passengers. An aerial dog fight using flare guns was great fun, too. A group also performed at an air show near a French chateau for war orphans, dropping candy to the youngsters as they made their passes. A few days later, a letter written by a nun at the chateau thanked the glider pilots, noting the orphans considered them heroes.

The nuclear bomb over Hiroshima, Japan, on August 6, 1945, ended the gliders' era. Most of the glider pilots had headed home following victory in Europe, their official discharge coming a few months later. More would follow from the Pacific, though some would receive orders for occupied Japan. Some opted to remain in the Air Force Reserve and later were recalled to active duty. A few made the military their primary career.

The journey home for some glider pilots had begun in May after they had been liberated from their prisoner-of-war camps deep inside Germany.

Flight Officers Steve Odahowski and William Jew had been prisoners of war since their capture in Normandy. They were among more than fifty glider pilots who were captured and sent to POW camps hundreds of miles to the east in Germany and Poland.

The camps for Allied officers were primitive at best. Several who had been sent to Stalag Luft III in Poland suffered from chilblains, the painful swelling of feet and hands from prolonged exposure to cold.

In late January 1945, as Soviet troops had pushed westward the Germans evacuated several camps. Odahowski, Jew, and others were given one hour's notice to prepare for what would become a two-week death march from Stalag Luft III toward Moosburg, Germany. For many, hope of survival faded as they scavenged frozen turnips and carrots in farm fields covered by midwinter snow, spent days stuffed in railroad cattle cars that sat on railroad sidings as inviting targets for Allied aircraft, and then faced another forced march, all totaling more than 350 miles.[2]

They endured long stretches of almost no food or water. One day, glider pilots and thousands of others marched sixteen miles on a quarter loaf of sawdust-packed bread per man. If they were lucky, they slept a few hours on straw in a drafty, unheated barn. For some, standing in packed railroad cars became horrifying as they listened for the growl of approaching Allied aircraft. Groups of fifty men in each cattle car, nearly all of them starving and many of them sick, could only wait and search for a zephyr of hope.

Stalag VII-A at Moosburg offered scant relief. Vermin infested the dilapidated buildings. Five hundred men were crammed into buildings designed for 200. A Red Cross food parcel intended for each soldier had to be shared by several. More than 100,000 prisoners made Moosburg Germany's largest POW camp.

Salvation had finally arrived at Moosburg on April 29, when one of General Patton's tanks bulled into the camp, dragging a barbed-wire fence in its wake. In the span of about a week, other Stalags across Germany were liberated as well. Before long, the former prisoners of war would embark on a long trip home. Their war was over.

Only eighteen months later, the Army Air Forces had shrunk from 2.3 million personnel to 340,000 and a single glider infantry unit. Surplus gliders in their five shipping crates had been sold to the public for as little as $75, mostly for the crates' 10,000 board feet of Grade A lumber. Enough lumber for a small house, a cabin, barn, or a bedroom, dining room, and balcony addition.

The gliders' fabric could be used for insulation. The steel tubing was reworked into barnyard feed bins. Cockpit Plexiglass became windows. Glider wheels were ideal for livestock and harvest trailers. America's glider force was cannibalized to the extent that only a handful remained and nearly none had been set aside for museum display.

Yet in their final, postwar chapter, some unusual circumstances called for the use of gliders.

Beginning in February 1946, Canada tested its ability to move a military force 3,000 miles above the Arctic Circle in midwinter. The three-month exercise placed a premium on continuous deliveries of supplies along the troops' route. Gliders were part of that mission, delivering mail, fuel, rations, and other supplies to supply stations. Gliders landed on gravel deposits and frozen lakes across the tundra. In one instance, a C-47 used the snatch pickup to return a glider to base.

On December 9, 1948, a C-47 crashed in Greenland. Four days later, a B-17 crashed as well, while attempting a rescue. The Air Force turned to gliders to rescue the aircrews. But a snatch pickup attempt of a CG–15 glider carrying the stranded men was unsuccessful when the tow rope broke under the strain of the fully loaded glider. A second attempt with another glider similarly failed.[3]

Finally, twenty-one days after the first crash, a C-47 equipped with "jet-assisted" auxiliary power rescued the aircraft and glider crews from temperatures that had dropped to forty degrees below zero and in winds that had approached 100 miles per hour with a deadly chill factor. (As late as 1975, the two gliders were still visible in the snow from the air.)

Only six days after the initial crash in Greenland, another C-47 ran out of fuel and crashed on a frozen river in the Yukon Territory near the Alaskan border. Once again, below-zero weather threatened the aircrew. The next day, a glider was towed to the site of the wreck, released, and came to a stop within 100 yards of the six survivors. Within an hour in the midwinter twilight, a snatch pickup device was erected. After four practice passes only ten feet over the riverbed, a C-47 snatched the glider and its passengers off

244

the frozen tundra and successfully delivered them to an Air Force base in Alaska a short time later.

In February 1950, a glider supplied rations to a team of scientists and fourteen volunteers living in remote tents for ten days in Alaska. They were testing a new midwinter daily ration of 475 calories in temperatures that dipped to thirty degrees below zero. The glider landed on a frozen arctic lake to deliver equipment and supplies for the successful experiment.

Despite the success of these missions, predictions of glider use in commercial aviation never got off the ground. Lewin Barringer, the man General Arnold had brought to Washington to lead the development of gliders, had grand plans for their postwar future. He envisioned tow planes pulling six gliders at once, each filled with cargo, from coast to coast. Over a single glider's city destination, that glider would release and land at the nearby airport while the tow plane would continue toward a pickup station, descend, and slow to 120 miles per hour to execute a snatch glider pickup to join the remaining five on tow, and then continue then on to the next city on the itinerary for another release-and-snatch.

One documented attempt to realize Barringer's vision took place in April 1946 when Winged Cargo, Inc., launched a glider cargo business. A glider filled with cargo was towed from Philadelphia to Georgia and then returned the same day with a load of young tomato plants. Nine months later, however, a C-47 flown by the company's passenger division crashed in Costa Rica, killing all seven on board. Meanwhile, trucking and railroads demonstrated both could deliver greater quantities of cargo less expensively, dooming any meaningful rebirth of military gliders in commercial aviation.

The military moved on from gliders as well. Despite their structural integrity once production issues were resolved, the remarkable track record of the glider pilots could not mask the reality that gliders were vulnerable to groundfire, required both airspace and massive numbers of tow aircraft, needed adequate room for landing, were limited in their capacity, and were expensive for what usually became a single mission. Shortages of tow planes and aircrews, dependency on good weather, and landings that were not always concentrated added to the gliders' tactical shortcomings. Further, when paratroopers preceded gliders into battle, glider pilots may have paid a disproportionate price from the loss of total surprise. On some missions, the proportionate share of casualties suffered by glider pilots exceeded that of powered planes' aircrews.

Nearly 400 glider pilots gave their lives, almost equally divided between combat and in the line of duty (training) in World War II. Though the CG-4A proved remarkably stout, it was often overloaded and forced to land at faster-than-prescribed speeds. Away from the battlefield, weather and bad luck sometimes were just as deadly. "Tow rope broke during a sudden encounter with bad weather ... killing pilot, co-pilot, and seven passengers." "The USAF states the crash was due to KCRGC (Killed in Crash Ground Collision)." "We cannot say that the mission was a complete success ... for we lost our glider operations officer and his assistant, two of the most well-liked and respected officers in the squadron." "... last seen when landing his glider on the LZ... The glider was found with the other glider pilots lying dead beside it. No further word has been heard of LT. Phillipson." "But suddenly, the glider struck a large pine tree, whirled in a circle and slithered to the ground. Ferguson was unharmed, but Haas was badly smashed. By the time he was freed from the wreckage, he had died." Clinical Army reports as impersonal as an autopsy painted a dire picture of the postwar future of gliders.

Gliders and their pilots became orphans when the US Air Force was created in 1947. Long-range strategic bombing, including nuclear weapon delivery, became the order of the day at the dawn of the cold war. Ten-thousand-mile bombing missions trumped 200-mile troop mobility in groups of thirteen. Meanwhile, the Army remained ground-combat centric. Not surprisingly, three of America's highest-ranking postwar officers, Generals Matthew Ridgway, Maxwell Taylor, and William Westmoreland, had led airborne divisions. Paratroopers and the advent of more capable helicopters left gliders in their wake despite the development of larger gliders.

Research into more powerful and larger-capacity gliders had continued throughout the war and beyond. One model had the same wingspan as a B-24 Liberator bomber and could carry sixty troops. Some glider versions had engines. But only one saw extended life as the C-123 Provider, the first jet transport that served until 1980.

The gliders' obituary was written in 1952 by the Joint Airborne Troop Board. "Gliders, as an airborne doctrine, are obsolete, and should no longer be included in airborne techniques, concepts and doctrine, or in references thereto."[4] In the 1930s, the Army had prohibited its men from flying in sailplanes, yet in the 1940s combat gliders had been invented and their pilots were sent into combat. But by the early 1950s, glider pilots had met the same fate on the battlefield as the cavalry.

"We fell through the cracks," grumbled more than one glider pilot after the war. "[Army Air Forces] thought the Army would be handing out the decorations while the Army, in turn, thought the [Army Air Forces] should be taking care of us." *Good luck with that,* others thought. *If you didn't fly a plane, shoot down the enemy or bomb him, you weren't a real combat pilot.* With a few exceptions, the rank of major was the highest rank that glider pilots reached.

Others resented that General Patton received all the credit for delivering supplies to the surrounded troops at the Battle of the Bulge when gliders and troop carrier groups had played a critical role.

Over the decades, however, glider pilots took pride when a glider captured national headlines and even commanded live news coverage. NASA called its Space Shuttle a "high-tech glider" that slowed from 17,300 miles per hour to 250 miles per hour when landing.[5]

Against that backdrop, only in recent decades have glider pilots received the recognition of their valor and sacrifice they deserve.

Captain Charles Gordon and four glider pilots received the Silver Star for their actions at the Battle of Burp Gun Corner in Germany. Although Gordon had recommended Bronze Stars for all members of the 435th Provisional Glider Pilots Infantry Company, the war had ended in Europe only two months later. None were issued. The paperwork was resubmitted in the 1990s and, in 1995, the Air Force awarded a Bronze Medal to every member of the company who reached the battlefield, including power glider pilots like Lee Whitmire who had cross-trained for glider duty and who had fought at Burp Gun Corner.

But only a relative handful of the original provisional combat team's 288 glider and glider power pilots were still alive. Presentations were made to those attending a glider pilot reunion ceremony and individually to others across the country in homes, ballrooms, and community centers in front of family, friends, and sometimes the local news media. Some were given to surviving family members and the remainder were sent to the Silent Wings Museum in Lubbock, Texas, for the day when family members might be located. (As of 2022, the museum still held approximately fifty Bronze Medals. Its affiliated National WWII Glider Pilots Association has tracked down at least 25 family recipients and has developed an extraordinary body of historical knowledge for museum use.)

Like many World War II veterans, sporadic recognition of glider pilots came decades after their service to America, just as many were beginning to share their war experiences toward the end of their lives.

But the men they delivered to the battlefield in Europe carried a reverence for glider pilots from that day forward.

I have the greatest respect and admiration for the guys who sat in the pilot seat of those gliders. Here they were, without a weapon, they had no defense mechanism aboard the plane themselves, they were flying a powerless aircraft. They had only one way to go which was down. There was no escape mechanism ... they knew they were going into enemy territory... I think they were remarkable people ... they not only trained to do this very thing, they were prepared to turn around and do it again and again, as often as they were told to do it.

War correspondent Walter Cronkite[6]

13

Epilogue

One of the most painful tragedies of war is death off the battlefield. Men who have braved enemy fire only to lose their lives after the enemy's guns have been silenced. Perhaps the most heartbreaking deaths came when those men were headed home to their families.

On July 23, 1945, nine glider pilots climbed aboard a B-24 bomber in Wales under a leaden sky and drizzle. They expected to fly over Scotland and then Iceland on their way home. As they approached Scotland, an engine caught fire. Perhaps a fuel leak fed the reddish glow that drew the attention of witnesses on the ground. The plane lost altitude as it made a broad, sweeping turn toward shore. As it crossed the Scottish coast, a wing melted. An engine slammed into the tail, breaking it off the plane. The bomber quickly nosed over and disappeared in a fireball when it hit the ground, killing all aboard. The crash had occurred so suddenly that no emergency call had been made before impact.

Flight Officer Edward Grzesiek had flown into enemy fire in Normandy, southern France, Holland, and into Germany. Flight Officer Wilber Titus had been wounded in Normandy. Flight Officer George Baker had flown three missions, had been wounded in Holland, and would have celebrated his twenty-first birthday in two weeks. But instead of stepping off a plane in America, they died two months after the war in Europe had ended. Four bodies were brought home for burial in cemeteries from California to Michigan. The other five remain buried on a grassy slope at

Cambridge Military Cemetery in England along with more than 3,800 other Americans – one of twenty-six permanent American military cemeteries in seventeen countries.

Death surrounded glider pilots far from the front line. Robert Horr had completed his first mission, a personal nightmare in Normandy. He had heard that his good friend "Buck" Jackson had died, had counted eighty bullet holes in his glider, had killed an enemy soldier, and had lived on canned food for three days spent in enemy territory. Horr had figured that if he received any medal he would give it to Buck's mother. A month later, Horr died in a routine glider tow accident in England. He never knew that his pal had survived his wounds and returned to the States.

Some glider pilots could not return home without first knowing what had happened to friends who had been listed as missing in action. Irwin Morales, Thomas Ahmad, and others had held off a German force near Graignes for several days following the Normandy invasion. When they finally had to withdraw from a church where townspeople hid and wounded were being treated, Ahmad had volunteered to stay behind to help protect the civilians. He never reported back to the Allied beachhead.

After the war in Europe ended in May, Morales borrowed a jeep and returned to Graignes. The surviving residents told him that, after the Americans had been driven out by the Germans, they had counted nearly 500 dead German soldiers. In retaliation, the Germans executed two priests and two nurses who had been caring for wounded Americans. They also set most of the houses in town on fire and shot more than thirty citizens.

Twenty-five airborne soldiers, including those lying wounded in the church, had been taken to a small farm where they were executed. Their bodies were thrown into a ditch near a pigpen. Morales was quite sure Ahmad had been among those shot in the head. He found Ahmad's grave in a temporary military cemetery nearby.

In the year following the end of World War II, thousands of other glider pilots blended back into America as silently as they had landed in enemy territory. Some married, others went back to school, a few made the military their life's work. Some returned as alcoholics and doomed marriages. Mothers warned their children that "we do not talk about the war." And as one military doctor told a glider infantryman, "All men who go to war die, son. Anyone who comes back, comes back cheated."[1]

Many charted a new course for the first time in their lives as an adult. Their destinations varied: bush pilot, county judge, minister, banker, well dowser, intelligence officer, postal clerk, dentist, aviation inspector, accountant, mechanic, helicopter pilot, border patrol officer, insurance agent, cartoonist, salesman, entrepreneur, construction foreman, industrial designer, and photographer, to name a few.

The carousing "Goldie" Goldman established a Baptist church in New Mexico and pastored for more than forty years. Hugh Nevins, who had assigned glider pilots to overnight combat duty in Holland, became a horse breeder in Colorado. Charles Gordon, who had led glider pilots in combat after crossing the Rhine, started a computer manufacturing company and served as a town's mayor in Tennessee. The meticulous notetaking Elbert Jella, who had fired his bazooka at a tank, forcing it to withdraw in the Battle of Burp Gun Corner, became a cartographer for the US Geological Survey.

Harry Loftis, the boyhood pal of "Goldie" Goldman, had held another friend from the States as he died in his arms on the battlefield. After he was discharged, years passed before he could share his experiences. "Finally, one day I sat down, and we had a talk [with his wife, Margaret]. 'You ask me anything you want about the war, and I'll tell you just exactly like it was. And then I don't want you to talk to me about it ever again.'" Loftis built a successful career as a lawyer, district attorney, county judge, community leader, and Sunday school Bible teacher in Tyler, Texas, where he and "Goldie" had first met.[2]

Some were in a hurry after years away from home. Guy Gunter, who had crashed off the coast of Sicily, returned home, and asked his girlfriend, Evelyn, to marry him "next Saturday." They forged a life together in Georgia as he built an appliance company in his hometown.

Some glider pilots made pilgrimages to Europe in the decades that followed World War II. On the 50th anniversary of the Normandy invasion, 2nd Lieutenant Leo Cordier visited a cemetery there.

> Going through the cemetery at Omaha Beach, I spotted two of the crosses of two glider pilots who were buried there… I looked down at the ground and that could have been me … there was about 50,000 people there [for the anniversary celebration], an eerie silence about the area … a little shrine in the middle of the cemetery saying they [the dead soldiers] should forever be young. And that's how you remember some of your buddies who were interred there. That's a hallowed spot.[3]

For years, Samuel Fine, the glider copilot in Sicily who had fought valiantly with a British unit capturing a bridge, looked for his British glider pilot, Staff Sergeant Lofty Wilkner. In 1993, he learned that Lofty had been killed in the battle for the bridge. "It took fifty years to find out that my British glider pilot was with me at the bridge so near yet so far… In 1997, I had to visit the grave of my pilot, to say goodbye."[4]

Perhaps by luck or compassion, traces of some glider pilots were miraculously found and preserved in Europe. Glider pilot Jack Merrick had flown every major mission except *Varsity* when his glider was assigned to a friend at the last minute. His buddy was killed a few feet from the glider.

Earlier in southern France, Merrick had survived a hard landing in a vineyard. Shortly thereafter, twelve-year-old Pierrot found a helmet with holes cut in it for headphones, an unusual find in a French vineyard among the rubbish of war. Two years after Merrick had died in 2018, his daughter discovered her father had worn and lost that helmet in Operation *Dragoon*. It had been donated to a French online museum. She knew little about her father's mission and planned a personal pilgrimage to southern France at the first opportunity.

Some glider pilots who never came home were adopted. Gordon Chamberlain lies in the Netherlands American Cemetery.

On Memorial Day 1946, hundreds of Dutch citizens who had volunteered to adopt and tend the graves delivered flowers to the gravestones. The same day, Mary Knicknie wrote a letter. "I beg you to send me his [Chamberlain's] home address. For I think that the picture I made from his grave are great souvenirs for his family," she wrote.[5]

Chamberlain's white cross is one of more than 8,000 graves across sixty-five acres, together with a monument honoring more than 1,700 Americans missing in action.

General "Hap" Arnold, the founder of the glider program and ultimately the US Air Force, was a sick man by the end of World War II. He retired on June 30, 1946, and died of a fifth heart attack on his California ranch less than four years later at the age of sixty-three. He had served in uniform for forty-two of those years and today remains the only five-star general of the US Air Force.

As the decades passed, some glider pilots looked back fondly on the war, somehow immune to the horrors that haunted others and that would never be fully shared. Ralph Lester had cross-trained in CG-4As and C-47s and "did a lot of growing in those four years [of service]." "The army was the best experience of my life," reflected Roger Krey who married a girl he met in Britain in 1945.[6]

For others, it was a life's chapter devoted to America. A few years of revulsion, horror, camaraderie, courage, and heartbreak, and then on to the rest of a man's life centered on family and his life's work. Glider pilot William Brown had written a letter to his young son the night before his mission in Normandy, "I go with the prayer that I will be permitted to return to you and Mother, and if it should work out otherwise, it will have been the will of God that I make the sacrifice." It was never mailed. Brown survived Normandy, flew into Holland, and helped defend a German advance at the Battle of Burp Gun Corner in Germany.[7]

He returned home to his wife and "Little Robert," and served thirty years in the Air Force, including tours in Korea and Vietnam. He died on Christmas Day 2008, at the age of ninety-four, leaving two children, three grandchildren, four great-grandchildren, and one great-great-grandchild.

Their duty to country honored, their ultimate mission had been to survive, one day to the next, and come home. Hopefully unhurt, but to come home. Most had left as naive young men who had seen little more than a fistfight. They returned hardened, some bitter, and many haunted.

That, too, is the legacy of war. Along with scars that bind; memories that cripple; sights and sounds that remain as fresh as yesterday. And a new mission to keep them tethered in the place where only a man's nightmares live.

Today, few glider pilots remain among us. Yet their legacy has inspired each subsequent generation of Americans when their nation has called for a full measure of guts.

Acknowledgments

Acknowledging those who make a book possible is akin to missing a trip wire in a mine field. The risk of overlooking an individual or institution sends shivers down a writer's spine. So, I begin with an apology in case there is an oversight, as well as a profound expression of gratitude to the following.

Research team member Patricia Overman of the World War II Glider Pilots Committee truly made this book possible. The Committee is part of the Silent Wings Foundation which supports the unique Silent Wings Museum. Access to detailed glider and glider pilot documentation compiled by the museum's affiliated researchers truly was a godsend. The daughter of a power glider pilot, the depth of her knowledge is remarkable, and her review of the manuscript kept me on course. She truly served beyond the call of duty. The museum's curator, Sharon McCullar, was extremely supportive from the beginning (despite the museum's pandemic-forced closure), providing well-organized archival access when I could spend time there researching the museum's archives.

The Silent Wings Museum organization is a unique national treasure, and it was my honor to review its repository of World War II documents, personal collections of glider pilots, and even step inside a restored combat glider. Over the course of two years' research, I was given access to more than 100,000 files that spanned US Army narratives, reports and analyses, personal histories, and photographs taken by glider pilots as well as diaries and letters written to their families, official glider pilot accounts, research theses, contemporary newspaper and magazine accounts, videos, newsreels, documentaries, and other personal accounts.

It was a glorious treasure hunt filled with side trips up tributaries in quest of the next insight worthy of inclusion. As Pulitzer Award recipient and historian Barbara Tuchman once said, "Research is endlessly seductive, but writing is hard work."

Other historians were quick to respond and support seemingly endless requests. They included Doug Poore of the Greater Harrington Historical Society; Meredith Cummings of Ramsey County Historical Society; Peter van der Linden who documented the Dutch underground's remarkable association with American glider pilots; Ian Murray who may well be Operation *Ladbroke*'s foremost authority; Richard Chancellor with his remarkable military aircraft photograph collection; Dimitris Vassilopoulos, Kriakos Paloulian, and George Chalkiadopoulos who assisted with glider pilots of Greek descent; Scott Nelson; and author/historian, Colonel Mark Vlahos, USAF, among others. Karl Zingheim, Adjunct Professor of Military History at San Diego State University's USS Midway Center for the History of War and Society, provided early guidance and critical perspective.

In several instances, family members of deceased glider pilots eagerly supported this project, sharing treasured documents and photographs. They included Mike Skidmore, Russ and Susan Jane Ramsey, Edward Colimore, Bob Grodin, Jack Goodnight, Terrell Parker, Chris Jella, Anne Hilber, and actor and freelance writer Christopher Warner, among others.

In recent years, a number of institutions have worked diligently to help preserve the legacy of World War II glider pilots via oral histories, written accounts, and primary-source document collections. They include the Silent Wings Museum, the Veterans History Project at the Library of Congress, The National WWII Museum, Air Mobility Command Museum, National Museum of the Pacific War, various county and state historical societies, and universities. Their archives proved indispensable.

Don Patton who established the World War II History Roundtable in 1987 which continues today has become a good friend and invaluable resource, both in terms of knowledge and contacts in America's military history community.

This book also stands on the shoulders of previous authors who have written detailed unit and glider program histories. They include Hans den Brok, Charles L. Day, G.J. Dettore, Gerard Devlin, James Fenelon, Michael Ingrisano, James Mrazek, H. Rex Shama, Colonel Mark Valhos, Christopher Van Valkenburgh, Colonel Charles Young, and several glider pilot memoirs, among others.

I will forever be indebted to my two muses, my literary agent Scott Mendel and military novelist Richard Setlowe. Scott has kept me on course in a journey which marks *Brotherhood of the Flying Coffin* as my 11th book. I value his guidance and perspective greatly. And Richard, an accomplished military history novelist, has opened my eyes to the art of storytelling. Like any successful military mission, each has played a key role, fulfilled his duty, and ultimately has made this book possible.

The team at Osprey Publishing (Kate Moore, Gemma Gardner, Anne Halliday, Clare Jackson and others) again proved invaluable in both guidance and in their creativity and detailed polishing that turned the manuscript into a gem of a story.

Finally, to my "morale officer" and inhouse editor, Marjorie. Her unwavering support throughout forty-three years of marriage has long been the foundation upon which I tackled the crazy idea of writing a book, then another, and another. Millions of written words later, I still can't settle on the best ones to truly convey how much she means to me.

Glossary

AA Antiaircraft artillery fire

AAF Army Air Forces

aileron Adjustable surfaces at the rear of each wing that control turning ability

Allied/Allies Principally the United States, Great Britain, and the USSR aligned against Germany and its Axis partners

bivouac A military encampment area

bridgehead A position established on the enemy's side of a bridge as a launching point for attacks farther into enemy territory

C-47 The workhorse military version of the civilian Douglas DC-3, used for paratrooper, glider, supply, and evacuation missions

CG-4A Also called a Waco glider, it was the Americans' combat glider. See "Waco"

command post Temporary battlefield location where tactical ground-troop decisions were made. Also referred to as CP

CPT Civilian Pilot Training Program

D-Day First day of several amphibious landings in World War II

D-rations Fortified chocolate bar designed to replace a meal in an emergency

D+1 The day following an invasion which is designated D-Day. Format also used as D+2, D+3, etc., as well as D-1, D-2, D-3

drop zone Designated area on the battlefield where paratroopers, pathfinders, and supplies were dropped by troop carrier groups. Also referred to as DZ

elevator Adjustable surfaces on either side of the tail's rudder to control rise and descent

Eureka Ground-based transponder placed by ground troopers to guide inbound aircraft

feet dry When an aircraft crosses the coast and proceeds inland

flak Antiaircraft shells exploding high in the air. Sometimes referred to as "black roses" with a red center

flak battery Mobile or permanent antiaircraft artillery position

flak wagon Antiaircraft gun mounted on a vehicle, sometimes towing a trailer filled with ammunition

flaps Hinged panels on wings to control lift and descent

glider infantry Combat troops assigned to ride by glider to the battlefield, as opposed to paratroopers who used parachutes

Griswold nose Metal tube brace structure retrofitted onto gliders' noses to reduce damage to the glider's nose and cockpit upon landing

hedgerow Concentrated stand of trees alongside or enclosing a field

Horsa Larger British glider made of plywood, otherwise similar to the American CG-4A

intel Commonly used shorthand for intelligence report

landing zone A designated landing area for gliders on the battlefield. Also referred to as LZ

marshaling pattern Choreographed alignment of tow planes and gliders at one end of a runway in a configuration that emphasizes serial takeoff speed and efficiency

Operation *Bluebird* Morning glider mission in support of Operation *Dragoon*

Operation *Chicago* Normandy D-Day early-morning glider mission in support of Operation *Neptune*

Operation *Detroit* Normandy D-Day early-morning glider mission in support of Operation *Neptune*

Operation *Dove* Early-evening glider mission in support of Operation *Dragoon*

Operation *Elmira* Normandy D-Day late-afternoon glider mission in support of Operation *Neptune*

Operation *Galveston* First second-day Normandy glider mission in support of Operation *Neptune*

Operation *Hackensack* Subsequent second-day Normandy glider mission in support of Operation *Neptune*

Operation *Husky* Allied invasion of Sicily

Operation *Keokuk* Normandy D-Day late-afternoon glider mission in support of Operation *Neptune*

Operation *Ladbroke* Gliders' mission as part of Operation *Husky*

Operation *Market Garden* Assault into Holland: *Market* signifying the airborne phase and *Garden* signifying the ground phase

Operation *Neptune* Gliders' and airborne's mission as part of Operation *Overlord*

Operation *Overlord* Allied amphibious landing in France at Normandy

Operation *Repulse* Airborne relief missions in the Battle of the Bulge

Operation *Varsity* The airborne assault across the Rhine River into Germany

panzer division German armored division

paradrop A delivery of personnel or supplies by parachute

parapacks Heavy-duty canvas bags or canisters packed with various supplies dropped by C-47s to ground troops

paratrooper Infantryman trained to land behind enemy lines by parachute

pathfinder Advance paratroopers who were the first to land behind enemy lines and establish navigation aids for incoming paratroopers and glider pilots

prop wash Turbulence to the rear of aircraft generated by propeller engines

RAF Royal Air Force (Britain)

ration Military meal

recon Shorthand for reconnaissance, often in the context of reconnaissance photos used to brief glider pilots in advance of their mission

GLOSSARY

Rommel's asparagus Wood poles (often six inches wide and fifteen feet tall) buried upright as deadly obstacles in potential glider landing zones. Some were wired together and mined to inflict more severe damage and casualties

rudder Adjustable panel on tail to control turns

salient A bulge along a battle line extending into enemy territory

serial Several aircraft flights in a group at a specific time interval

Skytrain Alternative name of the C-47 aircraft

slip When a glider is steered into the equivalent of a partial sideways slide, either in the air or on the ground when landing, to slow its speed

small arms Commonly used reference for rifle and pistol fire

SPAAF South Plains Army Air Field, at Lubbock, Texas, the primary glider pilot training facility in World War II

spoilers Panels on the back side of aircraft wings that, when engaged, reduce lift and speed

TCG Troop carrier group, a unit of C-47s assigned to deliver gliders, paratroopers, pathfinders, or supplies to drop zones and landing zones. Comprising squadrons, multiple troop carrier groups are organized as troop carrier wings

Tommy gun Soldiers' shorthand for the Thompson submachine gun, capable of firing at least 700 rounds per minute

tracers Self-illuminating bullets, typically every fifth round in a machine gun belt, enabling the operator to adjust his aim as he is firing

troop carrier group See "TCG"

troop carrier squadron Basic unit of combat pilots. Multiple squadrons comprise a troop carrier group

troop carrier wing The overall troop carrier commands of airborne operations

Waco Abbreviation of Weaver Aircraft Company which designed the combat glider most widely used in World War II. See "CG-4A"

windmilling When an aircraft's propellers continue spinning from air flow after its engine has stopped running

Selected Bibliography

BOOKS

Abbe, Donald R. *South Plains Army Airfield*. Charleston, SC: Arcadia Publishing, 2014.

Astor, Gerald. *June 6, 1944: The Voices of D-Day*. New York: St. Martin's Press, 1994.

Barnett, Correlli. *Hitler's Generals*. New York: Grove Press, 2003.

Craven, Wesley. *The Army Air Forces in World War II, Volume Six*. Washington, DC: Office of Air Force History, 1983.

Dank, Milton. *The Glider Gang*. New York: J.B. Lippincott Company, 1977.

Day, Charles. *Silent Ones WWII*. Self-published, 2001.

den Brok, Hans. *440th Troop Carrier Group in Operation Varsity*. Self-published, 2018.

den Brok, Hans. *Battle of Burp Gun Corner*. New Orleans: Walka Books, 2014.

Dettore, G.J. *Screaming Eagle Gliders*. New York: Stackpole Books, 2016.

Devlin, Gerald M. *Silent Wings*. London: W.H. Allen, 1985.

Ellis, L.F., and Warhurst, A.E. *Victory in the West: The Defeat of Germany*. London: Naval & Military Press, 1968.

Fenelon, James M. *Four Hours of Fury*. New York: Scribner, 2019.

Ferrin, James. *For Us "Der Var Ist Over."* Tempe, AZ: Desert Hills Publishing, 1987.

Flanagan, Edward. *The Angels: A History of the 11th Airborne Division*. Washington, DC: Infantry Journal Press, 1948.

Galvin, John R. *Air Assault: The Development of Airmobile Warfare*. New York: Hawthorn Books, 1969.

Grim, J. Norman. *To Fly the Gentle Giants*. Bloomington, IN: AuthorHouse, 2009.

Ingrisano, Jr, Michael. *Valor without Arms, A History of the 316th Troop Carrier Group*. Bennington, VT: Merriam Press, 2012.

Knickerbocker, W.D. *Those Damned Glider Pilots*. College Park, GA: Static Line Books, 1989.

Lowden, John L. *Silent Wings at War*. Washington, DC: Smithsonian Books, 1992.

Lynch, Tim. *Silent Skies, Gliders at War*. Barnsley, South Yorkshire, Great Britain: Pen & Sword Books, 2008.

Masters, Charles J. *Glidermen of Neptune*. Carbondale, IL: Southern Illinois University Press, 1995.

Mrazek, James E. *Airborne Combat*. Mechanicsburg, PA: Stackpole Books, 2011.

National World War II Glider Pilots Association. *World War II Glider Pilots*. Paducah, KY: Turner Publishing Company, 1991.

Shama, H. Rex. *Pulse and Repulse*. Austin, TX: Eakin Press, 1995.

Spiller, Roger J. *Combined Arms in Battle Since 1939*. Fort Leavenworth, KS: US Army, 1992.

Van der Linden, Peter. *Escape and Evasion*. London: Osprey Publishing, 2014.

Van Valkenburgh. *History of the 306th Troop Carrier Squadron, 442nd Troop Carrier Group 1943–1945*. No publisher listed: 2018.

Wolfe, Martin. *Green Light! A Troop Carrier Squadron's War from Normandy to the Rhine*. Washington, DC: Center for Air Force History, 1993.

Wurst, Spencer. *Descending from the Clouds*. Philadelphia: Casemate, 2005.

Young, Charles D. *Into the Valley*. Dallas, TX: PrintComm, Inc., 1995.

ARTICLES, ESSAYS, VIDEOS, AND HISTORICAL DOCUMENTS

Anonymous:

Airborne Missions in the Mediterranean 1942–1945. Washington, DC: USAF Historical Division, 1955.

Bastogne: Supplied on a Wing and a Prayer. Film produced by the National World War II Glider Pilots: December 18, 2017.

The Battlebook: The Battle of the Bulge. US Army Europe, undated. *Combat reports of the IX Troop Carrier Command, 1943–1945*.

Combat reports of the 82nd and 101st Airborne Divisions, 1943–1945.

Combat reports of the 313th, 314th, 315th, 316th, 317th, 318th, 319th, 375th, 433rd, 434th, 437th, 438th, 439th, 440th, 441st, 442nd Troop Carrier Groups, 1943–1945.

Development and Procurement of Gliders in the Army Air Forces 1941–1944. Washington, DC: Army Air Forces Historical Office, 1946.

DZ Europe: The Story of the 440th Troop Carrier Group. United States Air Forces, 1946.

Enemy Assessment. 62nd Troop Carrier Group, August 13, 1944.

Ever First! 53rd Troop Carrier Wing. Paris: Stars & Stripes, 1944–1945.

Flight Operating Instructions CG-4A Glider. Army Air Forces, December 31, 1942.

Glider Tactics and Technique, Air Forces Manual No. 3. January 1944.

Glider Training and Operational Procedures. Army Air Forces, September 8, 1944.

The Glider Training Program 1941–1943. Washington, DC: US Army Air Corps, 1943.

Handbook of Assembly Procedure, CG-4A Glider. Cessna Aircraft Company, undated.

Historical Data Headquarters, 435th Troop Carrier Group. March–April 1945.

History of the 38th Troop Carrier Squadron 14 February 1942 to 14 April 1944. Air Force Historical Research Agency.

Interrogation Check Sheets by glider pilots following each mission.

Iron Mountain News. Iron Mountain, MI: Ford Motor Company, 1942.

Narrative of Operation Market. HQ, First Allied Airborne Army, October 9, 1944.

Report on Glider Mission DOVE. 64th Troop Carrier Group, August 21, 1944.

Silent Wings. The American Glider Pilots of World War II, video released 2007.

Suicide Missions: Silent Wing Warriors. The History Channel, 2010.

Technical Manual Advanced Glider Training. Army Air Forces, December 17, 1942.

Brereton, Lieutenant General, Lewis. Correspondence with General "Hap" Arnold, November 4, 1944.

Buffkin, Ronald M. "Assault Gliders: A Reexamination." Master's thesis, US Army Command & General Staff College, 1991.

Ellis Jr, John T. *The Airborne Command and Center Study No. 25*. Army Ground Forces, 1946.

Fetters, Rolland. *Overseas Assignment for the Investigation of Army Air Forces Glider Program in European Theater of Operation*. Army Air Forces, 1943.

Garner, Christian A. *Forgotten Legacies: The U.S. Glider Pilot Training Program and Lamesa Field, Texas, During World War II*. Denton, TX: University of North Texas, 2016.

Huston, John W. *American Air Power Comes of Age: General Henry H. "Hap" Arnold's World War II Diaries*. Maxwell Air Force Base, AL: Air University Press, 2002.

Jenkins, Timothy. *The Evolution of Airborne Warfare: A Technological Perspective*. Birmingham, Great Britain: University of Birmingham, 2013.

Lemna, Samantha. "To Battle by Glider and Parachute: The Airborne Forces of the Second World War." Honors thesis, University of Lethbridge, 2014.

Lindley, John. *Villaume Builds Gliders in World War II*. Ramsey County Historical Society: Winter, 2007.

Lowe, James P. *The First Successful Airborne Operation*. Baton Rouge, LA: Louisiana State University, 2004.

MacDonald, Charles B. *U.S. Army in World War II European Theater of Operations*. Washington, DC: Department of the Army, 1973.

Manion, Michael H. "Gliders of World War II: The Bastards No One Wanted." Thesis, School of Advanced Air and Space Studies, Air University, Maxwell Air Force Base, 2008.

Martin, Jr, Lawrence Michael. "Fighters or Freighters: U.S. Troop Carrier Aviation, 1941–1945." Master's thesis, University of Nebraska, 1993.

McAuliffe, Kathleen. *On Silent Wings*. Washington, DC: Smithsonian, June 1994.

McCullough, John W. *Breedlove: An Empire of the Air, 1939–48*. Texas Tech University, 2017.

Miller, Charles E. *Airborne Doctrine*. Maxwell Air Force Base: Air University Press, 1988.

Murray, Ian. "Operation Ladbroke." Accessed May 2, 2020. https://www.operation-ladbroke.com.

Noetzel, Jonathan C. "To War on Tubing and Canvas." Thesis, Air University, Maxwell Air Force Base, 1992.

Ortensie, R. Ray. *Gliders: From Wright Field to the Netherlands*. Air Force Material Command History Office, 2019.

Rose, Don. "We Bought a Glider." *Flying Magazine*, February 1947.

Sargent, Sparky Barnes. "Silent Targets." *Flight Journal*, August 2014.

Sheehan, Thomas J. "World War II Vertical Envelopment: The German Influence on U.S. Army Airborne Operations." Master's thesis, U.S. Army Command & General Staff College, 2003.

Spencer, Leon. "They Flew into Battle on Silent Wings." Silent Wings Museum, undated.

Spencer, Leon. "U.S. Army Air Force Combat Glider Program." Silent Wings Museum, undated.

Stetson, Conn. *Mobilization in World War II in 1938–1942*. Office of the Chief of Military History, 1959.

Warren, John C. *Airborne Operations in World War II, European Theater*. USAF Historical Division, Research Studies Institute, 1956.

PARTIAL LIST OF FIRST-PERSON, DOCUMENTED ACCOUNTS

Among others, Noel Addy, Roger Airgood, Johnny Alison, Gale Ammerman, George Anderson, Joseph Andrews, Elgin Andross, Stratton Appleman, Lieu Arnold, Samuel Baker, Tim Balley, Herbert Ballinger, R.E. Barthelemy, Albert

Barton, Andrew Bates, James Bellah, Henry Benefiel, Sven Berg, Claude Berry, Robert Bisch, Edwin Blanche, Herb Bollum, Warren Bradley, George Brennan, William Brown, Pete Buckley, Joe Burrell, John Butler, Robert Cable, Pershing Carlson, John Casagrande, Clayton Cederwall, Gordon Chamberlain, Lloyd G. Clark, Joe Clowry, Kenny Coffman, Earl Cole, James Colimore, Benjamin Constantino, Leo Cordier, Corky Corwin, Milton Dank, Fred Daugherty, John Devitt, James Di Pietro, Ernest Dutcher, Louis R. Emerson, Jr, Gillespie Erskine, Oliver Faris, James Ferrin, Rolland Fetters, Samuel Fine, Richard Fort, John Fox, Joe Fry, Arthur Furchgott, Jr, Paul Gale, Joseph Gallimore, Harold Goldbrandsen, J. Curtis Goldman, Neil Goodnight, Charles Gordon, Zane Graves, Leon Gumley, Guy Gunter, Wallace Hammargren, John Hanscom, Joseph Harkiewicz, William C. Hart, John Heffner, Joseph Hesse, John Hill, Henry Hobbs, Arnold Holt, Arthur Hopper, William Horn, Robert Horr, Verbon Houck, Philip Howland, Bruce Hutton, Philip Jacobson, Elbert Jella, Denby Jones, Les Judd, Jr, David Kaufman, Tom Kilker, W.D. Knickerbocker, Roger Krey, Lawrence Kubale, Bill Lane, James Larkin, Jack Lavern, Ralph Lester, Richard Libbey, Harry Loftis, Fred Lunde, Otto Lyons, Jr, Don Manke, William Marks, Donald Martin, William McCormick, Tom McGrath, William Meisburger, Jack Merrick, Irwin Morales, Elden Mueller, John Neary, Major Hugh Nevins, Verne Ogden, Dale Oliver, Frank O'Rourke, Stephen Painter, Bernard Parks, Tom Pleger, Walter Raby, Tip Randolph, Jacob Reddick, Richard Redfern, Clinton Riddle, Shelton Rimer, Theodore Ring, Bless Rusk, Michael Samek, Thornton Schofield, Howard Schultz, Rex Shama, Mike Shapiro, Byron Sharp, Meyer Sheff, Charles Skidmore, Jr, Frank Slane, G.M. Slaughter, Bernard Smith, Leon Spencer, Leonard Stevens, Mac Striplin, David Suffrin, Charles Sutton, James Swanson, Robert Swenson, George Theis, Arthur Vogel, William Waggoner, Gordon Walburg, Ed Walters, Ben Ward, Tom Warner, Vic Warriner, Darlyle Watters, Ray Welty, John Whipple, Kenneth White, George Williams, Doug Wilmer, Norman Wilmeth, Robert Winer, Marty Wolfe, and Arnold Wursten.

Endnotes

PREFACE

1 Others have included *Honor Before Glory* about a remarkable World War II Japanese-American combat team that became the most-decorated unit of its size in the war and *New York Times*-bestselling *Surgeon in Blue*, a biography of pioneering Civil War surgeon Jonathan Letterman.

INTRODUCTION

1 Glider Pilot Citation: Silent Wings Museum Glider Pilot Papers Collection.

CHAPTER I: GUTS AND GLIDERS WANTED

1 Richard Libbey personal account: Silent Wings Museum Glider Pilot Papers Collection.
2 Harry Loftis personal account: Silent Wings Museum Glider Pilot Papers Collection, various written accounts, Veterans History Project, Library of Congress.
3 Jack Merrick personal account: Silent Wings Museum Glider Pilot Papers Collection.
4 Earlier generations of Arnolds had fought at Gettysburg and had served under General George Washington.
5 Major General John Huston, *American Air Power Comes of Age* (Maxwell AFB, Alabama: Air University Press, 2002), 6.
6 Ibid., 5.
7 Ibid., 23.
8 Walter Boyne, "Hap," *Air Force Magazine*, September 1997.
9 War experience would show that "transport gliders" in reality would become "combat gliders," given the battlefield conditions they faced

and the roles many glider pilots filled once they unloaded their troops or cargo.

10 The respondents were Bowlus Sailplanes, Inc., St. Louis Aircraft Corporation, Frankfort Sailplane Company, and the Waco Aircraft Company.

11 Gerald Devlin, *Silent Wings* (London: W.H. Allen, 1985), 47.

12 "Soaring," *Journal of Air Law and Commerce*, September 1938, 97–106.

13 "The Air Force on the Eve of World War II," *Air Force Magazine*, October 2007.

14 *The Glider Training Program 1941–1943*, 2–3.

15 "Origins of Airpower," *Airpower Journal*, Winter 1996, 70–92.

CHAPTER 2: CRASHING IS A LONELY SOUND

1 Guy Gunter personal account: multiple oral histories, Kennesaw State University archives.

2 Noel Addy personal account: Silent Wings Museum Glider Pilot Papers Collection, Chandler Museum archives.

3 Stetson Conn, *Highlights of Mobilization, World War II, 1938–1942*, 1959, https://history.army.mil/documents/wwii/ww2mob.htm.

4 "Gliders Play Important Role in AAF War Plans," *Army Air Forces Newsletter*, March–April 1942, 35–37.

5 Ibid.

6 By comparison, each C47 Skytrain that would tow gliders cost $50,000.

7 "Gliders Play Important Role in AAF War Plans," *Army Air Forces Newsletter*, July 1942, 5–7.

8 "Troop Gliders," *Flying and Popular Aviation*, February 1942, 118.

9 The Civilian Pilot Training Program had been established in 1939 to provide pilot training for 20,000 college students annually to create a pool of potential military pilots.

10 Starting in September 1942, the two tracks were revised and consolidated to include preliminary pilot training, elementary dead stick training, basic training in two- and three-place gliders, and advanced training in the CG4A combat gliders.

11 J. Curtis Goldman, *Silent Warrior* (Springfield, MO: 21st Century Press, 2008), 91.

12 Gunter personal account.

13 Don Manke personal account: Poynette Area Public Library archives, Silent Wings Museum Glider Pilot Papers Collection.

14 *The Glider Training Program, 1941–1943*, 21.

15 By employing his glider wings' spoilers, a glider pilot could increase the glider's sink rate to 1,600 feet per minute.

16 "Glider Pilot," *Wings*, December 1989, 52.

17 Charles Day, *Early U.S. Army Glider Training Programs*, Silent Wings Museum, undated.

18 Leon Spencer, *U.S. Army Air Force Combat Glider Program*, Silent Wings Museum, undated.

19 *The Glider Training Program, 1941–1943*, 20.

20 *Development and Procurement of Gliders in the Army Air Forces 1941–1944*, 29.

21 Ibid., 43.

22 Leon Spencer, *They Flew into Battle on Silent* Wings, Silent Wings Museum, undated, 2.

23 *Development and Procurement of Gliders*, 81.

24 $1.7 million in 1943 equates to $27 million in 2022 dollars.

25 Ibid., 95, 98–99.

26 Charles Day, *Silent Ones WWII* (self-published, 2001), 85.

27 "Villaume Builds Gliders in World War II," *Ramsey County Historical Society*, Winter 2007, 22–27.

28 *Development and Procurement of Gliders*, 125.

29 *The Glider Training Program, 1941–1943*, 36.

30 *Development and Procurement of Gliders*, 130.

31 George Brennan, Edward Cook, and David Trexler, *World War II Glider Pilots* (Paducah, KY: Turner Publishing Company, 1991), 16.

32 James Ferrin, *For Us "Der Var Ist Over"* (Tempe, AZ: Desert Hills Publishing, 1987), 8, 55.

33 John Butler personal account: Veterans History Project, Library of Congress, Silent Wings Museum Glider Pilot Papers Collection, Palm Springs Air Museum archives, American Air Museum.

CHAPTER 3: "PREPARE TO DITCH"

1 John Lowden, *Silent Wings at* War (Washington, DC: Smithsonian Books, 1992), 49.

2 Milton Dank, *The Glider Gang* (New York: J.B. Lippincott Company, 1977), 73.

3 W.D. Knickerbocker, *Those Damned Glider Pilots* (College Park, GA: Static Line Books, 1989), 48.

4 Paul Gale personal account: Operation *Ladbroke* https://war-experience.org/events/operation-ladbroke/.

5 There were no pathfinders, the advance troops in future invasions that would land ahead of the gliders' arrival and mark landing and drop zones with homing beacons, brightly colored signal panels or lights.

6 Gale personal account.

7 Michael Samek personal account: memoir, Silent Wings Museum Glider Pilot Papers Collection.
8 Kenny White personal account: Silent Wings Museum Glider Pilot Papers Collection.
9 Samuel Fine personal account: Silent Wings Museum Glider Pilot Papers Collection. He was recommended for a Silver Star, but it was rejected by General Mark Clark. Many glider pilots felt that Army headquarters believed that glider pilots were incapable of such heroism on the battlefield.
10 Ian Murray, Feat of Arms, http://www.operation-ladbroke.com.
11 Gunter personal account.
12 Murray, Feat of Arms.
13 Samek personal account.
14 Devlin, *Silent Wings*, 93.
15 A sixth, Captain Tracy Jackson, perished as an observer in a C-47 on a July 11 mission during *Husky II*.
16 Samek personal account.
17 Two of the American glider pilot flights were aborted and damage to the other two gliders that crash-landed prevented their cargo from being unloaded. Three of the four American glider pilots on the mission would not survive the war.
18 "Hitler Probably Chewing a Rug," *New Castle News*, July 12, 1943, 5.
19 "Glider Troops Crack Sicily Resistance," *San Antonio Light*, July 18, 1943, 2-A.
20 Samek personal account.

CHAPTER 4: PEA PATCH SAVIOR

1 Overseas Assignment for the Investigation of Army Air Forces Glider Program in European Theater of Operation (1943), 2, 17.
2 Ibid., 2–6.
3 *Summary of Exercise Bigot*, 3.
4 "Rommel Driven in Full Retreat," *East Liverpool Review* (Ohio), February 24, 1943, 3.
5 Dank, *The Glider* Gang, 56.
6 Elbert Jella personal account: Silent Wings Museum Glider Pilot Papers Collection.
7 *Development and Procurement of Gliders*, 60.
8 Ibid., 80.
9 Charles Young, *Into the Valley* (Dallas: PrintComm, Inc., 1995), 574.
10 Ibid., 575.11 *The Most Common Short-Comings in the Training of Battalion and Regimental S-2 Personnel, and Some Suggestions to Overcome Them*, 1–2.

11 "Rommel Driven in Full Retreat," *East Liverpool Review* (Ohio), February 24, 1943, 3.

12 Drew Pearson, "Washington Merry-Go-Round," *Port Arthur News*, August 10, 1943, 4.

13 "Defects Found After St. Louis Glider Crash," *The High Point Enterprise*, December 16, 1943, 5-A.

14 Leon Spencer, *The Fatal Tow Plane/Glider Accident of 15 September 1943*. Silent Wings Museum Archives.

15 General Arnold appointed duPont's brother, Major A. Felix duPont, Jr, who was serving in the AAF's Transport Command, as Richard's replacement.

16 *Development and Procurement of* Gliders, 82.

17 Young, *Into the Valley*, 574.

18 "Attack by Glider," *Flying Magazine*, November 1943, 26–27.

19 Clayton Cederwall personal account: Silent Wings Museum Glider Pilot Papers Collection.

20 One glider pilot was killed during the demonstration when his glider hit a solitary tree stump in the landing zone.

21 Edward Flanagan, *The Angels: A History of the 11th Airborne Division* (Washington, DC: Infantry Journal Press, 1948), 3.

22 Dank, *The Glider Gang*, 93.

23 Martin Wolfe, *Green Light!* (Washington, DC: Center for Air Force History, 1993), 54.

24 Ferrin, *For Us "Der Var Ist Over,"* 113.

25 Ibid., 62.

26 Sir Trafford Leigh Mallory, *Employment of U.S. Airborne Forces in Operation "Overlord"* memorandum, May 29, 1944, 1.

27 Dank, *The Glider Gang*, 102.

28 Tom Pleger personal account: Silent Wings Glider Pilot Papers Collection.

29 Butler personal account.

CHAPTER 5: POPCORN POPPING

1 Libbey personal account.

2 During the war, Britain was on "Double Summer Time," pushing sunset back two hours. It was not yet fully dark at 2300 hours.

3 Leigh-Mallory, *Employment of U.S. Airborne Forces in Operation Overlord*, 1.

4 Louis Emerson personal account: www.6juin1944.com/veterans/emerson.php.

5 "74 Years Later World Marks D-Day," *Sumter Item*, June 6, 2018, www.theitem.com/stories/74-years-later-world-marks-d-day,309367.

6 Goldman, *Silent Warrior*, 116.

7 Lowden, *Silent Wings at War*, 73.

8 Byron Sharp personal account: University of Utah Legacy Oral History Project.

9 Merrick personal account.

10 Andrew Bates personal account.

11 "Tow ship" and "tow plane" were used interchangeably by glider pilots.

12 John Hanscom personal account: Silent Wings Museum Glider Pilot Papers Collection.

13 Evans Ittner personal account: Silent Wings Museum Glider Pilot Papers Collection.

14 Hanscom personal account.

15 Andrew Bates personal account.

16 Just as Elkin reached the French coast on his way back, his right engine failed. Ditching seemed unavoidable. He climbed to buy time, but almost flew into an incoming glider formation. He dived for the water, told his copilot to switch fuel tanks, and the right engine miraculously restarted. He limped back to base, fighting vicious vibrations.

17 Most recon photos of Normandy had been taken when the sun was high in the sky. Without shadows to judge height, the field borders looked more like hedges than mature trees often growing on raised embankments.

18 Devlin, *Silent Wings*, 194.

19 Spencer Wurst, *Descending from the Clouds* (Philadelphia: Casemate, 2005), 41.

20 Dale Oliver personal account: Silent Wings Museum Glider Pilot Papers Collection, personal memoir.

CHAPTER 6: "THE GERMANS ARE COMING!"

1 Zane Graves personal account: www.6juin1944.com/veterans/graves.php.

2 Seven gliders had been lost in the cloud bank, five of which remained unaccounted for a month later. More were lost before reaching Operation *Detroit*'s landing zone.

3 Emerson personal account.

4 James Mrazek, *Airborne Combat* (Mechanicsburg, PA: Stackpole Books, 2011), 148.

5 Devlin, *Silent Wings*, 199.

6 Spencer, *U.S. Army Air Force Combat Glider Program*, Silent Wings Museum, undated.

7 Mrazek, *Airborne Combat*, 147.

8 Bob Horr personal account: Veterans History Project, Library of Congress.

9   Ibid.
10 Stratton Appleman personal account: Silent Wings Museum Glider Pilot Papers Collection.
11 Hanscom personal account.
12 Sharp personal account.
13 Glider Pilots Association, *World War II Glider Pilots*, 42.
14 Pete Buckley personal account: Silent Wings Museum Glider Pilot Papers Collection.
15 Addy personal account.
16 "Pilot Escapes After Killing 11 Germans," *Lincoln Journal*, June 12, 1944, 9.
17 Doug Wilmer personal account: Silent Wings Museum Glider Pilot Papers Collection.
18 Bill Adler, *World War II Letters: A Glimpse into the Heart of the Second World War* (New York: St. Martin's Press, 2002), 41.
19 Dick Hoag personal account: Silent Wings Museum Glider Pilot Papers Collection.

CHAPTER 7: "OUR MEN WERE LUCKY"

1   Enemy Assessment, 62nd Troop Carrier Group, 1.
2   Arnold Wursten personal account: Silent Wings Museum Glider Pilot Papers Collection. Richard McFarland, 32, left a wife and two children in Nebraska.
3   The Germans believed the amphibious assault would come either in southern France or northern Italy.
4   The invasion had been hotly debated among the Allies. At one point, it was planned to precede the Normandy invasion to draw German units from the north. But the ground war in Italy dragged into early 1944, a key factor to pushing *Dragoon* back to August.
5   Knickerbocker, *Those Damned Glider Pilots*, 164–165.
6   Young, *Into the Valley*, 225.
7   Knickerbocker, *Those Damned Glider Pilots*, 171.
8   Ferrin, *For Us "Der Var Ist Over,"* 130.
9   Lowden, *Silent Wings at War*, 90–91.
10 Young, *Into the Valley*, 221.
11 Ibid., 218. The passengers were members of the famed 442nd Combat Regiment Team, a segregated unit led by white officers that became the most decorated unit of its size in World War II. Their resolve and demeanor were legendary. One glider pilot was shocked to see his 442nd passengers taking naps on the way to their landing zone.
12 Ibid., 225. Richard Fort, personal account.

13 Miller had been a test pilot in Italy, at the controls of a glider towed by a P-47 Thunderbolt. Although Miller reported "smooth flying" behind a fighter-bomber that had a top speed of more than 400 miles per hour, Thunderbolts were never used to tow gliders that had a top towing speed of 130 miles per hour.

14 Leonard Stevens personal account: Silent Wings Museum Glider Pilot Papers Collection.

15 "Goldie" Goldbrandsen, Silent Wings Museum Glider Pilot Papers Collection.

16 Four months later, Leach was one of five men killed in an airplane crash on Corsica.

17 Joe Hesse personal account: Silent Wings Museum Glider Pilot Papers Collection.

18 Ben Ward personal account: Silent Wings Museum Glider Pilot Papers Collection.

19 Ferrin, *For Us "Der Var Ist Over,"* 183.

20 Young, *Into the Valley*, 222.

21 *Report on Glider Mission DOVE*, 3.

22 Loftis personal account.

CHAPTER 8: LIKE HORNETS AT A CHURCH COOKOUT

1 Several historians have been critical of General Browning's orders given to Gavin. They argue taking the bridges first was more central to the mission of reaching Arnhem, but Browning was worried the Germans could counterattack from the *Reichswald*.

2 Devlin, *Silent* Wings, 235.

3 A post-mission analysis by the 1st Allied Airborne Army characterized drops as forty-three being "good," twenty-four "fair," and fifty "poor."

4 Lowden, *Silent Wings at War*, xi.

5 Ibid., xii.

6 T.C. Schofield personal account: Silent Wings Museum Glider Pilot Papers Collection.

7 Following *Market Garden*, Schofield wore an "A-frame" cast extending from his chest to his ankles. His rehabilitation spanned fifteen months.

8 In addition to LZ-N, a second landing zone, LZ-T was another destination for gliders, particularly on September 18.

9 Lowden, *Silent Wings at War*, 108.

10 James Swanson personal account: Silent Wings Museum Glider Pilot Papers Collection.

11 Herb Bollum personal account: Silent Wings Museum Glider Pilot Papers Collection.

12 Bill Lane personal account: https://thehousinghour.com/general/greatest-generation/.
13 George Anderson personal account: New York State Military Museum, Silent Wings Museum Glider Pilot Papers Collection.
14 Pilots were trained to land against the wind, using its resistance for greater control.
15 Fred Lunde personal account, memoir, interview, Silent Wings Museum Glider Pilot Papers Collection.
16 Goldman, *Silent Warrior,* 188.
17 Michael Ingrisano, Jr, *Valor Without Arms* (Bennington, VT: Merriam Press, 2012), 181.
18 Goldman often sought excuses to travel to Paris to visit the Folies Bergère, noting "for a country kid from east Texas, I was really chopping in high cotton."
19 Rex Shama, *Pulse and Repulse* (Austin, TX: Eakin Press, 1995), 95.

CHAPTER 9: THEY WERE INVISIBLE

1 Dank, *The Glider Gang,* 187–188.
2 If the tow rope was nearly straight, that could indicate an air speed of close to 150 miles an hour, nearly the maximum speed for towing a glider.
3 James Di Pietro personal account: Air Mobility Command Museum archives.
4 Buckley personal account.
5 Kenneth Coffman personal account: Silent Wings Museum Glider Pilot Papers Collection.
6 Lawrence Kubale personal account: Veterans History Project, Library of Congress, Wisconsin Veterans Museum.
7 *Narrative of Operation Market*, HQ, First Allied Airborne Army, 10.
8 "Memories of Market Garden," *Silent Wings Museum Newsletter,* September 1990, 1–8.
9 Major Hugh Nevins personal account: Silent Wings Museum Glider Pilot Papers Collection, first-person published account in *World War II Glider Pilots,* Silent Wings Museum, 56.
10 Elgin Andross personal account: Silent Wings Museum Glider Pilot Papers Collection, first-person published accounts in *World War II Glider Pilots,* Silent Wings Museum, 53.
11 Guy Anderson personal account: Silent Wings Museum Glider Pilots Papers Collection.
12 Ibid.
13 *Narrative of Operation Market*, HQ, First Allied Airborne Army, October 9, 1944, 22–26.

14 Ingrisano, *Valor Without Arms,* 185.

15 Ibid., 182.

16 Glider pilots typically reported to their intelligence officer after a mission to complete an interrogation check sheet that summarized their experience and included their recommendations.

17 *Air Invasion of Holland,* IX Troop Carrier Command Report on Operation *Market,* January 1945.

18 442nd Troop Carrier Group after-action report.

19 *Narrative of Operation Market,* HQ, First Allied Airborne Army, 3.

CHAPTER 10: THE HOLE IN THE DONUT

1 Edward Zinschlag account in the *Journal Gazette,* Mattoon, IL, December 1985. He received the Silver Star for his heroism at Bastogne.

2 One division had only forty percent of its authorized tanks and one regiment relied on bicycles for transport.

3 U.S. Army Europe, *The Battlebook: the Battle of the Bulge,* 95.

4 Troops at Marcouray were in dire straits and those at St. Vith soon would have to retreat from the German onslaught.

5 Shama, *Pulse and Repulse,* 172.

6 Ibid., 185.

7 The glider likely had seen action in Holland three months earlier. Gliders left on the battlefield often were subject to scavenging by local residents.

8 Young, *Into the Valley,* 350.

9 Charles Sutton personal account: Silent Wings Museum Glider Pilot Papers Collection.

10 Wallace Hammargren personal account: Silent Wings Museum Glider Pilot Papers Collection, video, multiple published accounts.

11 "A battered World War II hero of Bastogne get a new home, and a museum built around it," https://www.washingtonpost.com/news/retropolis/wp/2017/08/03/a-battered-world-war-ii-hero-of-bastogne-gets-a-new-home-and-museum-built-around-it/.

12 Richard Fort personal account: Silent Wings Museum Glider Pilot Papers Collection.

13 Resupply Troops at Bastogne, *Silent Wings Museum Newsletter,* March 1991, 9.

14 Shama, *Pulse and Repulse,* 236.

15 Young, *Into the Valley,* 351.

16 Chuck Berry personal account: oral history, Silent Wings Museum Glider Pilot Papers Collection.

17 Young, *Into the Valley,* 86.

18 *Hangar Digest,* AMC Museum Foundation, October 2011, 10.

19 Shama, *Pulse and Repulse*, 288.

20 Estimates of the number of wounded housed at the makeshift garage during Operation *Repulse* ranged from 700 to 1,000. The 101st Airborne listed nearly 1,700 wounded men by January 6, 1945.

21 Antony Beevor, *Ardennes: The Battle of the Bulge* (New York: Penguin Publishing Group, 2016), 290.

22 Young, *Into the Valley*, 351.

23 Meanwhile at home, the families of glider pilots were reading newspaper reports such as one in the *Telegraph-Herald* in Dubuque, Iowa, on the day of the 50-glider mission that the 101st was "… in complete control of the situation, well-equipped with food and ammunition, and killing plenty of Germans."

24 Young, *Into the Valley*, 372.

25 Ibid.

26 Multiple glider pilot Interrogation Check Sheet reports following Operation *Repulse*.

27 Dank, *The Glider Gang*, 224.

CHAPTER 11: BEYOND COMMENDATION

1 Young, *Into the Valley*, 393.

2 In a double-tow alignment, one glider pilot was towed by a 425-foot nylon rope, the other by a 350-foot rope. Both pilots had to maintain proper altitude as well as horizontal separation, despite their tow plane's prop wash.

3 Young, *Into the Valley*, 384.

4 Ibid., 383.

5 A ten-foot deceleration chute on a twenty-five-foot leader could reduce a glider's speed from 150 to 75 miles per hour and add 500 feet to its descent in thirty seconds.

6 Elden Mueller personal account: Silent Wings Museum Glider Pilot Papers Collection.

7 Frank O'Rourke personal account: memoir essay. Glider pilots were dressed for combat on this mission, so the "dress shoes" comment might have referred to a C-47 pilot. It remains a mystery.

8 *World War II Glider Pilots*, 61.

9 Dick Redfern personal account: memoir essay, Silent Wings Museum Glider Pilot Papers Collection.

10 James Larkin personal account: memoir, published accounts, Silent Wings Museum Glider Pilot Papers Collection.

11 Roger Krey personal account: Silent Wings Museum Glider Pilot Papers Collection.

12 Ibid.

13 Oliver Faris personal account: Silent Wings Museum Glider Pilot Papers Collection.
14 *435th Troop Carrier Group Unit Narrative*, 1945, 6.
15 Redfern personal account.
16 Edwin Blanche personal account: Silent Wings Museum Glider Pilot Papers Collection.
17 Theodore Ring, Jr, personal account: Silent Wings Museum Glider Pilot Papers Collection.
18 Goldman, *Silent Warrior*, 204.
19 According to glider pilot "Goldie" Goldman, Hulet had volunteered to fly the mission in place of a married pilot. A newcomer, the pilot had begged off the mission and Hulet had volunteered in his place.
20 Hans den Brok, *Battle of Burp Gun Corner* (New Orleans: Walka Books, 2014), 43.
21 Arnold Holt personal account: Silent Wings Museum Glider Pilot Papers Collection.
22 Gordon, Jella, and two others ultimately were awarded Silver Stars for bravery. Fifty years later, Bronze Stars were awarded to every participant, too many of them received posthumously by their families.
23 Frank Slane personal account: oral history, Silent Wings Museum Glider Pilot Papers Collection.
24 Howard Schultz personal account: memoir essay, Silent Wings Museum Glider Pilot Papers Collection.
25 Thomas McGrath personal account: Silent Wings Museum Glider Pilot Papers Collection.
26 Bernard Smith personal account: Silent Wings Museum Glider Pilot Papers Collection.
27 Moore died forty-three years later in 1988.
28 Donald Martin personal account: memoir essay, Silent Wings Museum Glider Pilot Papers Collection.
29 *Operation Varsity*, IX Troop Carrier Command, April 15, 1945.
30 Lt Gen Lewis Brereton correspondence, March 29, 1945.
31 "One-way ticket: 'Pandemonium – WWII glider pilot recalls operations in Germany," US Army Public Affairs, May 12, 2011.
32 Dank, *The Glider Gang*, 17.
33 Gunter personal account.

CHAPTER 12: WORLD WAR II'S ORPHANS

1 Some accounts state only thirty-two reached the "Broadway" landing zone.
2 Soon other POW camps in the Soviets' path would be evacuated as well, their prisoners facing forced marches and railroad livestock cars bound for other POW camps.

3 The CG-15 was an improved version of the CG-4A with increased capability and protection. It arrived too late in the war for deployment in Europe.

4 John Galvin, *Air Assault: The Development of Airmobile Warfare* (New York City: Hawthorn Books, 1969), 264.

5 On one occasion, glider pilots received an autographed photo from a Space Shuttle crew. A handwritten note said, "At least the natives were friendly where we landed."

6 *Silent Wings: The American Glider Pilots of World War II*, video released 2007.

CHAPTER 13: EPILOGUE

1 Thomas Wood, *All Men are Casualties* (UK: Boleyn Bennett Publishing, 2018), 159.

2 Loftis personal account.

3 Leo Cordier personal account: memoir essay, oral history, Silent Wings Museum Glider Pilot Papers Collection.

4 Fine personal account.

5 Gordon C. Chamberlain Individual Deceased Personnel File, National Archives and Records Administration.

6 Ralph Lester personal account: Silent Wings Museum Glider Pilot Papers Collection.

7 William Brown personal account: Silent Wings Museum Glider Pilot Papers Collection.

Index

About the Author

Scott McGaugh is a veteran journalist and published author of *Honor Before Glory* (Da Capo/Hachette, 2016), the *New York Times* bestseller *Surgeon in Blue* (Arcade, 2013), *Battlefield Angels* (Osprey, 2011) and *Midway Magic* (CDS/Perseus, 2004). The latter became the basis for the History Channel's *Hero Ship: The USS Midway*, featuring the author, and *Honor Before Glory* was optioned for film development. McGaugh served as the founding marketing director of the USS *Midway* Museum in San Diego, the most visited floating ship museum in the world. His television appearances include the History Channel, Travel Network, and Discovery Channel, among others. Radio appearances include NPR's Weekend Edition. He lives in San Diego.